Straighten Up and Fly Right...

A book of stories about flying planes and hot-air balloons.

Brian Smith

Straighten Up and Fly Right...

Brian Smith

ISBN: 978-1-8384341-1-3

Published by Brian Smith Publishing in conjunction with Writersworld. This book is produced entirely in the UK, is available to order from most book shops in the United Kingdom and is globally available via UK-based Internet book retailers and www.amazon.com.

Copy edited by Ian Large

Cover design by Jag Lall

www.writersworld.co.uk
WRITERSWORLD
2 Bear Close Flats
Bear Close
Woodstock
Oxfordshire
OX20 1JX
United Kingdom
☎ 01993 812500
☎ +44 1993 812500

The text pages of this book are produced via an independent certification process that ensures the trees from which the paper is produced come from well managed sources that exclude the risk of using illegally logged timber while leaving options to use post-consumer recycled paper as well.

The title: *Straighten Up and Fly Right* seems to describe my ambitions. I picked a couple of idioms related to the title:

1. *To organize oneself, begin acting in a serious and mature manner, and start performing the way others expect of one.*

2. *To improve one's behaviour or attitude and perform better.*

In 1943, Nat King Cole had a hit with a song titled *Straighten up and Fly Right*. He and Irving Mills wrote the lyrics. Nat played the piano and sang the song. Using 'Straighten up and Fly Right' as the title of this book is to pay tribute to a fine singer and a great man.

CONTENTS

Brian's first flying lesson –
Trafalgar Square, London 1944.

PREFACE

"Just tell stories..."

I have noticed that many books I have read start with a Preface or an Introduction. My book is written during the coronavirus pandemic of 2020. My wife Cecilia and I, due to our age of 70 plus years, were classed as vulnerable! This meant being confined to the house for a number of months. With time on my hands, I decided to write this book. I have been given lots of advice, for which I am most grateful. When my wife and I were on a lecture cruise we became friendly with Peter Hobday, a very experienced broadcaster, and he too gave me much good advice. "Just tell stories," he said.

Mike Riley, a former British Airways Concorde captain said, "Write everything down, don't worry about the grammar." He kindly proofread much of the technical side of things.

I soon realised that trying to recall events starting in 1962 or earlier was to test my memory to the limit. I feel every chapter should start with *'As I recall...'* or *'If my memory serves me correctly...'* I have tried to include many events, dare I say, adventures, which made me smile. I hope you will smile too.

I have found listening to a piece of music triggers memories of significant events in one's life. I am sure when you hear a particular sound it takes you straight back there. As much as I have tried to describe in graphic detail some adventures, I am sure certain music might better set the scene. The following is a list of the music I would like to invite you to listen to before, after or while you read the relevant chapters:

Chapter 1. The Start Point. *'Singing to myself as I was flying long cross-country flights to gain my hours for my pilot's licence.'* Music: *Telstar* by The Tornados.

Chapter 10 Hot-Air Ballooning. Sub-chapter – Australia. *'On the long drive across Australia.'* Music: *Family Man* by Fleetwood Mac.

Chapter 11. Breitling Balloon Flight Round the World. *'Waiting in the cold night on the balloon launch site.'* Music: *Songbird* by Kenny G.

Chapter 13. The Albatross. *'Making an approach and landing on water in the Albatross.'* Music: *Albatross* by Fleetwood Mac.

Chapter 15. The Spitfire Simulator. *'We often play this piece of music with a profile view of the Spitfire. I have seen grown men cry.'* Music: *Nimrod* by Edward Elgar.

Brian Smith. Wheelers Farm, Sussex. May 2020.

1. THE START POINT

In July 1962, I joined British European Airways (BEA) as a bar steward (yes, the title still makes me smile). In 1991 I retired as a senior training captain with British Airways. I would like to tell you how this came about and recall some of the events along the way; I hope you will find some interesting and some quite amusing.

To define the exact start point for my dream becoming a reality has been difficult.

I was born in1938 in Plaistow, London. Not a good time to be born and the location was even worse. From 1939 onwards, over 5,000,000 children were evacuated from large city areas, most from London. John Anderson, a young and brilliant civil servant oversaw this huge operation. I was evacuated twice. My first evacuation was to Gloucester, with my mum as I was only two years old. The second time, I was sent to Staffordshire on my own.

If you see photographs of groups of children standing on a railway station with address labels pinned to their coats, I was part of a similar group.

I recently discovered the labels only gave the addresses of the 'holding place', not to a home. The children were taken from the destination train station to a town or village hall. They were lined up and host families would then choose a child.

You can imagine the pitiful state some of these children were in, having spent most of the day travelling, with little, or no toilet facilities or hot food.

My host family in Staffordshire were farmers with ten children, so one more did not faze them one bit.

After four years of rationing in London, life on the farm was wonderful. Milk straight from the cows and fresh vegetables were a treat. I believe I was there for about two years. I would recommend Ben Wick's book, *No Time to Wave Goodbye*. He gives a detailed account of the life of the evacuees and host families during this long and tragic period of the war. I was lucky.

Meanwhile, my mum and dad had moved from Plaistow to Seven Kings on the east side of London. The war was still on. I can remember my dad and brother building an 'Anderson Shelter' in the back garden. Anderson Shelters were named after Sir John Anderson, the same man who organised the mass evacuation of children into the countryside. Now, as the Lord Privy Seal in charge of air raid precautions, he commissioned engineers to design a bombproof shelter. The council supplied the shelter kit, leaving the families to build it themselves! Many people chose to incorporate the shelters into their gardens, planting vegetables and flowers on top of them. Some residents held competitions for the best display.

I feel the slogan **'Keep Calm and Carry On'** sums it up perfectly.

Mum watering the flowers.

The shelters were constructed using blocks of concrete buried about four feet deep with a curved corrugated iron roof, finished with a covering of soil about a foot thick. They were quite small structures, measuring about six feet by four feet. The siren would sound and we would all go to the shelter until the 'All Clear'. If a bomb had fallen on top of the shelter, it would have been flattened... we too. Several shelters nearby received direct hits, all inside were killed.

My father, who had survived World War One, would not join us in the shelter. During The Blitz he was on fire watch in London. He said he felt safer standing on top of a tall building with bombs falling all around him.

As any small boy growing up in bombed out London during World War Two, I was more interested in what was going on in the skies above than on the ground below.

My brother Johnnie was in the RAF on air sea rescue launches, and I listened to all his stories and the stories of visiting pilots that his team had pulled out of the water.

I joined the RAF in 1956 and trained as a physical training instructor (PTI). My dad wrote a letter for me to open on my first day. He was a sergeant in the Royal Horse Artillery in WWI and was awarded the Military Medal.

Of course, I wanted to fly, but I thought that with little or no education, and National Service coming to an end, I wouldn't stand a chance.

I was in the RAF, based in Germany. I had some leave and flew to London on a British European Airways (BEA) Viscount. I sat next to a BEA first officer who was positioning home. He was also a passenger. I introduced myself and the conversation quickly turned to flying. He said, "Have you thought about going down the civil aviation route?" He then went on to say the airline business was expanding and if I joined BEA or BOAC on ground duties, I could learn to fly at the Airways Aero Club, gain my Commercial Pilot's Licence (CPL) and get a job flying airliners. Simple...

After we landed at Heathrow on that occasion, I immediately phoned the Airways Aero Club and spoke to Archie Cole, the chief flying instructor (CFI). He listened to my plan and said the first step would be for me to come and have a flight with him.

Sunday 27. 5. 56.

Dear Brian,

Glad to hear you arrived safely & that you have already met someone you know, Well thats Great, because at first in strange company one is really glad to have another person with them & that should help you a lot in settling down, and getting kitted up. Dont forget to keep your ears & eyes open now because what you learn in the first few weeks will be very valuable later on. Well Son we are all well here, Mumm was somewhat distressed on Thursday as you can imagine but is gradually getting used to it. Write to us at least once a week & tell us all the news, which we eagerly await & if there are any problems let us know also if you want anything sent. So Son I will close with Fondest Love from us all

Your ever loving Father.

I drove over to White Waltham Airfield in Berkshire. There I met Archie and we flew in a Chipmunk aircraft to complete an 'assessment flight'.

The Chipmunk was designed and built by de Havilland Canada and first flew in 1946. It was a primary trainer for many air forces throughout the world.

The flight went well and, in Archie's words, "I don't think you'd be wasting your time, or more importantly MY time. Go for it!"

I needed to gain 200 flying hours for an attempt at the CPL exams. I set myself the goal of completing this within two years, although I quickly realised the mammoth task I had undertaken.

Chipmunk aircraft photographed by Adrian Pingstone in July 2008.

A big thank you goes to BEA for employing me as a steward. My whole plan hinged round the fact that I could hire an aircraft from the Airways Aero Club at a much-subsidised rate for employees of BEA and BOAC.

Coming from a military lifestyle to life in 'Civvy Street' was a big change. The training I went through with BEA helped me considerably some time later when flying as a pilot. Although it was in a slightly different format, we were taught what is now known as Crew Resource Management (CRM). To describe CRM in detail would take several chapters. My understanding of it is: As a crew you use the resources of people, equipment and procedures, such as communication, situation awareness, decision making and team work to safely complete a task. Personally, I would like to add one more component: A sense of humour!

I really had to pull out all the stops to try to reach and maintain the high standards BEA asked of their cabin crew. How lucky I was to be working with gorgeous girls and boys, always immaculately turned out, full of fun, and very professional. When any of them learnt of my flying dream, they were very encouraging, as were most of the pilots I flew with.

As my flying training progressed, I found putting every penny towards it quite a strain. A change started to take place. I found I looked forward to going to work as a relief. I really enjoyed my working environment. I just wasn't very good at it! As you will see...

I got the reputation as a 'Cockpit Clara', another name for a member of the cabin crew, mostly girls, who spent more time in the cockpit than working in the cabin. Alan Longhurst, a chief steward I flew with many times, always took over my duties so that I could spend time 'up the front'. First Officers Doug Stafford, Mike Riley and Cliff Phillips all offered advice and encouragement. I flew with them when I was a captain on the B707 years later. Small world...

After a day working on the Vanguard or Viscount aircraft, I would return to my minivan in the staff car park and drive round the perimeter track that surrounded Heathrow Airport. I would then spend an hour or two parked up (you could do that in 1962) watching the aircraft take-off and land. I did not collect registrations or aircraft types, but I could visualise exactly the procedures and instructions in those cockpits. 'Set power! Positive climb! Gear up!'

One of my stewarding duties was to charge the soda siphons with a CO_2 sparklet bulb. On one occasion, with my mind more on flying aeroplanes, I suddenly realized I had forgotten this simple task. Little did I know that Alan had already 'charged' the siphon. I whacked in another one. Now there was a potential 'bomb' waiting to go off... one of the first-class passengers was asking for soda. The standing order was to always test the siphon before you operated it. In my haste I just pointed the 'bomb' at the passenger's glass of whisky and pressed the trigger. The result was quite spectacular. The soda shot round the rim of the glass, leaving the whisky untouched, and sprayed all six first-class passengers. Fortunately, they all saw the funny side of it. No marks for good CRM that day!

I had digs in London, and a minivan to get around. To help pay for the flying lessons, I sold the minivan and bought a scooter and a caravan. Buying and setting up the caravan deserves a mention. I found a company in Sussex selling very cheap, second-hand caravans. A friend of mine said, "Why are they so cheap... because they are crap." One was advertised for £90. Too good to be true... and it was. I drove to the caravan site in a borrowed 1939 Ford Anglia saloon with Jim Kelly, an Irishman, who I met on the BEA steward's course.

A couple of weeks previously I had told Jim of my flying plans, and why every penny I had was spent on paying for my flying lessons. He decided to take up the challenge and also learned to fly at White Waltham. We became good friends. We arrived at the caravan site. The whole place looked like the set for the TV comedy series *Only Fools and Horses*. The salesman completed the picture, clad in sheepskin coat and flat cap. Pound notes were handed over and the caravan was ours.

"What vehicle are you going to tow it with?" enquired the salesman.

Jim looked at me, I looked at the salesman. "No!" the salesman exclaimed, pointing at our car. "You cannot tow it with that." Jim's command of the Irish blarney kicked in. He talked him into welding a tow hook to our car... no wiring for brake lights or indicators! Off we set, leaving the salesman shaking his head in disbelief.

With all the weight on the tow hook it meant the front wheels were barely touching the ground and so we unintentionally spent as much time on the right-hand side of the road as the left!

We had arranged with a local farmer to park our caravan in his yard, as it was close to White Waltham Airfield. He was there to greet us. He was a kindly old man, and, as we discovered, very tolerant of our antics with the caravan.

Although the caravan was conveniently positioned such that we could be at the airfield at the drop of a hat, that was its only advantage. It was very, very small, with two tiny single beds separated by a small space, a wardrobe, a tiny washbasin and an Elsan type toilet.

Jim and I shared this caravan for two years, and we are still friends! He retired as a senior captain with Singapore Airlines. Small world...

I devoted all my time to flying and the flying hours steadily increased. My first training flight in an Airways Aero Club Chipmunk was on 24th July 1962 with Joan Hughes. Joan had been a pilot with Air Transport Auxiliary (ATA), ferrying many aircraft types, including Spitfires during WWII. In 1940, ATA Headquarters was at White Waltham. In 1943, the women pilots and the men were given equal pay – a first for the government. ATA was disbanded on 30th November 1945. Lord Beaverbook gave a moving tribute to ATA at the closing ceremony at White Waltham:

"Without the ATA the days and nights of the Battle of Britain would have been conducted under conditions quite different from the actual events. They carried out the delivery of aircraft from the factories to the RAF, thus relieving countless numbers of pilots for duty in the battle. Just as the Battle of Britain is the accomplishment and achievement of the RAF, likewise it can be declared that the ATA sustained and supported them in the battle. They were soldiers fighting in the struggle just as completely as if they had been engaged on the battlefront."

Joan must have been about 70 years old when she flew the little Demoiselle aeroplane in the film *Those Magnificent Men in their Flying Machines.* Joan had great difficulty remembering names. She called everyone 'Thing'. She would say, "Hello old thing, is thing coming in later?"

I did several training flights with Joan. She was a very good instructor. Joan and Archie Cole became more like friends. Once a month, Archie, the CFI, used to take two or three of us into

Maidenhead and treat us to a sausage, egg and chips lunch.

The landlord and landlady of the Bridge House pub near White Waltham were very kind to Jim and me. They were full of enthusiasm for our flying plans and were very encouraging just when we needed it. Jim and I did get down in the dumps from time to time. After all, it was the 'Swinging Sixties'. Our friends and colleagues knew how to party and, although they thought Jim and I were 'strange', they were also quite understanding. We were often asked, "How many hours now?" referring to our flying hours gained towards our pilot's licence, or, "Keep going, you can do it!"

Once a week we would treat ourselves to an evening in the cosy Bridge House pub. If a customer offered to buy the hosts a drink, they would pour a half a pint of beer, but not drink it, passing it along the bar to us. At the end of the evening they would make up a 'pilot's platter' of bread, cheese, pickled onion and crisps – compliments of the house.

A Link trainer.

Around this period, I met Tony Angel. Tony was a BOAC flight simulator instructor. He had installed a Link trainer in a small room at the end of the clubhouse at White Waltham. It was a basic machine, but a very cheap way of learning to fly on instruments. Invented by Ed Link in 1929, it was used extensively to train pilots to fly on instruments. During the Second World War it is estimated that over 500,000 US pilots were trained on Ed's machines. From the outside, it looks like a cartoon-style light aircraft, However, when you are completely enclosed, with the hood and door closed, it doesn't seem quite so funny.

The photo above was taken in the 1950s, hence the hazy picture. It shows a Royal Naval Lieutenant RNVR pilot instructor monitoring the student's flight path by a crablike device that drew an ink trail on the desktop.

I remember it was very claustrophobic with the hood down. Pneumatic organ-type bellows drove the whole contraption. The original parts came from Ed's dad's piano and organ works based in Binghamton, New York. The more you struggled to keep on the correct track, the more the bellows hissed and bellowed... No wonder the simulators that followed on from Ed's pioneering work were known as sweat boxes.

Tony Angel became our guru. He took us under his wing (no pun intended). We used to go to his house in Maidenhead for tuition on radio aids and top tips for the Civil Aviation Authority (CAA) ground exams. The evening included a bath and dinner, in that order...

The winter of 1962/63 was severe. In January 1963, the average temperature was -2, the coldest recorded since 1814. All flying was cancelled for two months or more. We went to the flying club anyway as it was cosy and warm. The only heating in our caravan was a tiny paraffin stove. The nights were so cold the paraffin started to freeze over. Some mornings we had to pour hot water around the edge of the caravan door to get it to open. In order to get warm, we found it easier to have 20 minutes sparring (boxing) in the yard. One day, when we were going at it, the old farmer appeared, waving his arms and shouting, "Don't fight boys, don't fight, it's not that bad."

At the flying club one day, Archie said, "You are getting under my feet, why don't you go and fly where the weather is good."

"But, where?" we replied.

"Go to Spain, of course."

It was to be some time before we launched off on our 'epic' trip in the club's Terrier, G-ARZU. The Terrier was an upmarket Auster, easy to fly and ideal for touring.

The launch date was 22nd August 1963. The complete trip took two weeks, with 30 hours flying to record in our logbooks. The Terrier had side-by-side seating. Each sector we flew as a training flight. The handling pilot or captain sat in the left-hand seat and the co-pilot on the right. We would change seats on the next sector. We used 'borrowed' flight crew checklists from a BEA Vanguard.

We flew from White Waltham to Le Touquet via the low-level

Channel crossing, cleared customs and commenced our trip. The 'co-pilot' was responsible for the navigation and catering. The catering consisted of baguettes, cheese and a bottle of milk. This was served on every sector. As qualified BEA stewards, this arrangement did not tax our catering skills too much!

Our Terrier.
Photo courtesy The Peter Keating Collection(c) A Flying History Ltd.

Beers or wine were reserved for post flight. Most of the airfields we visited had a bar next to the control tower or flying club. A wonderful way to end the day was with a glass of wine, looking across a grass airfield, watching the sun go down. Henry Nicholls, a farmer friend had a saying for such a time: "You can't put a price on it." We would discuss the day's events and make plans for the morrow.

My logbook shows stops at Dinard, Bordeaux, Toulouse, Barcelona, Deauville, Le Touquet, and La Baule... not necessarily in that order. The leg from Perpignan to Barcelona was navigated using a BEA passenger flight guide. Well... aeronautical charts are expensive! Jim Kelly was navigating this sector. Under the circumstances he did a good job finding the gap in the Pyrenees at Carcassonne.

The weather was good throughout our trip, with long days flying over the beautiful French countryside, it was a sheer pleasure.

On the way home we landed at La Baule Airfield in Brittany. Its 100th anniversary was in 2017. We particularly wanted to visit this historic airfield. During WWII the Germans requisitioned the airfield. The Saint-Nazaire pocket, including La Baule was the last region of France to be liberated in May 1945. General De Gaulle visited the airfield in July 1945.

When we arrived there, we had run out of money, and this was in the days before credit cards. The club's flying instructor found a place for us to sleep, fed us, refuelled the aircraft the next day and even checked the weather for us. We thanked him and said we would refund him when we got back home… and we did.

When I was in the RAF and based at Martlesham Heath in Suffolk, most weekends I would drive down to Brighton in a borrowed 1939 Ford Anglia to stay with my sister Joan and her husband Clem. It became a tradition that at the end of the day on Sundays, I would drive up to London, park in the middle of London Bridge at midnight and wait about half an hour to give a lift to any stragglers who had missed the last train back to base. It was a long drive. I thought this little act of kindness would be rewarded by some sort of company on the four-hour journey through the night. How wrong I was. Some nights, four figures literally staggered out of the darkness, jumped in and fell fast asleep.

Martlesham Heath was a historic airfield. The airfield opened in 1917. It housed the RAF's Experimental Flight. In 1940, during WWII, Group Captain Douglas Bader DSO, DFC served there. The airfield closed in 1960 and the old control tower at Martlesham Heath is a now a museum.

Many acts of kindness also came from people like my sister Joan and her husband Clem. Right from Day One, when I told my sister Joan my flying plans, she was full of encouragement, both financially and morally. She was horrified when I said I was going to live in a caravan. "Darling," she said, "you are going to starve to death. I will teach you to cook." Joan and Clem had a beautiful house in Brighton. I loved spending time down there with them, overdosing on TLC, and learning to cook.

Joan was 18 years old and working in London when WWII started. At night she would join my father on fire watch. When an air raid was taking place and the bombs were falling, my sister and father stood on top of a high office building in the middle of the city of London and made a note of where the bombs fell. A report was made to the Fire Brigade or an Air Raid Warden. As you can imagine, it was extremely hazardous work. When they had finished their duties, or the 'all clear' was given, they would walk home through the bomb-damaged streets. They would have to walk three miles or so as there was no transport.

Joan had a boyfriend who was a B17 pilot in the US 8th Air Force. When the war ended the crew of the B17 took their English girlfriends for a trip in their bomber to Paris. Joan went there and back in the bomb bay of a B17!

In 1963, when I gained my Private Pilot's Licence (PPL), I phoned Joan to say a big thank you for all the support, and I would love to take her up for a flight. She expressed great interest, but her husband Clem told her, "Don't you go up with Brian, he has only just got his licence." Joan, however, was not going to be fazed by a short hop in a light aircraft. Plans were made. I flew from White Waltham to Shoreham Airport where I met my sister.

I said, "How about we just make a short flight to the Isle of Wight and back?"

"OK," she said, somewhat nervously. Her husband was standing there, arms folded with a disapproving look on his face.

I was flying a Chipmunk aircraft with tandem seats. Joan sat behind me. We took off and headed for the Isle of Wight. We had been flying for just about ten minutes or so when Joan called me on the intercom from the back seat. "Hello darling, it is lovely, but I think that's enough. Shall we go back now?"

When I was in my teens I said to Joan, "What was it *really* like in London during The Blitz?"

Photo of my sister Joan taken during WWII.

She said, "The parties were wonderful." There were soldiers, sailors and airmen from all over the world. The girls could not believe their luck, neither could the men. One night she was at an underground party. The bombs were falling and all the lights went out. Candles were lit and everyone carried on dancing and drinking. An Air Raid Warden appeared, shone a torch around and said, "Anyone hurt in here?"

"No," they all replied.

He persisted. "Is there anyone pregnant here?"

A girl's voice from the back of the room replied, "Give us a chance mate, we've only just arrived!"

During WWII, the Glenn Miller Band was playing in London and my sister was introduced to Glenn himself. A couple of days later, on 15th December 1944, Glenn was due to fly to Paris in a UC-64 Norseman light aircraft. The band was to give a series of Christmas concerts.

A UC-64 Norseman aircraft. Acknowledgements to USAF Museum.

Sadly, on the night of the flight, the aircraft disappeared, and to this day no trace of the aircraft, the crew, or Glenn has been found.

Many years later, I drove my sister to West Malling Airfield where Glenn's younger brother Herb and the Herb Miller Band were playing under the wing of a B17. We were part of a huge crowd held back by a rope surrounding the aircraft. We pushed our way to the front. I asked one of the guards if my sister could just say hello to Herb.

"Sure," he said, and raised the rope barrier.

Joan rushed up to Herb and said, "I met Glenn a couple of days before he disappeared."

Herb put his arms round her and said, "Well, why didn't you hang on to him?"

My sister would often ask my daughter Kerry to sing Glenn

Miller's tune *Moonlight Serenade*. There wasn't a dry eye in the house!

I studied for the ground exams at the Sir John Cass College in Aldgate. A branch of this school was originally designed to teach merchant seamen for their master's certificate. In the 1960s it started teaching aviation subjects and I joined one of the first courses. There was no space to fit us in at their main school in Aldgate, so a room was found for us in a tiny building by the Tower of London. Although it was small, we were delighted to share the building with the art students. One day, an art student appeared, a very attractive young lady, and asked if any of us wanted to join the student union. Technical books were slammed shut and we all volunteered to join.

Eventually, I was back to serious studying. Avigation Ltd was another college specialising in a tutorial system when you were cramming for the ground exams. There would be a daily programme posted of subjects that would be covered that day. You could just turn up and choose a subject, and at the appointed time join the class. There was always a teacher available to provide guidance or assistance.

One teacher I remember very well was Mr Podmore. I was told he was a veteran of WWII, having served as a navigator in the Merchant Navy, mostly in the North Atlantic convoys. On one occasion, when I was struggling to master the art of magnetism and compasses, I put my hand up for his help. He pulled up a chair, sat down and produced a propelling pencil. He was very proud of this pencil and spent some time getting it to a fine point. He lit his pipe.

"Now," he said with a sigh, "let's have a little look." With one hand he swept all my work onto the floor. He then produced a large sheet of clean paper, laid it on my desk as if it were a bed sheet, rather like a conjurer, and drew several lines very quickly. He turned to me and said with a smile, "Well?"

As if by magic, his 'few lines' turned into a working drawing of a compass and cleared up all my confusion. Everything was crystal clear. Pure genius! I passed all the technical exams. Thanks to Mr Podmore.

On one occasion, I left the college at the end of a long day spent studying meteorology. My brain was full of warm fronts, cold fronts and dewpoints. The highs and lows and depressions were getting to me. Wearily, I boarded the underground train. It was very crowded; I was jammed against the end door of the carriage. I reached down and took a book from the briefcase at my feet. It was a large, buff-coloured book, with the title *The Handbook of Aviation Meteorology* in bold print on the cover. I opened the book and started to read. After a couple minutes, I looked up. Right down at the far end of the carriage was a man reading the same book! He looked up and gave me a huge wink, and a thumbs up, then carried on reading.

On 10th March 1964 I took my CPL check flight in a Chipmunk aircraft at Stansted with Dan Thomas of the CAA. One of the exercises was to make a short field landing. This is a demanding exercise to be used when the length of the runway or landing area is relatively short. The final approach is flown at a slow speed, close to the stall. On touchdown in a tail dragger the correct technique is to hold the stick hard back, followed by relatively hard sustained braking.

I braked so hard the Chipmunk nearly tipped on to its nose. Although he did not show it, Dan was taken by surprise and quite rightly I was only given a partial pass. I retook the test with Dan (nerves of steel) on 23rd March. A full pass was awarded.

My pilot's logbook showed a total of 205 flying hours and 15 minutes in 23 months. I felt I had completed my first task. I posted my application form for a UK Commercial Pilot's Licence to the CAA, with the appropriate fee. A couple of weeks later my licence arrived in the post. I tore open the envelope. I looked at this document, which consisted of two sheets of paper, bound in a blue coloured cardboard cover, tied up with string. I did not know whether to laugh or cry. After all the blood, sweat, tears and considerable cost, was this it?

Of course, I did see the funny side of it and with a Commercial Pilot's Licence in my hand I started to look for a job. I made a start by looking in the Situations Vacant section of *Flight* magazine. I say 'look', as I did not purchase a copy, but would pretend to be browsing in WHSmith. After quickly noting any jobs, I would replace the magazine.

At that time, the aviation industry seemed to be going through a three-year cycle of employing pilots. This cycle of 'feast or famine' made it the luck of the draw regarding finding any type of employment. I scoured the magazines, but no opportunities appeared. Until one day...

2. MY FIRST JOB

An advert in *Flight* magazine showed Tube Investments (TI) were advertising for a co-pilot. They were operating a Heron 2E as an executive transport. It said to apply in writing. I was desperate to secure my first job, so I decided to use the phone and managed to get through to their operations room.

The chief pilot, Jack Goodrum, answered the phone. He said, somewhat tersely, "It says 'apply in writing'."

I poured out my story.

"Well, when can you come for an interview?"

"Right now," I replied.

"OK, let's see how much you really want this job, how soon can you get here?"

I just jumped on my scooter and set off for Birmingham as fast as I could. It was pouring with rain. Out of 42 applicants I got the job. Good result! I started flying for TI on 15th June 1964. It was a wonderful first job.

All the team were great people and the aircraft was a joy to fly, with four engines and retractable gear. We mostly carried Lord Plowden, the chairman, to visit many of TI's factories. This meant operating into small, sometimes disused, airfields. We used Decca Navigator as our primary let-down aid. It had an early version of a moving map display. From this information we made up our own let-down patterns.

During this time, I gained my Instrument Rating. This required two trips to Stansted Airfield. Both of these experiences showed me the worst and best of examining. How not to do it, and how it should be done. Although I was very inexperienced as a pilot, I was a trained instructor, having been through an instructor training system in the RAF, which was very advanced for its day.

The day at Stansted Airfield dawned, grey and overcast with a strong crosswind. I reported to the reception in the CAA building and was pointed to the briefing room. The detail consisted of a flight in the CAA's Dove aircraft. The forward windscreens were blanked out with a type of venetian blind, angled such that the examiner could see out, but the candidate could not.

A De Havilland Heron 2E, similar to the Tube Investments aircraft.
Photo from AirTeamImages.com.

The idea was to complete all manoeuvres purely by reference to the flight instruments – a holding pattern, an Instrument Landing System (ILS) and go-around, all completed to very fine accuracy or limits. In the briefing room I was engrossed in the information supplied by the Met Office. It was to be my decision to call the flight on or off.

The briefing room door swung open with a crash and there stood my examiner, a giant of a man – all gold braid and beard. "Name?" he boomed. "Are you ready to take the test?"

I replied that I was concerned that the crosswind might be outside my limits.

He rolled his eyes and snorted impatiently, "Are you ready to take this test or not?"

I meekly replied yes, and off we went, out to the aircraft. I failed the ILS part of the test. With my head down, I shuffled out of the crew room.

Photo of the Dove cockpit from The de Havilland Aircraft Museum.

The receptionist said, "There is a slot available tomorrow, would you like to take it?" My spirits were low, and so was the money in my pocket. The thought of further expense, a night stop in Bishop Stortford and a retest did not appeal. But, I said, "Yes" ...and thank God I did.

The next day dawned with cloud and visibility OK – defined as cloud ceiling above 5,000 feet and visibility more than ten kilometres – CAVOK (Ceiling And Visibility OK). Wind calm. Perfect conditions for flying.

After my experience of the day before, I went into the briefing room like a condemned man. There was a knock on the door and it swung slowly open. The examiner stood there with his hands in his pockets. "Hi," he said, "it's Brian isn't it? Looks a nice day for flying. Let's go and knock this old ILS on the head, shall we?"

I flew the best I have ever flown and passed the test. Maybe you suspect a slight exaggeration of the two characters, but when I became an examiner, I used that example of the 'bad' and 'good' CRM many times.

About this time, I had a phone call from my friend Jim Kelly to say he had secured a place on a cadet course with Aer Lingus, the Irish airline. I said I had just secured a flying job with TI. Things were looking up! Huge smiles all-round. Both Jim and I were well aware of how the cards had fallen for us. We resolved to never forget our beginnings.

We both had some free time for a couple of days and decided to go back to White Waltham and say hello to Archie Cole, our chief flying instructor (CFI.) We arrived at the airfield in the afternoon on a gorgeous spring day; light winds with just a few fair weather clouds. Archie was there to greet us. "Just the men I was looking for," he said with a wry smile. "I have sent a student off to complete his solo cross country. He has got himself lost and has been flying around the Gloucester area for some time, eventually landing at Staverton Airfield. He said he does not want to fly ever again, and wants me to fly over and pick him up. How about you boys come with me. I will pick him up and fly him back. You can both bring his aircraft back. Let's go. Oh, by the way there is a party in the clubhouse tonight!"

Jim and I both said, "Sure, why not?" After all, we thought we were proper commercial pilots now... Pride comes before a fall!

The three of us climbed into a four-seater Gemini aircraft and off we went. When we arrived at Staverton Airfield, the student was looking pale and shaken. He ignored Jim and I, and immediately jumped into Archie's aircraft. Archie shrugged his shoulders and said, "See you back at White Waltham, don't forget the party!"

Somewhat hesitantly we said OK. We were left standing on the tarmac, with our mouths open, no money, no flight bags, just the clothes we stood up in.

We checked in with air traffic control, then went to the aircraft and started the pre-flight checks. Nothing appeared amiss, until we tried to start the engine. It eventually fired up, but it was running roughly and the magneto check confirmed it was not flyable. Our guess was that he had been flying around with the throttle closed, engine at idle, and the plugs may have oiled up. We set off to find a mechanic who would clean or change the plugs. However, we had forgotten it was Saturday night and the airfield was about to close. We tried calling Archie on the radio, but he was out of VHF range. From the control tower, we put a call through to White Waltham Airfield to request Archie to phone us as soon as possible. Eventually, Archie called. "I cannot come to pick you up *now*."

The sun was setting and, of course, the party was about to start. Lucky Archie. Tough on us! However, he did say, "Stay the night in a hotel and fly back tomorrow, send the bill to the Flying Club." The air traffic controllers took pity on us and booked us into a hotel and gave us the money for the bus to Cheltenham. The bus stopped outside a very smart hotel. I cannot remember the name. The receptionist asked if we had any ID, and how were we going to pay?

This was before the days of credit cards and we did not have a single penny between us. I said, "Not to worry, all expenses would be covered by the Airways Aero Club." The receptionist was not impressed with an Englishman named Smith, and an Irishman named Kelly. She said she needed something in writing to secure payment. Things weren't looking good, and were about to get worse. I said confidently, "If I can use your phone, I will call our chief flying instructor. He will vouch for us."

The club's phone rang and rang. I concluded everyone, including Archie, were partying. Right on schedule it got worse. The receptionist called the manager. He said we could stay the night if we would be able to contact Archie in the morning and payment made. We reassured him all would be fine in the morning. By this time we were very hungry and ready for dinner. We approached the dining room only to be stopped by the very smart headwaiter.

"Sorry gentlemen, the rules are jacket and tie required." We rapidly poured out our story. Eyebrows were raised, and the nose was looked down. He phoned the manager. "Follow me," he said. He quickly escorted us down to the waiters' changing room where he selected two waiters' jackets and two bow ties for us. The jackets were bright red with gold braid collars, and hugely oversized. We looked as if we were the comic turn for the evening's entertainment as we shuffled to our table. You can imagine the look on the other diners' faces.

The next morning we phoned Archie, and he phoned the hotel and arranged payment. The plugs had been changed on the aircraft and we flew back to White Waltham. It was a beautiful summer's morning. We had no maps on board, but we knew the way, and visibility was unlimited. It was an unforgettable weekend.

On my return to Birmingham there was a note to say the chief pilot of TI wanted to see me first thing in the morning. What could it be about? I wondered. I entered the office.

The chief pilot looked over his specs, saying that he did not think it quite fitting for the co-pilot of the TI executive aircraft to be seen pottering about on a scooter. How would I like to have the car which one of the ground engineers wanted to sell? He paused, still looking over the top of his specs, and said in a gruff voice like Winston Churchill's, "I suggest you buy it." I was delighted. It was a bright yellow Ford Anglia.

I had digs in Solihull with Mrs Smith, no relation. She was a very kind person. Every night she would cook dinner for me and the other young lodger. I tried to explain there would be many nights when I worked shifts and would not be back until late, so would not require dinner.

"Oh, no problem," she said, "I will just leave it in the oven for you."

By the time I came home, sometimes via the pub, my dinner had been in the oven several hours, and was inedible. I did not want to offend Mrs Smith by not eating the dinner she had prepared for me, so I developed a routine. I would take the plate out of the oven, read the newspaper for a couple of minutes, then scoop my dinner, which was by now cool, into a paper bag, which I carefully put into my briefcase.

The next morning, on my way to the airfield, I would open the car window and throw the bag over a hedge. I felt it was OK as it was biodegradable. Do cows eat cottage pie? I did this over a period of a year! I fully expected that one day the farmer might appear with a shotgun, and shout, *"Got yer, yer bugger!"* and let me have it with both barrels.

Life was good with TI, and I had learned much from Jack Goodrum, Ken Young and 'Jeep' Holmes. One day, I asked Jeep how he came by his nickname. *"Because I can fly anywhere and fly anything, a completely general purpose sort of bloke!"* was the laconic reply. He could not only do it, he made it look very easy. I felt, rightly or wrongly, that I should move on and join an airline. My last trip with TI was on 23rd August 1965 with Captain 'Jeep' Holmes.

Shortly after I left TI, I heard the following story: It was the time of the prestigious Annual Toy Fair in Nuremberg and TI flew a group of their executives in the company Heron to Nuremburg from Birmingham. The founder of another company, JCB, also based in Birmingham, was Joseph Cyril Bamford. In 1945 he added a hydraulic digger to a conventional tractor and they sold in their millions. JCB had an HS125 eight-seater business jet aircraft. They also flew to the toy fair.

Both aircraft were to spend the day there and were parked side by side on the tarmac by the control tower. It was an extremely hot day. The JCB aircraft had an Auxiliary Power Unit (APU). This provides power to the aircraft and runs the air-conditioning. The Heron did not have an APU and, as a result, it was very hot in the cabin.

The passengers on the TI Heron, who were hot and thirsty, sent their assistant James (not his real name) to the terminal to pick up some sandwiches and drinks for the flight back. James looked and behaved rather like Bernard, the Prime Minister's harassed private secretary in the 1980's TV series *Yes, Minister*.

James rushed off. When he came out of the terminal he was

clutching a pile of sandwiches and cold drinks. The Heron had disappeared... somewhat distressed, he ran towards the area where it had been parked.

The captain of the JCB aircraft waved to him. "Hello," he said, "don't look so worried, air traffic control called the TI aircraft to say can they start up NOW, otherwise they would have a two-hour delay to their departure. They have just taken off and are on their way back to Birmingham. You can come back with us."

James, somewhat shocked by the proceedings, climbed the steps into the air-conditioned cabin. An immaculately dressed stewardess showed him to his seat. "Would you like a cool drink, Sir?" she asked. "May I suggest a gin and tonic, and would you like me to take your packages?"

James quickly replied, "Yes to the gin and tonic, thank you, but I would like to hold on to the packages."

Halfway through an excellent dinner of steak and chips, the captain appeared and said, "I hope you are being looked after. You might be interested to know we passed the TI Heron five minutes ago."

After landing at Birmingham, James, still clutching the package of sandwiches and drinks, was told the TI Heron was due to land in 30 minutes. He waited patiently outside the terminal. Eventually, the TI passengers appeared, looking somewhat dishevelled, clearly hungry and thirsty. "Good evening gentlemen," he said, "I have your refreshments right here."

3. BRITISH UNITED AIR FERRIES (BUAF)

I was sorry to say farewell to Tube Investments and the friends I had made there. On 2nd September 1965 I joined British United Air Ferries as a co-pilot, based at Lydd on the Kent coast, flying the Bristol Freighter B170.

Silver City Airways started the cross-Channel car ferry in 1948. I often wondered, 'How did Silver City get its name?' A huge mine in Broken Hill, Australia started to mine silver. The silver mining grew and grew, until Broken Hill became known as the Silver City. In 1946, an airline to serve the mining industry was given the name 'Silver City Airways'. Eventually, the airline was transferred to Lympne in Kent, a former grass WWII airfield. In 1948 the airline inaugurated the first air ferry service from Lympne to Le Touquet.

A Silver City Airways Ltd poster, circa 1950s.

Once operations started, using heavy cargo aircraft, it proved impossible to operate on the grass runway in the winter months, so the operation was moved to Lydd, a purpose-built airfield a few miles south, at Dungeness. The airfield was built by Costain in six months, quite an achievement. This new location was ideal for short hops across the Channel to Le Touquet, Ostend, Calais and Deauville. At one time it was busier than Heathrow Airport.

The Duke of Edinburgh visited Silver City Airways Ltd at Lydd. He was to fly in the Bristol Freighter from Lydd to Le Touquet. The Duke had a reputation as a 'hands on' sort of person. He was invited to close the huge clamshell doors and put the locks in place. Unfortunately, the locks had been painted with red paint the day before and the paint had not quite dried. There were many red faces amongst the staff as well as red hands. The Duke saw the funny side of it though.

A typical working day would involve four, sometimes six, trips across the Channel. Le Touquet was my favourite destination. A visit to the airport bar and restaurant during the turnround was a must to get the true flavour of France. The décor was all polished wood with the wing of a 1930s aircraft over the top of the bar, like an awning, with waiters rushing about with plates of moules et frites. Although we could not have alcoholic drinks, we had time to sit and enjoy this happy scene before taking cars and passengers back to Lydd. We operated in pool with a French company, Compagnie Air Transport (CAT), operating Bristol Freighters based in Le Touquet. In the summer months, some of the CAT stewardesses, carrying sacks of moules and bottles of wine, would come over for a weekend in Greatstone-on-Sea, next to Lydd Airport. Happy days!

On one occasion I was due to fly with a captain who had just been posted to Lydd. He had already gained a reputation as a pompous type, who considered co-pilots inferior beings. We set off on our first sector to Ostend. In those days it was quite normal to smoke in flight. I asked the captain would he mind if I smoked. I explained I smoked a pipe. Much to my surprise he agreed, and added that he also smoked a pipe. I began to think all was going well, when he produced an ornately carved pipe, I believe it was called a Meerschaum. We puffed away happily.

In the roof of the cockpit there was a hole, designed to take an emergency Very pistol. The name Very pistol is derived from the name of the inventor, Lt. Edward W. Very of the US Navy. He invented a large-calibre single shot pistol, with a single action firing mechanism that could fire special flares into the air. The hole was always open; it gave an improved airflow in the cockpit.

As was the custom, when I finished my smoke, I held my pipe against the hole. With one tap it was clean. "What *are* you doing?" the captain asked.

I explained.

He nodded his head and proceeded to tap his pipe. There was a loud sucking noise, and the top of the expensive Meerschaum disappeared. To this day he believes I played a prank on him. The rest of the day's flying was completed in total silence.

I also flew with Captain Bert Hayes, former RAF Hurricane pilot. After the war, I understand he was employed by Silver City as a loader. He invented a wheel shackle, with a quick release mechanism for holding cars down in flight. The company was interested in buying the copyright from Bert. He negotiated a deal with them, but rather than pay for the copyright, they paid for Bert to obtain his Commercial Pilot's Licence, and to employ him as a pilot.

In the Lydd Operations Room, a large board had the latest NOTAMS pinned up. NOTAMS are 'notices to airmen', usually listing operational matters.

One day the following notice appeared: '*Filming is to take place at Lydd Airport over the next few days. This will involve film personnel and vehicles moving about the airfield. This should not cause any inconvenience or disruption to normal operations.*'

We learned that there was a film to be made called *That Riviera*

Touch, starring Morecambe and Wise, two famous comedians. Part of the film involved flying the stars to Le Touquet in a Bristol Freighter with their vintage car. At the last minute, a cost-cutting plan to convert Lydd Airport to Le Touquet Airport swung into effect. Clearly, cancelling all the flying sequences would save money. The day the filming started, we taxied out on a routine commercial flight to fly to Le Touquet.

We were surprised to see the filmmakers had taken down the Lydd Airport sign on the control tower and replaced it with a new sign saying Aéroport Le Touquet. To complete the deception a French registered Peugeot was parked on the tarmac, complete with a gendarme at the wheel.

A busy day at Lydd.

At Le Touquet we picked up our passengers and set off back to Lydd. When we landed and taxied towards the control tower, we remarked how all the new Aéroport Le Touquet signs were still there. We shut down the engines. This is usually followed by a moment of silence, as if the whole operation was giving a sigh at the end of a long day. Not this time, however. We became aware of much noise and commotion at the rear of the aircraft. We went to investigate and were met by our passengers. They were shouting and pointing at the sign on the control tower. No one could understand what they were saying, or why they were so angry. Eventually, it transpired that they thought we had been flying them around for half an hour or so, and then landed back at Le Touquet! Just when the interpreter appeared to have calmed them down, a French registered Peugeot was driven across the tarmac and the shouting started all over again.

I think it is fair to say that the B170 was not the most elegant looking aircraft ever built, but it did the job it was designed for and did it very well. The story goes that it flew to Canada in August 1946. Flying to Canada in 1946, in a twin-engine, unpressurised aircraft with minimum navigational aids was in itself no mean feat. It was a great distance, via Scotland, Iceland and Greenland on to Canada. This was the first leg of a 41,000-mile sales tour of North and South America. Although the following story is true, there is some doubt as to exactly where in the world it took place. Was it Gander, Canada or during the Berlin Airlift? Does it matter? It is a good story...

As the Bristol Freighter popped out of cloud on final approach, the air traffic controller said, "Say, what sort of airplane is that?"

The test pilot very proudly said, "It is a Bristol Freighter Mk170."

"Gee," came the reply, "you mean to say they had 169 goes and they came up with that!"

On another approach at a different airfield the controller asked, "What sort of airplane is that?"

The test pilot replied, "It is a Bristol Freighter Mk170."

Controller: "Wow, did you make it yourself?"

To save space here, if you take a look on YouTube for 'Bristol Freighter B170' you will find the full story of this remarkable aircraft.

The long-nosed Mk32 version (did they really have 31 goes?) could accommodate three cars loaded in through the front clamshell doors. There was a small cabin at the back of the hold for the passengers, complete with a stewardess to look after them. The pilots' flight deck was housed above the hold – B747 style.

The only means of communication from the passenger cabin to the flight deck was by intercom. In the side wall by the co-pilot's seat an amber light would flash when the stewardess wished to contact the pilots.

One day, as we taxied out, the amber light came on. The stewardess's voice came over the intercom. "Hello up there, I'm *not* ready for take-off."

"OK," I replied, "what's the problem?"

"Oh it's awful," she said, "I have forgotten my drawers!" Stunned silence. I understood the problem right away. The cabinets, which were stowed in the little galley, had drawers inside to carry the duty-free drinks. Part of the pre-flight checks was to open the drawers and check they were correctly loaded. We subsequently learnt she had just finished her training. It was the poor girl's first flight on her own, with a full complement of passengers. She had not checked her drawers!

The captain, who had been listening, recovered his composure, called the control tower to explain we had a problem and would have to return to the ramp as the stewardess had forgotten her drawers. I leave you to imagine the controller's reaction.

At a recent BUAF reunion, one of the former B170 captains I used to fly with asked if I had ever flown 'the sheep run to Ostend'. Yes. I remembered it well... on one occasion, approximately 120 sheep were jammed into the aircraft hold and transported to Ostend on a 'one way ticket'. On that very hot day, as the sheep were being loaded at Lydd, the ground engineer said to the captain, "The sheep have to arrive alive, or we don't get paid." It was particularly hot in the hold. The engineer went on to say, "Why don't we take out the emergency windows, they are only held in by four bolts." It was agreed and thus allowed the sheep some fresh air in flight.

"Good idea," said the captain.

The flight was uneventful. The aircraft landed and taxied to the side of the field, the clamshell doors were opened and the sheep disembarked. The agent, who was counting the sheep, quietly informed the captain that one sheep was missing. It had jumped out in flight!

The Bristol Freighter could carry horses and Dublin to Deauville was a regular run. One flight en route from Dublin it was carrying very expensive racehorses, and a huge stallion went berserk. It started kicking its stall to pieces. The whole aircraft started to shake. One of the grooms hurried to the cockpit and explained to the captain that if they could land as soon as possible, it would be far better than tranquilising the horse. At the time, the aircraft was flying over an RAF station in Wales. The captain called the station on VHF radio and declared an emergency. Clearance was given to land.

After landing, the aircraft taxied to the edge of the parking area. The clamshell doors were opened and the stallion leapt out with two grooms clinging to his harness. Within seconds the horse was peacefully grazing on the grass at the edge of the tarmac. It was only then the grooms and the pilots noticed a large brass band and airmen lined up as if on parade.

An RAF officer came striding over, and shouted, "What the hell do you think you are doing?"

The captain started to explain. The officer cut him short and continued, "This band and airmen have not turned out to greet YOU and that bloody horse. Do you realise the Air Officer Commanding [AOC] has been flying round in circles waiting for you to land, so he could carry out his annual inspection of the station!"

It must have looked an incongruous sight. A very smart RAF wing commander, a civilian airline captain and co-pilot, two grooms in brown overalls and wellies, plus a horse. The horse must have seen the funny side of it, as it let out a huge fart, and then deposited a pile of manure on the manicured grass.

There was a roar of jet engines and the AOC's immaculate aircraft landed and taxied in. The band struck up and the airmen were called to attention. Out stepped the great man.

Instead of inspecting the parade, he came over, patted the horse and said, "Well done chaps, I have already heard all about this incident. I wasn't looking forward to today, all rather boring really. But you have put a smile on my face. I would invite you all for lunch, but I think I would be pushing my luck. Goodbye... and have fun!"

4. BOAC AND BEYOND...

Happy though we were with BUAF, my colleagues and I always looked at the situations vacant section of *Flight* magazine. One copy had a half page advert: *BOAC recruiting direct entry pilots.*

Decisions had to be made, and fast. To cut a long story short, all four of us were offered jobs. Personally, I was surprised that I had been selected. My background as a 'self-improver' with a measly 1,000 flying hours did not fit the mould of the other successful applicants.

It was some years later that I became aware of the BOAC interview procedure. One of the questions from the interview panel was, *'Do you know anyone in BOAC?'* I said I knew Tony Angel – BOAC simulator instructor. Nothing further was said.

I subsequently learnt that immediately after the interview they spoke to Tony to ask if he knew me and, in short, was I any good. Tony must have given me a good review. I passed the interview. I owe much to Tony Angel, as we shall see as the story unfolds.

I had about three weeks leave before I joined BOAC. Time to pause and reflect on what was, or what I thought was, to come. I hired a boat on the Norfolk Broads and in the peace and quiet spent some time there attempting to prepare myself for this momentous change to my life.

On my boat, I read Ernest Gann's book *Fate is the Hunter*. His description of life as an airline pilot in the 1930s, and as a civilian pilot in WWII is highly regarded throughout the aviation world. With the greatest respect, I have tried to emulate his style in writing this book. I also came to realise how fortunate I had been to listen and learn from my previous captains.

On 6th June 1966 I joined BOAC as a direct entry co-pilot. We started our extensive ground school to learn how the B707 worked. At first I struggled with the transition from the Bristol 170 to the Boeing 707. Everything was different, not difficult, but different – bigger and heavier, four jet engines, faster, and higher. My brain was overloaded with learning all about yaw dampers, Dutch rolls, Mach numbers and high-altitude flight. The list seemed endless. It was all what we called 'talk and chalk' in those days, no computers and we all found it hard work.

I became friends with two other pilots on my course, Clive Ritchie and Guy Stephenson. Clive was the most experienced, and a very capable pilot, having flown as a co-pilot with BKS, an independent airline. Guy was an ex-RAF instructor, given Grade A status all round. Two weeks or so into the ground school our instructor informed us that from next week we were to start our flight navigators' course.

"Whoa! Hold your horses," we all cried. "We have joined as co-pilots not navigators."

Our instructor patiently explained that every flight had two co-pilots and on the long oceanic sectors one would navigate and one would co-pilot. It did not take long to add up my education qualifications and I quickly realised I required more than one GCE in English to stand any chance of becoming a flight navigator.

Our flight navigation instructor was Mr Jones, who immediately became known to us as 'Jones the Star'. He stressed the need to study and get to know the stars and constellations if we were to succeed in astro nav and recommended a booklet: *A Field Guide to the Stars and Planets.* We rushed out and bought the book. He said the way to learn was to find a dark sky area, take a torch and a blanket, lie down and study the stars. Simple?

Clive took control and arranged for us to drive out to White Waltham Airfield. We walked onto the middle of the grass airfield, spread our blankets and lay side by side in the darkness, torch and book at hand. I could not contain myself any longer and burst out laughing.

"What's wrong?" asked Clive.

I said, "If a policeman comes along now, how do we explain, 'It's alright officer we were just looking at the stars!'" Clive did see the funny side of it.

The BOAC training was very thorough. We were scheduled for each session to fly as a pair. At the end of the first half you changed seats, one half handling, the other half co-piloting. I was paired up with Norman Britten, former Navy fast jet pilot, a character, and a superb handler of the 707. He was not fazed one bit by the 707, the new life in BOAC and all that went with it. However, Norman had had no experience as a co-pilot or working with other crew members using what we now call CRM, Crew Resource Management. When Norman was flying and I was his co-pilot we were a great team. All went smoothly. However, when I was flying, with the combination of my handling and Norman's co-piloting skills we quickly went from heroes to zeroes. However, Norman's career subsequently went supersonic and he ended up flying as a captain on Concorde – a very well respected pilot.

The flight simulator instruction was excellent and I must have cottoned on as we were allowed to go forward to base training. At last we were to get to handle the real aircraft. 707 Base Training took place at Shannon, Ireland. We were there for about a week. Our instructors were senior BOAC training captains. Shannon Airfield on the south-west corner of Ireland suited our requirements perfectly. It had a long runway, with very little other air traffic to interrupt us. The Emerald Isle lived up to its name – not that we had much time to gaze at the scenery as we flew round the circuit, green field followed green field, bordered by the mighty Shannon River and the Atlantic Ocean.

On a day off, I visited Foynes, near Limerick. There is an excellent museum there dedicated to preserving the memory of the golden age of the trans-Atlantic flying boats. There was one story the curator loved to tell you: One time the flying boat arrived from New York in the early hours. The passengers disembarked into the terminal. They were cold and hungry.

The airline agent said to the waiter, "Could you put something in their coffee to warm them up a bit?" The waiter poured a shot of Irish whiskey into each coffee. Eureka! Irish Coffee was born in Foynes, Ireland!

Flying the 707

As I recall, we explored many of the flight characteristics, including high-speed runs, the effect of flying controls in various configurations, and then on into the circuit to cram in plenty of landings.

It was a steep learning curve for me. To go from propeller power to jet power was a massive change. It may sound odd but I found the control loads on the 707 were similar to the Bristol Freighter. However, one of the very different characteristics was the wide range of speed. This emphasised the importance of keeping the aircraft in trim at all times – achieved by moving the horizontal stabiliser at the back of the aircraft, thus keeping the aircraft stable in pitch. As the speed changed, so did the pitch. The load could be trimmed out by toggling a 'pickle' switch on the control column with your thumb. This caused a large trim wheel right next to your knee to rotate rapidly with a very loud buzzing sound as it moved the stabiliser. It was quite alarming when heard for the first time.

Having come from an aircraft where everything to do with the handling was large, heavy and noisy, I learnt to like the trim system. I was taught to use the switch in little 'blips' to trim out the load.

From British Airways Archive Section.

On the Bristol Freighter the flight deck was located above the cabin, a similar height to the 707 flight deck, which helped to get my 'eye in' when landing. Our training captain, 'Dizzy' Neville had a wicked sense of humour. After every one of my landings, he would pointedly rub his back. To save time, and of course money, each landing was followed by an immediate take off. A procedure known as a 'touch and go'. Touch and goes were to play a significant part later in my life.

When I became a base training captain, I was placed on standby to take three command course candidates to Shannon for a touch and go detail. The 'command course' in BOAC included a base training session. However, for this the candidate had to demonstrate three times that he could land the aircraft safely in a 25-knot crosswind.

A considerable amount of time and money went into the setting up and running of this operation. A training captain and three candidates would be put on standby, while the Operations Department searched for an airfield with a 25-knot crosswind. The vagaries of the weather meant days would go by waiting for the wind to blow.

Late one evening, I received a phone call from Operations confirming there was a significant crosswind and rain showers forecast at Shannon and, by the way, there were now *six* candidates. Most sensible souls would have put the phone down, but I found myself saying, "Great, let's go."

When we arrived in Shannon at about midnight the weather was slightly worse than forecast, with heavy rain showers and a *very* strong crosswind. Not ideal, but just within operational limits. The sequence of actions to execute a smooth touch and go requires the following: The final approach is made with the aircraft pointing into wind but tracking down the centreline of the runway. Just prior to touch down the pilot uses the rudder to ease ('ease' being the operative word) the aircraft straight, and at the same time using aileron to stop the upwind wing coming up. It was very easy to scrape one of the under-slung engines on the runway. Now the real fun begins! After the landing (which could be more than one!) the training captain quickly stows the speed brakes, raises the flaps to the take-off position, repositions the stabiliser trim and slowly pushes the throttles forward to give reduced take-off power. And, most importantly, watches what was happening to the aircraft. Simple? The words *'working like a one-armed paperhanger'* come to mind. The workload was high and as the detail went on, I realised I was becoming tired. After all, it was 2am in the morning!

I was very pleased to have an experienced training co-pilot and a training flight engineer as part of our crew. They monitored every movement, particularly mine! If I was just the slightest bit slow in my actions, a quiet word of 'trim' or 'flaps' acted as a subtle prompt. The saying *'Just keep up, don't get ahead'* ran through what was left of my brain!

We had been flying around Shannon 'touching and going' for some time when the Shannon air traffic controller called us to say, "There's no need to call downwind."

"Thank you," I replied. I had a mental picture of the controller sitting with a pint of Guinness and smoking a pipe.

Then... "There is no need to call on base leg."

"Thank you."

"In fact there is no need to call on final approach... *In fact, there is no need to say anything at all, as you are the only silly buggers here tonight!*"

Initial Training

Back to my initial training. We then progressed to line training. This consisted of flying as a supernumerary co-pilot throughout most of the BOAC route structure.

The captain on my first trip was Tommy Dobson. Probably one of the most charismatic characters around at that time, and an excellent pilot.

In an age when many BOAC captains were regarded as sky gods, and often stayed in a smarter hotel than the rest of the crew, Tommy was a breath of fresh air. If we were staying in a different hotel to Tommy's, he would ask one of his co-pilots, "What time is the party tonight, and where?" Tommy flew with the Canadian Air Force prior to BOAC, not only was he a good pilot, he was also way ahead with how he looked after all the crew, years ahead of what we now call CRM – Crew Resource Management.

Also, on this first trip as a supernumerary steward was Ron Clatworthy. He had spent time as a steward on the oceangoing weather ships. It was a tough life on these small ships equipped with radar, positioned in the North Atlantic to act as radio beacons for shipping and aircraft. They were required to maintain their exact position for weeks on end. They achieved this by turning into wind and using the engines to keep station. To change from this harsh environment to the relative luxury of life with BOAC was reflected in his approach to life. As the 'new boys', Ron and I formed a bond. When sipping gin slings with the crew in Raffles Hotel in Singapore he would sometimes look over with a huge smile on his face and say, "Better than working!"

All good things must come an end and after a 16-day trip with the same nine crewmembers, stopping at Rome, Karachi, Hong Kong, Singapore and Sydney, we returned to Heathrow. I said goodbye to the team and Captain Tommy Dobson. I thanked him for my first trip and I quipped, "Prior to the trip I had never been west of Woodley or east of Epsom."

He said, "Ok, but, on your next trip your captain will be a right bastard!"

Notice of a trip would arrive by post. I opened the envelope, which contained a long strip of blue paper with the names of the crew and the itinerary. The captain's name was Tommy Dobson! Thank you Lord! I could not believe my luck. When I checked in, Tommy was there, leaning nonchalantly on the counter, his cap at a jaunty angle. "See, I told you your captain would be a right bastard!"

Flying the BOAC Route

It was a wonderful lifestyle. The trips were long. Some were 16 days or more. A trip to, say, Sydney and back would involve a number of stops along the way. At that time Pan-Am, our competitor, started to operate flights around the world. As a result, BOAC also started a round-the-world service.

'Clipper' was Pan-Am's call sign. Clipper1 would fly eastbound and Clipper2 would fly westbound.

BOAC first adopted the call sign 'Speedbird' from their logo, which was on the aircraft's tailplane. It was a stylised emblem of a bird, first designed in 1932 by Theyre Lee-Elliott, a graphics artist. Unfortunately, the logo was 'retired' in 1984.

BOAC B707 with the elegant gold and dark blue colours and the Speedbird logo.

I always thought 'Speedbird' was an elegant call sign. Just my opinion of course!

The call sign of the President of The United States, 'Airforce One', tops the bill though. It was rumoured that when Hilary Clinton was flying in the US Marine Corp helicopter, their call sign was 'Broomstick One', military humour at its best.

Every airline has their own call sign followed by a number. For example, 'Speedbird 123'. Nowadays all aircraft also carry a transponder. Air traffic controllers can interrogate this device and it then sends a signal in return, identifying that specific aircraft.

Round-the-world trips were very popular with our passengers, staying in exotic and interesting places. In the 1960s the flights were infrequent. Sometimes we would stay for three or four days in one place. This allowed time for all sorts of activities – golf, swimming, and of course shopping. The Flying Staff Recreation Club (FSRC) was formed. Sports equipment was positioned wherever the crews stayed. Sets of golf clubs in Delhi, bicycles in Prestwick. I believe FSRC fees are still only £4 a month!

Bermuda had a lovely little FSRC sailing dinghy. One day, three of us decided we just had time for one last sail before we were to be picked up from our hotel and fly back to London. It was winter in England. Bermuda was bathed in warm sunshine, ideal for sailing. We were about a mile off the shore when the wind suddenly dropped. It went completely calm. We were stuck, and time was ticking by. We tried to paddle with our hands, but to no avail. No shirts to wave, as we were only clad in swimming trunks. Our engineer volunteered to strip off and wave his trunks. I said, "No, no, don't do it, you might frighten the fish!" Being late for a flight was a 'hanging offence'. Just when I was beginning to think it was the end of my career, someone had seen us and whizzed out in a motorboat. We had to change into uniform in the taxi to the airport. We made it just in time.

Most hotels where we stayed were four stars. However, there was one place in Karachi that was very different: 'The Speedbird Rest House'. We were housed in bungalow-type accommodation, a former British Army barracks. The way it was run was like going back to the days of the Raj. The single rooms were very basic, but comfortable. A small bed with a writing table, a shower and a toilet. You would be wakened by a bearer (waiter) with a cup of tea. An Irish friend of mine once said the tea was so strong you could trot a mouse on it! The laundry was collected using a donkey and cart.

One evening, a captain, who was not well liked by his crew, went to his room and fell fast asleep. The crew got hold of the donkey, broke into the captain's room and left the donkey there all night. You can imagine the state of the room when the captain woke up!

The male members of the crew were housed in one section and

the ladies in another. The ladies' section was known as 'Virgin's Alley'. There was a communal dining room. All meals were taken there, it was open all hours. Bearer's Curry was in great demand and quite delicious.

Qantas crews also stayed there. The Qantas crews seemed to take a shine to the BOAC girls. One day, the BOAC crew were splashing about in the swimming pool when the Qantas crew appeared, ten males and one female. They had just arrived from a flight, and always looked immaculate in their uniforms. They all walked straight into the pool, fully clothed, and joined in the fun!

When we stayed overnight in Rome, the whole crew would visit a lovely little restaurant for lunch. We sat in the courtyard at one long table, dappled sunlight filtering through the overhead vines. All the Italian waiters were falling over each other to serve our girls. One very old waiter, looking much like Groucho Marx, approached the girl next to me and asked, "Would you, dear lady like-a-some cheese?"

"Oh, I would love some Gorgonzola," came the reply in her best Joanna Lumley voice.

He gave a loud groan, with tears in his eyes he grabbed her hand and with a big sigh said, "We donna have any Gorgonzola."

The girl played it beautifully. She said, "My dear man I have flown halfway round the world to dine at your restaurant, and now you are telling me you don't have any Gorgonzola!"

Still holding her hand, he cried, "For you... I make a-some." He rushed to the nearest deli, purchased the cheese and proudly presented it. Smiles all round!

A very popular trip was to St Lucia, in the eastern Caribbean. I believe we had a stay of three nights there. The airport is located on the very southern tip of this beautiful mountainous island. Our hotel was on the northern tip. This meant a minibus ride of over an hour, some 30 miles at night over hills and mountains. In order to take the pain away, the cabin crew would produce a two-gallon plastic container filled to the brim with spirits. At the end of a long day we were all quite tired, and the alcohol just went to our heads. You can imagine what state we were in by the time we arrived at our hotel.

The next evening was the Manager's Cocktail Party. This was a very nice gesture by the hotel, but it was a rather quiet affair. Most of the guests were elderly. The whole crew were invited. One of our stewards said to me, "There is a beautiful grand piano in the corner, and I can play."

Before I could reply, a stewardess said, "I can sing."

I approached the manager. "Could my crew play and sing a couple of songs for you?"

His eyes lit up. "Please, bring 'em on!"

It was like listening to Nat 'King' Cole and Diane Krall. The manager invited the whole crew to stay on when the guests went in for dinner. In the course of conversation he said, "Do you know all the hotel staff turn out to see the BOAC minibus arrive, the door opens and the captain falls out, straightens up and staggers into the hotel."

Room parties were all the rage. A room was nominated as 'the party room'; this was often the captain's room, as he invariably had a suite. The expression 'bring your own glass' was well known throughout the airline. Some nights there would be a fancy-dress theme. The rules, such as they were, you could only use what was available in the hotel for your costume.

One night it was a no theme evening. The phone in my room rang. It was our flight engineer. "Brian, I have a great costume for tonight, but I need your help, can you pop down to my room and give me a hand?" Somewhat curious I went along. He opened the door. He had decided to come as The Invisible Man. There he stood, trying to wrap toilet roll paper round his body. He wanted me to kneel down and hold the paper in place with sticky tape. The things you do for Queen and country! We all met up in my room for the prize giving. 'Fred' (not his real name), The Invisible Man, won first prize.

A room party in St Lucia.

A complete contrast to the Caribbean trips was a couple of days in Moscow. It was at the height of The Cold War. One sector was from Moscow to Tokyo. The average flight time was about nine hours each way. Most of the flights were at night, flying over the vast, sparsely inhabited space of Siberia. As well as the usual Met briefing, we were also given a comprehensive briefing on the political situation, and what to do in the event of having to make a landing in this inhospitable area. We had a list of Russian military airfields that would accept us. Our callsign was 'Speedbird 007'. Geoff Nolan, a BOAC officer, decided on the service number. Clearly, he had a sense of humour.

Later, at a meeting in Moscow with the Russian ATC authorities, Hugh Dibley asked if they would prefer use of the callsign "Speedbird 7 or 007?"

The reply: "We like Speedbird 007."

On one flight we were flying over the middle of Russia, on our way to Tokyo. It was a pitch-black night, with wisps of cirrus cloud gently sliding by, and an outside temperature of -50° Centigrade.

We turned the flight deck lights down low, enjoying the peace and quiet, and watching the frozen land below drift by, when a radio call from Novosibirsk air traffic control came through. A husky Russian voice said, "Speedbird 007 you are 100 metres south of your track. Be careful!" Our only navigation guidance was an Inertial Navigation System (INS) unit. An on-board computer housed accelerometers and gyroscopes to determine our position. On long flights its accuracy tended to drift a little.

Normally, when flying at 35,000 feet, a track error of 100 metres would be considered quite acceptable, but we were in the middle of The Cold War! I looked at my co-pilot; it was his first flight on the Russian route. I said, "Maybe our call sign '007' tested the Russian controller's sense of humour."

A friend of mine who had been to Moscow a few times said, "Take two golf balls with you."

I said I did not play golf.

"No, no," he said, "There are no bath plugs. One golf ball is for the wash basin and one golf ball for the bath."

We were accommodated in a dingy hotel in the city. There was a 'dragon lady' receptionist sitting at a desk in the corridor of each floor. She gave you the key to your room.

One evening a crew were having a quiet soirée in the captain's room. When the flight engineer arrived, he said, "OK, do you know we are bugged?" Everyone told him to just sit down and relax. He started to look behind the paintings on the walls and in the bathroom. Suddenly... he noticed a round carpet under a large table in the middle of the room. He rolled back the carpet, and there was a wire, mesh dome with a brass surround, held in place by three large screws. "There! I told you, we will get to the bottom of this," he said. He then produced a large screwdriver and started to undo the screws. The rest of the crew looked on, thoroughly bored by the whole thing. The first two screws were extracted and, as the third unwound, there was a tremendous crash from the room below as the chandelier fell from the ceiling. A true story, and many years before the wonderful skit had it in the TV comedy *Only Fools and Horses*.

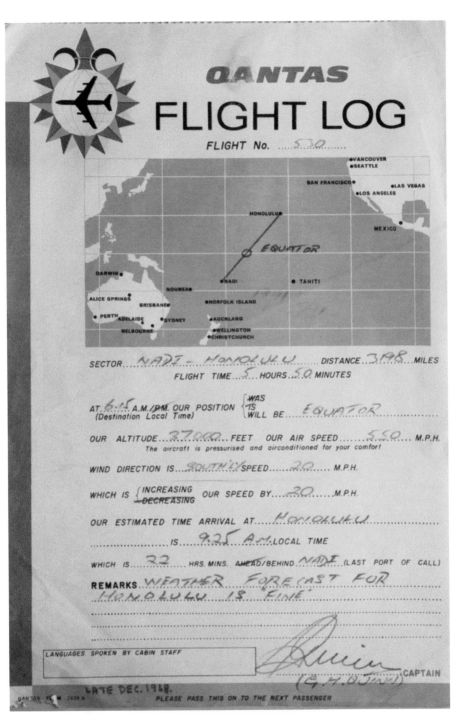

QANTAS
FLIGHT LOG

FLIGHT No. ....530.....

SECTOR.....NADI – HONOLULU..... DISTANCE....3198....MILES

FLIGHT TIME....5....HOURS....50....MINUTES

AT..6:15...A.M./P.M. OUR POSITION { WAS / IS / WILL BE } ....EQUATOR.....
(Destination Local Time)

OUR ALTITUDE....37,000....FEET OUR AIR SPEED......550....M.P.H.
The aircraft is pressurised and airconditioned for your comfort

WIND DIRECTION IS....SOUTH'LY...SPEED......20.....M.P.H.

WHICH IS { INCREASING / ~~DECREASING~~ } OUR SPEED BY....20....M.P.H.

OUR ESTIMATED TIME ARRIVAL AT....HONOLULU....

......IS....9.25 A.M...LOCAL TIME

WHICH IS....22....HRS. MINS. AHEAD/BEHIND....NADI..(LAST PORT OF CALL)

REMARKS....WEATHER FORECAST FOR
HONOLULU IS "FINE"

LANGUAGES SPOKEN BY CABIN STAFF

(G. H. OSMAN) CAPTAIN

LATE DEC. 1968.
PLEASE PASS THIS ON TO THE NEXT PASSENGER

A copy of a passenger flight log from a QANTAS flight.
December 1968.

I have listed just some to the 'goings on' down the route. I hope I have not given the impression that life was frivolous when not flying – relaxation was important too. It emphasises the difference in the way the crew got along in those days.

This harmony was mostly due to the fact that there was a small crew of nine or so, the flight deck was on the same level as the cabin, and the flight deck door was always open. Passengers were encouraged to visit the flight deck. I believe this was a big selling point.

The in-flight entertainment on the 707 was almost non-existent. The flight's progress was recorded on a duplicate pad with a map of the world. This passenger flight log was given to the flight navigator to fill in with a pencil line of our route, and any places of interest on the way, with our ETA at destination. The paper was given to a stewardess, who handed it to the first-class passengers. They were instructed to pass it on to those sitting behind them. As you can imagine, it was some time before the passengers sitting in the rear seats got the flight information.

In those days, one of the items in the seat pocket in front of you was a 'sick bag'. I recently flew as a passenger on a low-cost African airline. A notice on the back of the sick bag said, 'Get well soon!' I think British Airways missed a trick there.

For the youngest passengers there were the 'Junior Jet Club' books. This was in the form of a pilot's logbook. The captain signed each flight. When I signed these books, I was surprised at the number of flights recorded. This little procedure was normally followed by a visit to the flight deck.

Dear Club Member,

I should like to welcome you as a joining member of our Junior Jet Club, and hope you will be pleased with your own personal log-book. My fellow Captains will look forward to meeting you on many future flights, and will be delighted to help you build up your BOAC mileage.

We should like you to complete the enclosed Enrolment Card and hand it to your Steward or Stewardess to enable us to keep in touch with you from time to time.

With every good wish.

Yours sincerely,

Captain O. P. Jones.

Visits to the flight deck were numerous. Although I met many people, I cannot claim to have met many celebrities. I do remember Spike Milligan though. He sat on the jump seat the entire flight from Singapore to Sydney. He made that long night flight all too short.

On one flight from Gatwick to Malaga the stewardess casually asked me if the flight deck was open for visitors? I said, "Yes."

Unbeknown to us 'up the front', she had told all the passengers, "When Captain Smith lands at Malaga he is retiring. If anyone would like to visit the flight deck and wish him a happy retirement, please do so." One hundred and fifty passengers came up, shook my hand and wished me a happy retirement!

The co-pilot and I hatched a plan to 'get her back'. After landing, we shut down the engines. It was normal for the captain to use the PA to say goodbye to the passengers, wish them a safe journey and thank them for flying with BA. I added, "I would like to thank all those passengers that wished me a happy retirement. In fact, today is a double celebration, as Miss Jones is also leaving to join the prison service!" The flight door opened and Miss Jones wagged her finger, pointed at me and said in a loud voice, "Do not eat or drink anything on the flight back!"

Time for an Upgrade

After nine months or so as a second officer, I was notified I would be upgraded. To achieve this promotion I had to demonstrate I could complete three safe landings. On 31st March 1967, a training detail was organised and a training captain, Peter Mains-Smith and three co-pilots, including myself, set off to Stansted Airport. I was the first to fly. As we lifted off after my first touch and go, a rubbing or scuffing sound came from the nose wheel area. Eyebrows were raised, all instrumentation was checked but nothing appeared amiss. After the second touch and go, when the gear was selected 'up', the noise level increased substantially. Still all appeared in order. It was decided to continue. As we turned onto final approach and selected the gear down, instead of three green lights confirming that both main landing gear and the nose wheel were down and locked, there were only *two* lights. The nose wheel was jammed in the 'up' position. The air traffic controllers watching from the tower confirmed this.

Much consultation took place between the captain, our flight engineer, and by radio link to the maintenance base at Heathrow. My part in all this drama was to fly the aircraft safely in a holding pattern, and not get otherwise involved, or distracted from this task. Several accidents had happened to other airlines with all the crew trying to solve a minor failure, and no one flying the aircraft! However, I was aware that several attempts were being made to lower the gear. The emergency gear lowering procedures were carried out. The aircraft was then put into a steep dive followed by a sharp pull up to try to free the nose wheel. All to no avail. As a last resort our flight engineer climbed down into the electronics bay below the flight deck, knocked a hole into the nose wheel covering to reveal the nosewheel tilted to one side. It was jammed on the edge of the door. It should have been lined up in a straight line. It was deemed impossible to lower it.

An emergency was declared and we were granted clearance to

return to Heathrow for an emergency landing without a nosewheel. I was still flying the aircraft, and under the circumstances glad to be given a task rather than be involved with the stressful technical problems that the captain and flight engineer were having to handle. The captain made a calm and thorough briefing. I was to continue flying the aircraft onto final approach, then he would take control (much to my relief!) and land the aircraft. We would plan to deploy the door exit chute and leave though the main passenger door.

In by a nose! Photo courtesy of BA Archive Section.

The captain made a very smooth landing. All was normal until, at about 80 knots, the nose lowered slowly onto the runway. The aircraft came to a juddering stop, the engines were shut down and all crew exited by the main passenger door... except myself. I had suddenly thought that if the fuselage was twisted, maybe the main door would be jammed and we would be unable to get out. I quickly opened my side window and threw out an escape rope, thinking we could escape this way, plus I would be the first to leave! I turned in my seat only to see the aircraft completely empty! The main door had opened and everyone had shot out like greyhounds. Except myself... the rest of the team gave me a round of applause as I rather sheepishly appeared and slid down the slide.

The subsequent inquiry discovered our aircraft had been given a major overhaul prior to our flight. The nose wheel-centring cam, that should do what it says and centre the nose wheel as it retracts, was not working. The nosewheel was at an angle as it retracted and remained jammed in the nosewheel housing bay.

An expensive incident, but no one hurt.

Reliability

The airline strove for reliability in all things, including the service to our passengers. One story relating to the 707 concerns its in-flight entertainment system. This consisted of two projectors suspended from the aircraft ceiling. One for the first-class passengers and another for the economy class. The projectors had gained a reputation among the cabin crew for their unreliability.

On one flight, Lucy Starling, a vivacious red-headed stewardess, came to the flight deck to report to the flight engineer (who could fix anything!) that the projector in the first-class cabin had stopped working. Tim Westcott immediately entered the cabin to take a look at the broken projector. Within a very short time he appeared in the galley and said to Lucy, "Are you wearing stockings or tights?"

Lucy raised her eyebrows. "I beg your pardon," she replied.

"Oh, don't mess about," said Tim, "we need to fix this damn thing, and fast."

"Well," she said, "as it happens, I am wearing stockings."

"Excellent, I need one."

Lucy obliged and off he went. The projector's fan belt had broken and was repaired using Lucy's stocking. The headline in the papers the next day read, 'LUCY PULLS IT OFF!'

5. CECILIA

I was navigating across the North Atlantic on what I thought was to be a routine flight, when it turned into a life changing experience. I feel a small introduction to this moment is required. On long flights the stewardess would serve food to the pilots. The captain would choose from the first-class menu (naturally!). The navigator's table was so small – and usually covered with a chart – that it was impossible to accommodate a food tray. To have anything to eat or drink the 'navigator' relied on the stewardess. On this flight I noticed a small plate of sandwiches appeared on my table, then a cup of coffee. I also noticed the stewardess who placed these much-appreciated items was 'drop dead gorgeous'.

Cecilia.

When we made landfall the navigator's job was done... I seized this moment to wander back to the galley and, doing my best impression of James Bond, I spent the next ten minutes or so chatting to this lovely girl. I went back to the flight deck on cloud nine as I had obtained the all-important home telephone number.

However, as we were both scheduled on long haul flights, when Cecilia was away on a trip I would be home and when Cecilia was home I was away... a year went by before we had our first date.

I had sold the yellow Ford Anglia and now had an MGB roadster. I booked a table for two at the prestigious Monkey Island Restaurant near Maidenhead. I polished the MGB and put the hood down. I was going flat out to make an impression on our first date.

I picked Cecilia up from her flat in Richmond and we headed out west towards a glorious sunset.

Just as I was thinking all was going very well... my world was about to fall apart. Monkey Island is approached by crossing a bridge over the River Thames, with weeping willows touching the water. We sat in the bar. When I put my hand in my pocket to pay for our drinks, to my horror I found I had not a penny with me. Earlier that day I had returned from a trip and just had time to change from my uniform into my smart clothes for our first date. I must have left all my money in my uniform pocket. I rushed to the nearest phone and called Tony Angel, who lived nearby. His wife Shirley answered. She told me that Tony was working and she had just spent all the money in the house on a week's shopping.

I explained the situation as calmly and carefully as I could to Cecilia. I fully expected her to get up and leave me standing with my mouth open. Instead, she simply said that the only money she had were Canadian dollars... Bless. I went to see the manager and explained my predicament. He did not appear concerned and said, "Mr Smith, if what you say is true, I am sure your companion knows the exchange rate better than I do. Why don't you have a lovely dinner and come and see me at the end of the evening and pay in Canadian dollars." Lucky me.

Round-the-world trips were very popular with our passengers – staying in exotic and interesting places, however, it was rumoured that you would not be scheduled to fly with your girlfriend. Cecilia would come back from a trip and say she had flown with Guy or Clive – my friends – but never with me! On one occasion our flights crossed paths in Fiji. Cecilia was on the eastbound flight and I was on the westbound. We were all staying in the same hotel.

The weather was perfect. Dinner was served on a huge veranda that opened out to a beautiful garden, with palm trees swaying in the breeze and Fijian girls dancing to a local band, how romantic...

Cecilia and Brian in Fiji.

I was determined to take advantage of this romantic scene. The first thing was to book a table for two.

All the Fijian waiters were very friendly. I had got to know the headwaiter, named Kelly. I asked him if he would reserve a table for two that evening right at the front of the restaurant. He gave me a huge smile, and a wink and said, "No problem."

When Cecilia and I arrived for dinner we were met by Kelly. "Come, come," he said. He quickly led us to the prime spot at the front, weaving our way though the other guests, including the rest of our crew. We felt like royalty. When we arrived at our table, Kelly had put a large hand-drawn notice on it: *Reserved for Lord and Lady Smith.*

On 19th December 2020 Cecilia and I celebrated 50 years of happy marriage! If anyone asks how long I have been married, my standard reply is, "I have been married three times." Invariably, eyebrows are raised. The truth is, I *have* been married three times... to the same person.

Cecilia is a Baha'i. The Baha'i Faith is a new religion, teaching the essential worth of all religions, and the unity of all people. Founded in Persia in 1863, it grew until it has now become established worldwide. We had the Baha'i marriage ceremony in Rhodesia on 19th December 1970.

The following day we had a Church of England ceremony at St Luke's Church in Greendale, Rhodesia, and the third Registry Office ceremony took place on 19th March after we had returned to the UK, as will be explained later.

Cecilia's father kindly lent us his lovely Oldsmobile car and we had our honeymoon in the eastern districts of Rhodesia where we checked into the famous Troutbeck Inn for a few days, and then on to a game lodge for a couple more days. We planned to spend some time exploring the beautiful Rhodesian countryside, so we studied the hand-drawn map placed in our African hut, or *rondavel* as it was called. A dirt track would lead us to our next stop. We could see from the map there was a large lake crossing the track. Much to our surprise, a car ferry was marked. We followed the track to the car ferry departure point.

As we approached the ferry ramp, we parked close to a flagpole. There was a box at the base. Written on the box was a hand-drawn notice: *'If ferry required, raise flag.'* We remarked that that seemed a very simple and effective way of attracting the attention of the ferryman on the other side of a very large lake. We could see the ferry was moored on the other side of the lake, so we raised the flag and walked back to the car. We had not seen anyone since leaving the camp some two or three hours earlier. We sat in the car looking at the flagpole and across the lake.

Suddenly we heard a loud rumbling... Out of the bush appeared a huge rhinoceros. It walked slowly over to the pole and started to scratch itself. The pole was waving back and forth as the rhino continued to scratch. No one could fail to see the waving flag.

The ferry set out from the far shore. What was going to happen next, we thought? The rhino continued to scratch. The ferry neared the shore. A voice from the ferry came loud and clear, "Stay exactly where you are." We were not intending to move. Twenty minutes or so passed. The rhino continued to scratch.

Finally, the rhino stopped scratching and lumbered off into the bush and we safely boarded the ferry.

About a month later we returned to England. At a party we were hosting, a friend of ours asked, "Do you think you are legally married?"

I replied, "I hope so, as Cecilia is pregnant."

He persisted. "Well, you were married in Rhodesia which has unilaterally declared its independence from the UK (UDI) and has now been declared an illegal state. You really ought to check. Your insurance might not be valid and if anything happened to you Cecilia could be left without a penny. My advice would be to have a registry office marriage, just as a sort of 'belt and braces'."

I phoned a solicitor to ask his advice. He had offices in Midhurst. He said he agreed the best move would be to have a registry office ceremony. He also advised me I would need two friends as witnesses. We agreed to meet on 19th March at 3pm. I must admit I was amused by the whole situation. I then thought, why not make a day of it. I asked Harry and Jeannie, good friends of ours, to be our witnesses. I booked a table for lunch at 12.30 in the lovely restaurant of The Spread Eagle Hotel in Midhurst.

Then things started to get complicated. Harry was on flight standby for BA and explained he would be late. Then the solicitor phoned to ask if we could have the ceremony a little earlier. I was determined not to let these minor hitches spoil the day. We met and had a glass or two of champagne in the bar, then went in to lunch. Time was ticking by. We had just finished the main course when our time was up. I called the headwaiter and said, "We have just got to go over the road to get married... can we come back for the sweet and cheese?"

He took a deep breath and said, "That will be perfectly alright, Sir."

This was in the days before credit cards. I had booked the table in my name – Smith, and I had not paid a deposit. I am sure the headwaiter must have thought to himself, 'Are they really going over the road to get married, with two women that are clearly so pregnant?'

Cecilia, Jeannie, Harry and I staggered across the road to his office and stood in front of the registrar in a ragged line. Harry had got the hiccups. When the registrar asked Cecilia, "Do you Mrs

Cecilia Smith take Mr Brian Smith to be your lawfully wedded husband?" it all dissolved into farce… we did go back for the sweet and cheese, and paid the bill.

Some time later, after I had met a chap a couple of times in our local pub, one night he said, "Why don't I bring my wife down and you bring Cecilia, I am sure we would all get along really well."

We arranged to meet up the following Friday. Cecilia and I arrived a little early. One of the regulars said in a loud voice, "Hey, Brian, tell us that story about you being married three times."

I had not noticed but Jim and his wife Frances had come into the pub and were standing behind me. Frances turned to Jim and said, "If that is the man you want me to meet, and he has been married three times, I do not want anything to do with him, take me home immediately." And they left.

After a little while Cecilia said, "I wonder what happened to Jim and Frances."

The following night, Jim was in the pub, when one of the chaps said, "Brian, tell Jim that story about you being married three times." I told the story.

Jim looked at me and said, "Don't move." He rushed off to phone Frances and explain the whole misunderstanding. We became good friends, and often laughed about how we all met.

Some years after our first date, I was on board a booze cruise full of air traffic controllers sailing along the River Thames from Richmond to Maidenhead. As the boat turned round at Monkey Island to return, I was standing with the organiser and thanked him for a great event.

He said, "Not so great, we are about to run out of beer and there will be a riot any minute."

"No problem," I said, "I know the manager of Monkey Island." We organised a whip round and soon had a pile of folding money. As we approached the shoreline the waiters came running across the lawn, followed by the manager, all ready to shoo us off. Luck kicked in once again and I remembered the manager's name. "Hello,

Mr Middleton," I said.

He stopped in his tracks. "Oh no," he exclaimed, "not Canadian dollars!" I waved a fist full of crisp pound notes. The next moment crates of beer were being loaded onto the boat and pound notes handed over in exchange. Happy days!

Navigating

I settled down to a routine of long-haul flying. Flights were divided between co-piloting and navigating. My astro navigation had improved, mostly through practice I feel. On many of the oceans there were no navigational aids, therefore navigating by the stars became the norm. No GPS in those days.

I was to fly a charter flight from San Francisco to Tahiti and, hopefully, back. It required a long flight of nine hours or so. The other co-pilot, Terry Hall, tossed a coin to decide who was to navigate to this tiny island in the middle of the Pacific. I lost the toss. It was a daylight flight, no stars to be seen. I sat at the navigator's table to check by opening all the many charts that were required to cover this route over the largest ocean in the world. They were all blue...

The navigator's station on the 707 consisted of a tiny table on one side of the flight deck behind the captain's seat. I had to start navigating as soon as we took off, as we were immediately over the ocean. Initially, this involved making several calculations by reference to huge manuals called Sight Reduction Tables. These tables were designed to reduce the time spent working out azimuths, declinations and hour angles, and obtain all the information to 'shoot' the stars.

A periscopic sextant was stowed in a box under the navigator's table. You took it out and pushed it up through a pressurized hole at the back of the flight deck roof. Unless you were 6' 10" or more, you had to use a small stool to stand on to be able to reach the sextant. Two handles each side were pulled down, you then climbed on the stool and screwed your eye up against a small window in the sextant. If your calculations were correct, a star or planet would be seen. The star was kept in view by using a rocker switch on one of the handles for a couple of minutes. This worked out another set of calculations for you. You then used this information to draw lines in the form of a cross on a chart (map) and obtain a 'fix'. It was an extremely laborious and time-consuming operation. If you are still reading this, several minutes will have passed.

The 707 was speeding along at approximately eight miles a minute. Unless you were very quick, the fix you drew on the chart was where you had *been* several miles ago, not where you were *now*.

The pinnacle of my flight navigating skills was reached on this flight, when I successfully completed a circumzenithal fix using the sun. Sounds like a rather nasty medical operation! As I remember it, if you crossed the Equator with the sun in a position directly overhead the aircraft, it is possible to take three 'shots' with the periscopic sextant using the sun, and thus plot a fix.

Right on schedule Tahiti island appeared dead ahead. What a wonderful piece of navigation... and *luck*. Phew! I had time to reflect that I had navigated to Tahiti probably using the same method Captain James Cook had used to find Tahiti in the 18th century!

On another flight, it was my turn to navigate. I was standing on the stool with my hands resting on the handles, one eye screwed into the eyepiece, and the other looking towards the curtains that were the entrance to the first-class cabin. I was just wondering what would happen if a passenger appeared – I looked like a U-boat captain. All I needed was my cap on back to front to complete the picture. Suddenly, the curtains were thrown open and there stood Spike Milligan dressed in his pyjamas. He took one look at me, leapt to attention, and said, "Fire one. You fool!" and collapsed with laughter. "What on earth are you doing?" he enquired.

I was a great fan of Spike, he would always reduce me to tears, and that was exactly what he did that night. I explained to him that I was trying to navigate.

Trying to navigate with Spike Milligan on board was not easy.

"Oooh," he said in his best Goon Show voice. "Can I have a look?" He climbed on the stool and rocked the sextant around, climbed down shaking his head. He spent the rest of the flight sitting on the jump seat behind the captain. He told us a story of how the Goons first met. The story goes, during the Second World War, Harry Secombe was serving in the Royal Artillery in North Africa. Harry was in charge of a gun, positioned on the top of a cliff. He fired his gun, a four-ton howitzer. Unfortunately, someone had forgotten to apply the handbrake. The gun toppled over the cliff and landed on the road below. Spike was in a tent about one inch from where it landed. It could have killed him outright. Harry came scrambling down the cliff and said in his silliest/crazy Goon show voice, "Ullo! Anybody seen my gun?" He started his crazy giggling and the rest is history. Spike and his stories made the long flight feel quite short.

There were several ways an astro fix could be interrupted. Flying in turbulence made it difficult to keep the star you were 'shooting' in the cross hairs in the eyepiece.

On the long oceanic flights at night, it was quite normal for a member of the cabin crew to pop up to the flight deck for a cigarette and a sit down for a few minutes. It was a haven of peace and quiet. The only lighting was from the flight instruments; the only sound was the humming of the engines. The workload was low for the pilots and flight engineer, mostly consisting of vigilance and monitoring the aircraft's instruments.

In the 1960s there were few other aircraft flying the oceanic areas. As a result, calls to and from air traffic control were infrequent. The navigator, however, was always busy plotting the course, and standing up to take a fix with the sextant every few minutes. If the sextant was hanging from the roof, it was easy for anyone moving about to bang his or her head on it. This gave the more adventurous members of the cabin crew an opportunity to have some fun – putting black boot polish on the foam rubber ring of the eyepiece. Only when you looked in a mirror did you see the joke. You were particularly vulnerable if you were standing on the stool with both hands on the handles, facing the cabin, with the flight deck door open. Your trouser zip could be undone and your shirt pulled out. It was a considerable distraction...

6. IN COMMAND

Clive Ritchie phoned to say we were to be paired up to start our command course shortly. This course was to check we were suitable to become captains. It had gained a reputation as tough to pass and there had been several pilots who had failed the course.

I was confident that I was paired up with one of the most competent pilots I had ever met. This feeling was confirmed by Clive's gruff observation. "Now, listen Smiffy, we are not only going to pass this bloody course, we are going to pass it with flying colours."

We spent many days, prior to the start of the course, studying all the emergency procedures. We set up a back room in my cottage as a B707 cockpit and would sit for hours flying the 'cardboard bomber'. For a break, we would take my dog for a walk and verbally brief the dog on all the procedures, until we were word perfect. Surprisingly, he did not bite us once.

After much blood, sweat, toil and tears we were successful. I visited the uniform stores to pick up my captain's uniform, and I headed home for a grand parade in full attire, to the cheers of my family.

Life was very good, but as a junior captain I spent quite some time on standby. This involved being at home, near a phone, and if the company called you were required to be at Heathrow within an hour and half, and possibly fly off for a two-week trip. Just before Christmas I was called out to fly a 707 cargo aircraft to Sydney. The rest of the three-man flight crew, and our steward, were also newly married with a young family.

The last sector of the trip was to Hong Kong where we were to have 24 hours rest, then travel home as passengers to arrive in the early hours of Christmas morning.

Whilst 'stopping over' in Sydney, I received a call from operations. The freighter's schedule had become disrupted and our aircraft would be arriving in Sydney 24 hours late and we would now be scheduled to be home on Boxing Day, instead of Christmas

Day as originally planned. I passed this information on to the rest of my crew. There was disappointment all round.

Photo courtesy of Ron Batchelor.

British Airways Archive Section.

The next day we were flying to Hong Kong – our last stopover. We set off. I looked round the flight deck at my crew, everyone was looking gloomy. I suddenly had a thought. "Wait a minute, why do we need to spend 24 hours in Hong Kong?" A BA747 was scheduled to leave for London about two hours after we arrived in our freighter. "Why don't we just jump on this flight to arrive in London on Christmas morning?" We contacted operations in London on the long-range radio to ask permission to do this.

"Standby," was the reply. Hours seem to pass, and then the reply came though. "Permission given." Not normal procedure we were told... but it is Christmas. Smiles all round!

We landed in Hong Kong and headed for the customs hall. There to meet us was our handling agent, an immaculately dressed Chinese officer from Jardair. He introduced himself, grabbed our bags and headed for the exit. "Hold it!" we all cried. "We are not staying overnight, but catching the BA747 flight departing for London in 90 minutes."

"I understand completely," he calmly said. "First I take you to hotel, you freshen up and I pick you up in one hour."

Parked outside the terminal was a large black shiny limousine. We sank into the plush seats, relaxed, and were whisked off to our hotel. We had exactly one hour to do our Christmas shopping. What better place than Hong Kong!

One hour later, my crew and I assembled in the hotel foyer. I introduced myself to the 747 captain who was standing with his crew. We were to fly as passengers on his aircraft. I should say by flying BA707 freighters we were looked down upon as third-class citizens by certain crewmembers that were flying more prestigious larger jets. The 747 captain looked down his nose and said in a loud voice, "Ah yes, I have heard about you freighters boys. I suppose you would like a lift to the airport?" Parked outside was the rather battered BOAC crew minibus, ready to take the crew to the airport. Next to it was our large black shiny limousine complete with our immaculate chauffeur.

"No thank you," I said, "we have our own transport," waving a regal hand in the direction of our limo. The look on the 747 captain's face kept us smiling all the way to the airport.

We landed at Heathrow in the very early hours of Christmas morning. I drove home. Our families had been contacted by BOAC crew control some days before to say we would not be home until Boxing Day, but they were not given an update of our new arrival. I let myself in, tiptoed into the lounge, laid out their presents, and waited... Cymbeline, my youngest daughter, was the first to come downstairs. She shouted so loud when she saw me. Kerry, my other daughter, and Cecilia quickly came tumbling down the stairs. Tears and laughter followed. A Happy Christmas all round.

The 707 cargo trips were very popular with the crews. Although the schedule could be unreliable and trips long, they visited many interesting places. We also had the luxury of having a steward to look after us. Most of our stewards had been off flying duties due to illness and were delighted to be back flying. It made a nice foursome for a game of golf too!

One day a stewardess walked into the office where they scheduled trips for cabin crew. She said, "I would like to request a trip."

"Certainly, where would you like to go?" asked the officer.

"I would like to go to Sydney."

"Ah, the 707 doesn't fly to Sydney anymore," he replied.

The girl immediately smiled sweetly, and said, "Well, the freighter does." To be politically correct, stewardesses started to be scheduled to fly on the freighter.

On some of the long sectors, to relieve the boredom the girls would fly the aircraft, and the flight engineer did the cooking. The long trips quickly became a 'super-shopping trip' for the girls, with stopovers in Delhi, Sydney and New York. A notice board in the crew room at Heathrow was soon covered in messages with the best bargains and where they were to be had. *'Best tea sets in Pac Soo shop in Hong Kong. Cheap bicycles in Macy's in New York.'* The relaxed rules and regulations meant you could carry anything you purchased, put it in the aircraft hold and bring it home. Size and weight were not a problem. Fridges, lawnmowers, bicycles and baskets of fruit would all make the trip.

Hong Kong Airport

The approach and landing into Hong Kong's Kai Tak Airport was classed as 'special' by the UK Civil Aviation Authority (CAA.) There were several weather restrictions for the visual harbour approach, the visibility and cloud base had to be good enough for the pilot to clearly see the surrounding terrain. My first landing at Kai Tak was on 13th April 1967. As I recall, the start point was overhead Cheung Chau Island, fly straight to Green Island just off the northwest tip of Hong Kong Island and on to Stonecutters Island in the harbour, then turn right and head straight for a huge board on the side of a hill painted in large red and white squares, the famous chequerboard.

The landing checks had been completed earlier. Runway 13, the normal runway in use, was located nearly 90 degrees to the right, then a right turn was made to line up on the runway centre line. The installation of an Instrument Guidance System (IGS), similar to an Instrument Landing System (ILS), in 1974 meant use of the airport under adverse weather conditions could be greatly increased, and the visual harbour approach would rarely be used.

The runway was constructed from reclaimed land and protruded out into Hong Kong Harbour. To make an approach and landing on Runway 31, a reciprocal heading to Runway 13 involved flying through the Lei Yue Mun Gap, with Hong Kong Island close on your left-hand side, and steep hills to your right whilst pointing at the hills and high-rise buildings to the north of the runway.

Kai Tak Airport closed in 1998 and Chek Lap Kok became Hong Kong's main airport. Kai Tak was the original home of Cathay Pacific Airlines Ltd. I am sure it was just routine for their pilots to fly in and out of Kai Tak. However, I found flying into the airport in the BOAC B707 always exciting!

The Lady from Bloemfontein

When a BOAC aircraft lands and a crew changeover takes place, the on-going crew are standing by, lined up on the ramp, ready to take the aircraft to its next destination. It is called 'the handover'. The captain talks to the next captain and the chief steward talks to the next chief steward. The conversation includes any 'snags' the aircraft may have, catering arrangements, and general operational matters.

I was standing at the bottom of the steps, when the chief steward came down, shaking his head. "Hello Captain," he said, "Boy! Have you got some trouble ahead of you!" He continued, "There is a rather large Afrikaner lady in first class who has complained about everything, the cabin service, the food, and the fact that we are running 30 minutes late."

I then turned and greeted the off-going captain. He said, "Well Brian, I guess you have heard about the lady from Bloemfontein [as she became known to all the crew from then on]. She will want to see you straight away."

We started our pre-flight checks in preparation for the sector from the Seychelles to Johannesburg. Our chief steward came up to the flight deck. "I guess you have heard about the lady from Bloemfontein," he said. I nodded. "She has already given me a piece of her mind, and she is saying she wants to see you."

I said, "Thanks Pete, would you be so kind as to tell the dear lady I am busy, I will come and see her later."

"OK," he said, "she won't like that."

We settled down into the cruise, it was a beautiful evening, clear with smooth flying conditions. Eventually, I went back to the first-class cabin. The lady from Bloemfontein was standing in the aisle, swaying from side to side, holding a glass of wine. She started to rant in a very loud voice. I duly made my apologies and quickly scuttled back to the flight deck.

The original weather forecast we had for Johannesburg was 'slight mist'; the latest weather reports were that the mist had turned to fog. Our diversion airport was Durban. We had enough fuel to hold for about 30 minutes, then divert to Durban. We talked to BOAC Operations in Johannesburg on VHF radio. They would advise us of any improvements in the weather.

We started to fly a holding pattern over Johannesburg. The time was ticking away, with no improvement in the weather. We were a few minutes away from diverting to Durban, when Ops called to say could we wait a little longer and, if necessary, divert to Bloemfontein (BFN) about 200 miles closer than Durban. The weather in BFN was clear and forecast to stay that way.

The minutes ticked by, and there was still no improvement in the weather. The decision to divert to Bloemfontein was made. I informed the cabin crew and passengers of our intentions. I understand we were the first BOAC 707 to land at BFN. It became a busy time in the flight deck, checking for any special landing procedures.

These were the days before GPS and computer displays. Everything was written down on paper. The weather remained good and we landed at BFN.

We had just cleared the runway, when our steward appeared.

I said, "Not the lady from Bloemfontein again... surely!"

He laughed and said, "The lady from Bloemfontein fell asleep and you woke her with your landing."

As we flashed down the runway, she saw a sign on the terminal building that read 'Welcome to Bloemfontein'. She stood up and cheered in a heavily accented Afrikaner voice, "Man! These BOAC boys are bloody marvellous, you only have to tell them where you live, and they take you right there!"

7. A TRAINING CAPTAIN

On my return from a routine 14-day trip, I received a note to ask me to call in to the Flight Training Manager's (FTM) office. When I entered the office, I was met by the FTM, who I think was Captain Pete Royce at that time, and Captain Bob Simpson, a very senior and much respected training captain. This does not look good, I thought. I guessed I was in for a reprimand of some sort. Both Pete and Bob were held in high regard for their exemplary standards, combined with a natural ability to relate to, and encourage, the crews on their fleet. "Ah, good to see you Smith, we were just talking about you." I remained apprehensive. "We require more training captains, and your name is on the list." I thought to myself, don't panic! "It would depend on you passing not only the BOAC Training Captain's Course, but the Civil Aviation Authority [CAA] Type Rating Examiner's Course as well. What do you think?"

I was finding it difficult to think, but I must have replied, "Yes." (I managed to restrain myself from blurting out, "God bless you. Thank you! Thank you! Thank you," and furiously shaking his hand at the same time.)

Thus started the long process of being trained and checked out not only as an instructor, but an examiner. D.P. 'Dai' Davies's book, *Handling the Big Jets* became my bible. It was written by a pilot, for pilots. Explanation and advice pour from every page. I read it from cover to cover, numerous times... as the photo shows.

I enjoyed the instructing very much. Most of my training took place in the 707 simulator under the guidance and instruction of senior training captains. They were all first-class teachers, particularly Bob Simpson, Keith Meyers, Hugh Dibley, Phil Hogge, Pete Royce, Spud Tait, Laurie Harris and Jim Smillie.

The CAA's Type Rating Examiner's course, as it was called, was a more formal course. It took place at the CAA building at Stansted Airport. The simulator used was a mock-up of a DH125 executive jet, owned and built by Tony Angel, my original guru. As the computers were analogue, they required constant monitoring. This was Tony's task and he sat at the back of the cockpit. He was contracted to the CAA but was not part of it. He became so much more than a simulator operator. Tony acted as an air traffic controller; this made the whole detail more realistic. If he felt you were coping with everything, this gave him licence to expand his range of 'air traffic voices' and added a touch of humour to a sometimes stressful session. The radio waves would suddenly be full of Indian type voices jamming the air, asking questions such as *'Which is the best way to Bombay?'*

It may sound frivolous but it was all part of the course and carefully planned to pile on the pressure. All this was going on when you were trying to monitor how the CAA captain was flying the aircraft. We were taught how important it was to give a good pre-flight briefing. Then there could be no doubt as to *exactly* what was required.

The CAA captain sat in the left-hand seat and would act as if he were a candidate applying for his Instrument Rating. All commercial pilots have this rating as part of their pilot's licence. This confirms that they are able to fly an aircraft in cloud or at night solely by reference to the flight instruments. There were set parameters for each flying exercise. If the candidate strayed outside these parameters then he failed that part of the exercise. There were many exercises. If you were required to fly in level flight, for example, the tolerances would allow you to stray 50 feet above or below your assigned altitude. Speed control was also subject to tight limitations, such as plus 10 knots or minus 10 knots from the optimum airspeed.

The CAA captains flew the simulator very, very accurately. They were aware of the limits and from time to time would deliberately fly exactly ON the limit for just a few seconds. This was done to provoke much discussion. A wide deviation of a few hundred feet was much easier to spot and, therefore, much easier to mark the student down. The task was to note when this happens and make notes to be used at the debrief. It sounds like a game.

I quickly realized that the exercise was to train me to become a good observer. I was being trained and checked to be able to pick up the *slightest* deviation from the optimum flight path; this required absolute concentration. The high standard of observation required was driven home in the hardest way by the CAA captains.

My first two simulator details with them went well. I felt I had picked up most errors made by the captain being tested, and he agreed with my observations. However, at the end of detail three, when full of confidence, I pointed out various errors he had made. He changed into a demon, suddenly arguing quite violently, every point. "Prove it," he shouted. "Oh, no I didn't." I sat there in shock. He calmed down, lit a cigarette, and said with a smile, "You are going to meet someone like that. Write everything down, then there can be no argument." I was pleased and relieved when I passed the final CAA check flight.

My new role was training and instructing pilots new to the 707. I took over from the ground instructors and we moved onto the simulator syllabus. I eventually became a Base Training Captain, which involved teaching on the aircraft, mostly 'touch and goes' at Shannon or Prestwick.

One of the unusual jobs was to take an aircraft that had just been completely overhauled by the maintenance department and carry out a thorough check to see that it was ready to go into airline service. These 'Certificate of Airworthiness Test Flights', as they were called, were carried out flying over an area of the North Sea far away from the busy airways. There was always a full flight deck crew – captain, co-pilot and engineer, all experienced trainers. Engines were shut down and relit, pressurization checked, and so on. There was a long checklist of items to work through. I was scheduled to fly on one of these test flights when I received a call from operations and was told that Captain 'Bob' Simpson was due to retire and was to fly his last line flight to the Caribbean.

If you were approaching retirement, it was an unwritten tradition that you could choose your last working trip to anywhere in the world. The Caribbean was the most popular. However, he had to drop the trip as his mum had died. I really felt for Bob, the sadness of his mum's passing and, after a long and distinguished career, he was not going to be able to finish with just one last trip. That must have been hard. The phone call continued: "Is there anyway Bob could come with you as extra crew?" I immediately replied that not only would Bob be more than welcome, I would be delighted for him to be the captain and I would be his co-pilot. I then received a call to say that when we return from what was now to be Bob's final flight, we were to taxi in and park in the cul de sac in the maintenance area. Our FTM had arranged a surprise. All Bob's family and most of the training office staff would be there to greet him and wish him a happy retirement. What a wonderful idea!

About this time the company had the names of famous explorers sign written under the captain's window of the 747s, such as Sir

Walter Raleigh, Ernest Shackleton, etc. As Bob walked down the aircraft steps everyone came into view to congratulate him on his retirement. He was completely taken by surprise. A set of steps was positioned by the captain's window and with giant Letraset (large black sticky letters) the letters were stuck to the fuselage. We stood back to admire the handiwork. The sign read: *Sir Rupert Simpson* (Bob's real name was Rupert). Bob was delighted with it! The aircraft was subsequently sold to an African cargo airline and I believe *Sir Rupert Simpson* is still flying in Africa.

Command Course

When I joined BOAC, I was given a seniority number. At the time I felt it was just another number. The longer you served with the airline the more important this number became. Any pilots joining after you were junior to you. I worked my way up the seniority list as co-pilots became captains or retired. Talent did not play any part. All pilots were treated as equally talented, which we all know is not true. However, when the numbers decreed it, you were placed on a Command Course. This involved a period of training in the simulator and flying on the line in the left-hand seat. It was an intensive course, and rightly so, I feel. Probably, the final flight check is the most stressful.

One of the jobs I really enjoyed most as a senior training captain was the final flight check. It was the culmination of the command course. If the candidate passed this check flight, he or she became a captain. I mentioned Crew Resource Management (CRM) in earlier chapters. I would like to give an example of CRM at its best.

Senior First Officer Tony Pike was due to fly to Malaga and back as the final flight of his command course. Tony was required to act as the captain and sat in the left-hand seat. A management pilot, Captain Fred Rivett sat in the co-pilot's seat, and I sat in the jump seat. Fred and I were there as observers. We were to watch Tony Pike throughout the whole flight to make sure he was up to the required standard. You can imagine the pressure on Tony to have two pairs of eyes watching your every move. Both Fred and I were well of aware of this pressure and, more importantly, how to manage it.

Picture the scene: Prior to the flight the captain, in this case Tony, had to study all the information for that particular flight. Weather forecasts, notes for the route for the destination, and alternate, etc. This is done in a large room with many other crews all checking in for their flights. Not the ideal environment. Tony, Fred and I were sat at a table wading through the piles of paperwork. Captain John Macaulay, another training captain, walked by and said in a stage whisper, "Don't do anything stupid Pike!" The saying was taken from the popular TV series called *Dad's Army.* The scene is the one where the Home Guard have captured some German sailors. These sailors are very resentful and one of German officers points at one of the Home Guard and shouts, "*Vat iz your name?*" Quick as a flash, the Home Guard Captain Mainwaring shouts back, *"Don't tell 'im Pike!"* The phrase *'Don't tell 'im Pike!'* has become part of our language. This may sound trivial or even frivolous but it broke the ice throughout the day. Anything that required the captain's decision, in this case Tony's decision, was followed by a chorus of *'Don't do anything stupid Pike!'* It made the day. Tony passed with flying colours!

One day, I was busy working in the B707 flight simulator when I received a call from my friend Clive Ritchie. "Oi!" he said in his inimitable style. "The Farnborough Air Show is starting next week. I understand that the BA training office has some free tickets available. You're a training captain, can you get a couple of tickets for us?"

I said I would make some enquiries. I phoned Clive, "Sorry, mate, no go. They do not get free tickets now."

Clive was not to be put off. "Well, try Singer Link Miles the simulator company at Shoreham, you know their sales team quite well, don't you?"

I phoned Rolly, my only contact at Singer Engineering.

"Sure," he said, "how many tickets do you want, but you have to go tomorrow."

I said, "Thank you."

The next day, Clive and I drove to Farnborough Airfield; at the airfield entrance gate we picked up our free tickets. I said to Clive, "I think we should call into the Singer Link Miles hospitality marquee and thank them for the free tickets."

Standing at the entrance to the marquee was an immaculately dressed head waiter. "Good morning gentleman," he said, "please follow me." Clive and I shrugged our shoulders and did as we were told. We followed the man to the bar. "Harry," he said to the barman, "look after these boys, I will be back in a moment."

The head waiter returned. "I'm very sorry gentlemen, I don't seem to have you on my luncheon list." I thought, I'm not surprised; we are not supposed to be here. "Would you mind sharing a table?" he enquired.

I got a kick in the shins from Clive, and said, "Not at all."

We were shown to a table right at the front of the marquee, with a superb view of the air show. Sitting at the table were two gentlemen. They introduced themselves as Captain Brown and Commander Jones (not their real names), Army and Navy simulator instructors. We had a wonderful lunch. At the end of the lunch our two companions looked at each other and then said, "We have to make a confession, we are impostors. We are simulator instructors, and we were given free tickets. We called in to thank them, and that head waiter sat us down and gave us a free lunch."

Clive, rose to occasion. "Well!" he said in his best headmaster's voice, "I don't know what to say." They looked sheepish. Then he laughed and said, "We are impostors too!" There was a second or so of stunned silence, followed by much laughter and glasses raised to my friend Rolly and Singer Link Miles.

8. BEYOND 707s

Things were about to change.

Following the merger of BOAC and BEA to form British Airways, the airline had too many pilots and not enough work for them. The company was happy for some of us to stand down for some time, 'six months leave of absence' until the situation improved. I had vowed to keep in touch with my roots, so I started a variety of mixed, but very interesting flying. I feel the best way to cover this period is to write about my experiences, though not necessarily in chronological order.

Meridian Airmaps Ltd

I started working for Meridian Airmaps Ltd, based at Shoreham Airport, flying a Piper Apache.

The aircraft always flew with three crew. Pete Parsons was the only permanent member of the crew. He was responsible for organising the flying programme. This involved liaising with Ordnance Survey as to where and what they wanted photographed. Once we were overhead of the site, I would fly the aircraft at a specific height and speed in a long racetrack pattern. The cameraman, who sat behind Pete and me, switched on the camera and the sequence started.

The ideal weather was for a clear sky with no cloud shadows. If the weather allowed, we would fly from dawn to dusk, stopping only to refuel the aircraft and us. It demanded very accurate flying. I had to 'up my game' as Pete was a hard taskmaster. Any slightest deviation from the required flight path resulted in a whack over the head with a rolled-up copy of *The Times* newspaper... or was it *The Sun*?

Haywards Aviation Ltd

Pat Fry, a captain with Dan Air, started a company called Haywards Aviation Ltd. They used a De Havilland Dove on charter flights from Shoreham Airport. Pat, a highly decorated WWII pilot, was way ahead of his time as regards cheap air travel, way ahead of Freddie Laker of Laker Airways and Michael O'Leary of Ryanair. Pat started a regular service from Shoreham to Dieppe. He negotiated a deal with the Chamber of Commerce in Dieppe such that no landing fees were paid and fuel was at a much-reduced rate. Fares were also subsidised.

Shoreham Airport is the oldest civil airport in the UK. It opened in 1910. The first commercial flight from there was made in 1911. It was reported to be a cargo flight, from Shoreham to Hove, a distance of five miles, carrying a box of light bulbs! Clearly, they were not taking any chances with weight in those days.

First cargo flight from Shoreham Airport.

The flight took place on 4th July 1911. Captain Horatio Claude Barber was the pilot. He was offered £100 (about £8,000 in today's money), which he gave to The Royal Aero Club, who commissioned a trophy. The Britannia Trophy is awarded to aviators accomplishing the most meritorious performance in aviation during the previous year. Brian Jones, Bertrand Piccard and Sir David Hempleman-Adams have all won this award. Their exploits are recorded in this book.

The Haywards Dove was a light, twin, 11-seater. It was a delight to fly. The flying was varied and much of it was last minute. Pat recruited Harry Linfield, Dave Hawkins and me as the pilots. The jobs were ad hoc. I really enjoyed this variety of flying.

For example, on one occasion I was asked to fly as soon as possible to RAF Northolt to pick up four passengers and take them to Wick in Scotland – a distance of 700 miles! Wick Airport is located at the northeast tip of Scotland. A refuelling stop was made at Edinburgh, and I put a phone call through to Wick Air Traffic Control to make sure the airfield would be open when we arrived. The controller sounded like Dr Cameron from the TV series *Dr Finlay's Casebook*. "Dinna worry," he said, "I will stay open until you arrive." We arrived at Wick at sunset. I was dog-tired. Although I had packed an overnight bag, I had not given a thought as to where I might stay. I was securing the aircraft for the night, when a large Humber Super Snipe limousine (circa 1930s) pulled up; the air traffic controller was the driver. He said in his broad Scots accent, "I was just wondering if you were thinking of having a beer."

I replied, "I have been thinking about that for the past four hours." I jumped in the car, and we were off like a rocket! "Stop, stop," I said, "I haven't booked any accommodation."

"Dina fuss yerself man. I am taking you to the only hotel and bar in town," he said with a wink and a smile!

To sum up 24 hours in Wick… in the morning, when I went to the airfield control tower to file a flight plan, the milk had been delivered in a scotch whiskey bottle and the bottle was leaning against the doorframe! It says it all!

Pat Fry managed to secure a contract to fly parts of oil rigs to Stavanger in Norway. It was a long flight for the Dove and took place at night in winter.

I did the first flight. Harry Linfield was to fly the next day. He phoned and asked, "How did it all go?"

I said it was a long night of five hours or so, and the heater in the cockpit was not working, but the one in the cabin worked perfectly. The oil rig parts were kept warm, but I froze. Harry did the flight. I phoned him to ask how it went. "Everything was fine," he said.

"How about the heater?" I enquired.

"Oh, it was not working... so I stood in the cabin, reached forward and flew it from there." Being 6' 6" tall has its advantages!

One of the regular Dove flights was from Shoreham to Morlaix in France. The cargo was live lobsters. As the pilot, I had to get into my seat first; the cabin was then crammed from floor to ceiling with boxes of the little critters, and the door was closed. If there was a fire, I guess I would be the last to get out.

The local paper had an article about the flight. The headline was '*2,000 fly in an 11-seat plane!*'

Rhodesia

The stand down period looked as if it would be extended. Cecilia thought this was a great opportunity for us to both visit her family in Rhodesia, as it was called then. The country gained official independence as Zimbabwe on 18th April 1980. I hoped I would be able to fly in Rhodesia. It is such a beautiful country.

The Rhodesian government was running a cloud seeding programme. This involved flying into active thunderstorms, firing silver iodide pellets into the clouds to make it rain. I had heard about this programme.

Having been taught to avoid thunderstorms at all costs, it seemed crazy to deliberately fly into one, but I wanted a job flying. I went to Salisbury Airport to take a check flight for the cloud seeding job. I was briefed for the procedure and we walked out to an Apache aircraft, which looked if it was not in the first flush of youth!

2,000 fly in 11-seat plane

IF YOU THINK there is something fishy about a report of 2,000 passengers flying across the Channel in an 11-seater light aircraft, you're right— the passengers were live lobsters.

Pilot Brian Smith took off from Shoreham Airport yesterday to take his live cargo to Belgium.

The trip was arranged by Haywards Aviation, which operates Dove aircraft for passenger and light cargo air lifts from Shoreham and other airports.

Haywards Aviation, run by Dan Air pilot Capt. Pat Fry, has for the past two years been transporting live shell fish to the Continent from Portsmouth for Selsey shell fish merchant John Arrow. Yesterday's flight was the first from Shoreham.

—ABOVE: Capt. P. Fry (right) holds up two live lobsters to show pilot Capt. Brian Smith.

The check pilot, who was also a meteorologist, delivered the brief. He sat behind the pilot and, using a type of sawn-off shotgun bolted to the side of the aircraft, fired the pellets into the thunderstorms.

The ideal scenario was to 'seed' two or three thunder clouds, hoping they would amalgamate into one giant thunderstorm and it would rain. He said, "When you enter the storm, there will be severe up and down drafts. Only you will register whether we are going up or down. When you feel a strong up draught, shout as loud as you can 'NOW!'. I will then fire the pellets."

We took off and headed for a giant thundercloud. It looked like huge lumps of boiling cauliflower, the outside of which was in bright sunshine, but the centre looked the colour of slate, dark and foreboding. I took a deep breath, and in we went. Suddenly, all hell broke loose. Flashes of lightning and hailstones battered the aircraft. We were ascending at an alarming rate. I was scared and shouted "JESUS!" Bang! And off went the pellets. We shot out of the cloud completely covered in ice. 'What's next?' I thought.

The voice from the back of the aircraft said, "Good. Right ho, let's head back to Salisbury." He was as calm as could be. When we had left Salisbury a couple of hours before, it was bathed in sunshine, wind calm with unlimited visibility.

I made a call to ATC to advise them of our intention to return, and as a matter of routine I requested their latest weather report. The controller replied, "Wind 30 gusting 55 knots, visibility 1 mile in heavy rain, THUNDERSTORMS in the vicinity... AND YOU DID IT!"

This was not the end of it. The debrief followed. The check pilot said, "As I recall I briefed you to shout 'NOW!' as we started to ascend. This is an important call, by going up the silver iodide hangs in the cloud much longer. The pellets are very expensive, so do you remember my brief?"

"Yes," I replied, meekly.

"Then why did you shout 'JESUS'?" He then burst out laughing. "You've got the job. Let's go and have a beer." I have to say it took *several* beers for the adrenalin to subside and I saw the funny side of it.

Techair

The next night I received a call from Techair to ask if I wanted to fly for them. Although I did a couple more cloud seeding flights, I was not reluctant to leave.

Techair was an air taxi company operating out of Charles Prince Airfield to destinations all over Rhodesia. Charles Prince Airport, formerly Mount Hampden, was renamed Charles Prince after a previous airport manager. It is a general aviation airfield located northwest of Harare. After a comprehensive check flight, I was cleared to fly passengers to anywhere in Rhodesia. They operated mostly into remote grass strips, and local knowledge was a huge advantage.

I subsequently discovered that some of the management and training pilots were wary of employing airline pilots. They felt, rightly or wrongly, the airline-operating environment was not suited to 'bush flying'. I was determined, somehow, to prove the doubters wrong. An opportunity came my way quite by accident, flying to farm airstrips in remote areas.

My first passenger was a young farm manager who needed to visit several areas to pay his workers. When making my first approach the landing checks revealed only two landing gear green lights instead of three. Three would indicate the nose and main wheels were down and locked.

Standing on the roof of a battered Mk1 Land Rover was an African farm worker waving his hands in greeting. After making a low pass over the airstrip my passenger looked at me and nodded. He understood the problem with the gear. I moved the gear lever slowly up and down a couple of times. There were still only two green lights. My passenger asked for paper and pen. Was he going to write his will? I thought. He quickly scribbled a few words on the paper. In bold capital letters it read: 'IF ALL GEAR DOWN, RAISE YOUR ARMS OVER YOUR HEAD.' Genius... He took off a long sock, stuffed the paper in the sock and tied a knot in it. He then asked me to fly low right over the Land Rover. As we zoomed over, he opened a small window, and out went his sock. I banked the aircraft steeply and flew back towards the airfield. There was our man standing with both arms raised. Huge relief all round!

While the farmer was paying his men, I checked the circuit breakers, fiddled with the gear micro switch and the gear green light glowed beautifully. However, the fun had not finished...

We were running late. The weather had deteriorated. Maybe the cloud seeders had been at work! We were about 30 miles or so from Charles Prince Airfield when the weather really hit us. Heavy rain reduced the visibility; the cloud base was lowering at the same time.

I was about to divert to Salisbury main airport when I saw the railway line to Salisbury to our right beneath us and running parallel to our track. I knew the line forked just before our airfield. If we could see the junction we should be able to see the threshold of Runway 24 at Charles Prince Airfield. I instructed my very capable passenger to look out and tell me as soon as he saw the junction.

The thought, 'always have a plan and manual back up' came to mind. Plan A was to see the junction, drop the landing gear, turn right and land. Plan B, if we could *not* see the junction was to climb away and divert to Salisbury main airport. Plan C, er, we did not have a plan C!

The cry from the right-hand seat came loud and clear: "*Junction dead ahead!*"

I immediately lowered the landing gear and flaps. We landed in torrential rain. It was dark. I slowly taxied towards the hangars. As we came to a halt and shut down, I noticed the huge hangar doors were wide open with bright lights spilling onto the tarmac. People started streaming out, including many Techair staff. The check pilot Mr Rawson was there, he just gave me a big smile and a 'thumbs up'.

Unbeknown to me, the Techair staff had been quite concerned

as to my whereabouts. This gave support to the argument that airline pilots were not cut out for bush flying. Their genuine smiles and the welcome back made me feel I had redeemed the airline pilots and myself.

Rhodesia and the Civil War

Most of the grass airstrips were next to protected villages or forts. These villages were designed to keep local people safe, surrounded by barbed wire and guarded by soldiers, sometimes South African soldiers. A regular trip was to fly engineers to carry out maintenance at these forts. On my first landing it was a shock to see the grass strip lined with South African soldiers, all heavily armed. I was to spend the day there and return to Charles Prince Airport at sunset.

One of the managers of a fort I got to know well. Sadly, I can only remember him by his first name, Charlie. I believe he was a Greek Rhodesian, a striking looking man, completely bald, weighing about 20 stone. He was full of life, always laughing, mostly at his own ribald jokes.

One day, as we were leaving, he asked me if he could come back with me to Salisbury the next week, and could he bring a kitten for his girlfriend. I agreed.

So, the next week, as we were leaving 'Charlie's place', as I called it, he exclaimed as he was walking out of the door, "Oh, I've forgotten the bloody kitten!" There were many wild, stray cats around. He turned and grabbed the nearest kitten, stuffed it into a large wicker wastepaper basket and slammed the lid down.

Charlie, the kitten, two passengers and I climbed into a truck and headed out to the aircraft. It was extremely hot; you could fry eggs on the metal skin on the wing. As usual, the runway was lined with South African soldiers. They never acknowledged our presence in any way. I can only imagine they did not want to be there. The start-up and taxi out was carried out as quickly as possible. Due to the heat the passenger door was left open until we were ready for take-off. Charlie was sitting next to me in the right-hand seat, his gigantic body overflowing, almost on top of me. We shut and locked the door and took off.

Once we were safely climbing away, I shouted to Charlie to crack open the lid of the basket to let the kitten have some air. Charlie never did anything with *small* movements. He lifted the lid as high as he could. The kitten shot out and streaked over the combing like a Titan rocket. The poor little thing was terrified. It hid under the back seat. Charlie and the two passengers were shouting obscenities, waving their arms and trying to catch it. Eventually, peace and quiet descended and we proceeded on our way to Salisbury.

The following week I returned to the fort. The soldiers were lined up alongside the runway. One of them waved his hand clutching his rifle. "Hey MAN!" he said. I stood stock-still. "MAN, every week I see this aeroplane take off, it climbs away and turns towards Salisbury. Last week I watch the plane, it suddenly does aerobatics, zooming up, down, left and right. What the HELL was going on?" I shrugged my shoulders, implying it wasn't me guv. "MAN!" he said again and slowly walked away shaking his head.

I was very lucky to fly all over Rhodesia. All the airfields were interesting, some more than others. All the flights were day trips. We carried a variety of passengers, mostly farm managers and engineers. They had done the trips many times, and most importantly knew the lie of the land thoroughly.

I got to know them very well; they were great people to fly with. Although we were a civilian company and carried civilian personnel, we were well aware we were in a war zone.

Mukumbura

Mukumbura is a village in the far north-eastern part of Rhodesia. It had a grass airstrip long enough to take DC3s. It shares a border with Mozambique. It was known as a 'hot spot' during the bush war. I do not remember it very well, and my logbook has no particular entries.

I never felt apprehensive when I was there, but we never stayed very long, certainly not overnight. In 1977 Mukumbura was immortalized in the song *It's a long way to Mukumbura* by Mike Westcott and Leprechaun.

Marymount Mission

I found Marymount Mission rather spooky. With the many soldiers, both Rhodesian and South African, mixed with the local civilians there was an atmosphere that I could not really define.

Just before I flew there, there had been a firefight and many people, including priests, nuns and children were kidnapped and taken to Mozambique.

The place had been ransacked and was as silent as a cemetery. I flew an engineer in to fix a water pump. As soon as it was working, we left this sad place, and flew back to Salisbury in silence.

Chisumbanje Airfield

I remember Chisumbanje well as a strip of soil and gravel, rather than smooth grass. My flight there was delayed several days as the airstrip was waterlogged, plus communications with Chisumbanje were difficult to say the least. A call came through that the strip was open, so we took off immediately.

On landing we taxied to the parking area. The aircraft sat there all day in the hot sun. We came to leave just before sunset. A beautiful, calm, clear late afternoon. As I started the right engine, the aircraft slowly sank on to its right wing. I quickly switched off the engine, and more by good luck than judgment it stopped sinking, with the propeller parallel to the wing. No damage. We all disembarked and looked at the large muddy potholes, scratching our heads. I thought to myself, 'We ain't going nowhere.'

While we were all pondering what to do. The farm manager put two fingers to his mouth and gave a whistle that could have been heard in Salisbury over 100 miles away. Twenty or so African workers popped their heads over the airfield boundary hedge. The manager talked in rapid Shona and they took up position all round the edge of the airplane, shoulder to shoulder. "*Hey up,*" he must have said in Shona. With one collective grunt they lifted the aircraft out of the mud and even more astonishingly moved it forward to dry ground! We were on our way.

During my time flying in Rhodesia I realised the importance of hand flying the aircraft and keeping in touch with visual flying. Clearly flying the TI Heron and the Dove for Haywards Aviation had been valuable experience. Interestingly enough, base training in the 707 should be put on the 'keeping in touch' list as multiple touch and go training requires all the CRM components – good situation awareness, good communications, etc.

My six-month spell was up. I left Rhodesia with many happy memories, little knowing I was to return for more adventures.

9. MORE ADVENTURES

The 707 was coming to the end of its day. The airline was now flying B747s. The demand for low-cost travel favoured these wide-bodied jets. Concorde made its spectacular debut.

Training captains were in much demand. I was the most junior training captain on the 707 and watched on as these senior trainers went off to fly these new aircraft. I jokingly felt I was to be the one to turn the lights out in our 707 training office!

Kenya Airways

Almost overnight East African Airways ceased operations. The last flight was in January 1977. The legal battle was looking as if it might take some time to sort out as to who owned what. The Kenyans wanted to start operating straight away. Within four months Kenya Airways was formed, but what aircraft were they going to operate? British Midland Airways (BMA) immediately came to their rescue with the lease of two 707-321 aircraft. The inaugural flight was on 4th February 1977. However, BMA could only release a few pilots. They contacted BA, requesting a loan of about half a dozen pilots. I was soon on my way to East Midlands Airfield for a checkout flight prior to joining BMA/Kenya Airways. More touch and goes!

The next day I received a call from BMA operations. "Hello Brian, this is Ray here, how would you like to go to Nairobi tomorrow?"

"Ok. What's the deal?"

"You will report to the Excelsior Hotel at Heathrow at 22.00." The BMA/Kenya Airways crew rostering department was run by 'Old Ray' and 'Young Ray'. They were very diplomatic in dealing with such a mix of contract crews. They were true professionals and handled it as if they were conducting a huge orchestra in the Albert Hall. Their conversation started with, "Hello Brian, this is Old (or Young) Ray here. How are you? And the wife and kids OK?" followed by, "We would like to invite you to go to Nairobi tomorrow evening." It made me feel that if I did not take up their kind 'invitation', the airline would grind to a halt.

My first flight sounded very much routine. I was about to have a taste of life outside of BA!

It was late evening when I met the rest of the crew at the hotel. The first officer was from BMA. The flight engineer was formerly with BOAC but had retired some years ago. Our cabin crew were a mix of Kenyans and BMA stewardesses.

The first officer took me to one side and said, "Do you know we are going to Nairobi, via Frankfurt!" This was news to me. The Civil Aviation Authority regulates all airline crew's hours of operating. This was beginning to look like a very long night.

It was dawn when we landed at Nairobi some 15 hours later. The whole crew were completely exhausted. We shut the engines, and the passengers disembarked. A Kenya Airways liaison officer came onto the flight deck to brief us on our next trip. He sat on the jump seat and proceeded to read through reams of paperwork. He eventually realised how tired we were. To his eternal credit, he produced a bottle of scotch. From that moment on the liaison went smoothly.

On this contract the captain was given about £5,000 in cash to pay for expenses on the trip. On a layover in Nairobi I met another captain who asked me where I kept the £5,000. I replied I put it in my locked briefcase, locked in the wardrobe in my hotel bedroom. He laughed. "When you get back to your room the money won't be there." He showed me a money belt around his waist. "This is what you need." The next day he was walking in downtown Nairobi, and he was robbed at knifepoint! Away went his belt and about £5,000.

As it was early days in the formation of Kenya Airways, the route structure was quite small, but the duty days were long. We flew to various destinations including Cairo, Bombay, Karachi, Frankfurt, Rome, and Zurich. I really enjoyed my short time with Kenya Airways/BMA. They came over as a 'can do' company, getting the job done with a good team, which was reflected in all the folks I met.

Just when I thought it was safe…

707 G-AYSL

In 1978, British Airways leased a Dan-Air 707-321, registration G-AYSL. This aircraft was built in 1959! It was initially operated by Pan American Airways (Pan Am).

Newly painted – G-AYSL. It shows the rudder hard over to the right. It must have been on a training flight at Stansted.

The last two letters of their registration usually identify an aircraft, Sierra Lima (SL) in this case. SL had been flown by many, many airlines prior to coming to BA. The Dan-Air ground engineers kept calling it 'Spread Legs!' I asked one of them why? Came the gruff reply, "Well, 'cos every buggers 'ad 'er at one time or another!"

Why did BA lease this aircraft? Several Trident aircraft operated by BA short haul were found to have small hairline cracks in the wing root area, and after the necessary structural repairs the Tridents could no longer operate their long-haul sectors with a commercial payload. This left a gap in their scheduled services and needed to be resolved as soon as possible. A temporary lease of a 707 seemed the answer.

The problem was that BA had no spare 707s. SL was available from Dan-Air though. There was a certain amount of pressure to have this aircraft fully operational as soon as possible. The BA 707 Flight Manager, Hugh Dibley, flew with the Dan-Air crew on their last flight from Heathrow to Lasham to have it painted. About a week later, Hugh Dibley, Spud Tait and I went to pick up SL from Lasham Airfield in Hampshire.

The acceptance flight was from Lasham to Stansted. We had some Dan-Air engineers on board, and I believe one of their senior training captains. I do know there was a great deal of 'who is checking who' going on. We were all very pleased with the way such an old aircraft flew. I also think we got a tick in the box for our gentle handling of the old girl from the Dan-Air observers who discreetly observed every manoeuvre, and occasionally muttered, "Not bad, not bad!"

Two days later we carried out a base training session at Stansted and in three hours or so, several crews were checked out. More touch and goes! SL made its first commercial flight a few days later, resplendent in BA colours. SL became an institution. It was very popular with all the crews and ground engineers.

I used to joke; the amalgamation of BEA and BOAC to form British Airways was like trying to get Pan Am, an American company, and Aeroflot, a Russian company, together. However, SL proved it could be done. The mix of former BOAC long-haul pilots, complete with a flight engineer, together with former BEA short-haul cabin crew worked very well. But why did so many girls fall in love with the flight engineer?

One of our pilots described flying SL was like driving an old sports car or putting on an old sports jacket. Everything worked if you treated it gently. I discovered just before touchdown a slight whistling sound could be heard. Some of the pilots expressed an opinion that the sound came from the airflow off the tips of the flaps. Whether this theory is right or wrong I do not know. If I heard this sound I knew I was at the correct height to flare the aircraft and, hopefully, make a smooth touchdown. 'Every little helps!' Such was the feeling for this historic aircraft... a party was held after its final flight. T-shirts were worn stating: '*I flew Spread Legs and survived*'. Happy days!

"You're Real Cute…"

Heraklion Airfield on the island of Crete is considered 'difficult', suffering from strong crosswinds. All captains had to have a special briefing before they could operate into this airfield.

On one occasion a 707 landing at Heraklion in a strong crosswind scraped one of its engines on the runway. It was inspected and declared safe to fly back to Gatwick. Back at base, further investigations found several more defects. The aircraft was grounded for airline service. It was sold to Time Aviation in Tucson and we ferried it to the 'boneyard' in Arizona. The deal was, when we landed in Tucson and shut down the engines, the aircraft then belonged to Time Aviation. They had booked us into overnight accommodation at The Two Trees Motel in downtown Tucson.

John (Spud) Tait was the captain, and I was his co-pilot. Spud was very good looking and in his captain's uniform he looked every inch the perfect airline commander. When we walked into the motel, Spud was in the lead. The very young lady receptionist looked up at Spud. Spud played it perfectly. In his best English accent he boomed, "Good afternoon, my name is Captain John Tait, BOAC. I understand you have three rooms for us."

The girl put her hand on her chin and, wide eyed, gazed up at Spud. "Say," she said, "you're real cute, can you say summut else?" This incident went viral, as they say now. If any of Spud's colleagues happened to pass him in the corridors of the training centre they all said, "Hi Spud… say, you're real cute." Spud took it all in good part. He was an excellent training captain. Sadly, he passed away a couple of years ago.

Air Mauritius

Although Hugh Dibley was now flying 747s, he also had a brief to look after the dwindling 707 fleet.

One day, Cecilia received a phone call from Hugh Dibley. "Hello darling," he said in his inimitable style, "is Smith around?"

"Sorry Hugh, he is at White Waltham Airfield," Cecilia replied.

"Well, I may as well ask you. What do you think Smith would say if I asked him to go to Mauritius tomorrow?"

Cecilia calmly replied, "I expect he would say, 'What time does the flight leave?'"

Hugh then immediately phoned White Waltham Airfield. "There is a call for you Brian," shouted one of the engineers from the hangar. I picked up the phone.

"Ah, Smith," said Hugh, "what would you say if I asked you to go to Mauritius tomorrow."

"What time does the flight leave?" I replied.

In fact, it was two days later that Mark Capaldi, a co-pilot, and Colin Parker, a flight engineer, and I climbed on-board the Air Mauritius 707 flying as passengers to Mauritius. The operating crew were from Air India.

Air Mauritius had just started their blue ribbon route, Mauritius to Johannesburg and Durban. However, this was the time of Apartheid. The son of India's Prime Minister was visiting Mauritius and he was not happy that Indian flight crews were flying to Durban and Johannesburg. The crews had to stop flying and the operation ceased overnight. This left Air Mauritius without flight crews to operate their lucrative route. Air India gave notice that they would not be operating into South Africa forthwith. The very next day we operated our first flight as Air Mauritius crew. This was to start a long association between our two airlines. We were put up in a hotel for a week in Mauritius, and then we had to find our own accommodation.

We discovered there were French pilots flying DHC Twin Otters – robust, short take-off and landing aircraft, ideal for hops round the islands of Reunion and Rodrigues. We made enquiries from these pilots as to the best place to stay. They recommended Pointe d'Esny, a remote seashore area on the south-eastern coast, near the airport. At that time there were no estate agents on the island. We were advised to just walk along the beach and knock on the doors of likely looking bungalows and ask if any were for rent. Mark, Colin and I set off along the beach. Within no time we had found three places to rent.

I moved into my bungalow that evening. The back doors opened onto the beach. It was a clear pitch-black night, with stars you felt you could touch. I poured myself a drink and sat on the veranda looking out over the Indian Ocean. The only sound was the lapping of the waves on the shore. Suddenly, there was a terrific BANG on the front door. I froze in my chair. BANG it went again. I crept slowly and somewhat timidly to the door. What or who could it be? Putting on a brave face, I inched the door open. A small brown and white dog brushed past me, walked into the lounge, and curled up on the floor. He remained with us throughout our time in Mauritius.

We christened him 'Café Crème'. Our families came out to join us within a couple of weeks. When we had to return to the UK, our children were distraught at the thought of leaving the dog, but our landlord moved back into the bungalow and Café Crème stayed with him. Cecilia and I would give our daughters Kerry and Cymbeline lessons under a palm tree on the beach. What a life…

The Air Mauritius routes were expanding. Hugh Dibley, our flight training manager, thought we should be able to provide BA 707 crews for this expansion. After much negotiating we were able to crew the whole contract. Thanks to Hugh Dibley, a contract was signed and BA crews flew for Air Mauritius for quite some time.

Christian Pfeiffer, one of the French pilots, lived next door to us with his family. In the early evening he would stand on the beach, put his head on one side, rather quizzically, and say, "Alcohol?" We would sit and have a 'sun downer' together.

One evening he appeared. "I have something to show you," he said. We went into his kitchen. There on the table was a beautiful model of a sailing ship, complete in every detail. Mauritius is well known for making beautiful models of sailing ships. The name of this ship was the *Nereide*, complete with the French tricolour flying from the mast.

I was so taken with the model, the next day I visited the shop. I said to the owner, "My friend has just purchased a model from you and I would like to buy one."

"Ah yes," he said, "I remember, the *Nereide*, it was a ship operating off the coast of Mauritius. A British Royal Navy ship, the *Harvey*, also patrolling off the coast used to chase this ship." He then showed me a model. The name on the model was the *Harvey*.

"I'll take it," I said. I started to form a plan. I could not believe my luck. I hurried home as fast as I could and set the model up in the kitchen. I then stood on the beach outside Christian's house. I said, "Alcohol?" I continued in my best French. "J'ai quelque chose à te montrer." It made Winston Churchill's French sound good. I proudly unveiled the *Harvey*. Christian jumped up and down and shouted, "I knew you would buy it, I just knew it!" I still have the model of the *Harvey* in our dining room.

Christian gave me a flight in his aircraft, a DHC Twin Otter, to Rodrigues, a remote island 300 miles out into the Indian Ocean. As a thank you, I asked if he would like to come on a 707 trip with me to Johannesburg.

We flew to Johannesburg (JNB) via Durban and stayed overnight. The Air Mauritius handling agent in JNB is South African Airways. We were always assigned the same two ground engineers, Johannes Pretorius and Pieter Potgeiter. They were gentle giants who could only just fit through the flight deck door of the 707. They told us many times how much they hated the British. Maybe they thought we were Mauritian, for they were extremely kind to us, and kept us supplied with all sorts of hardware we could not obtain in Mauritius.

After our overnight stay, we had time in the morning to go shopping. All our cabin crew were Mauritian. It was a big event for them to shop and pick up various delicacies, which were not available in Mauritius. Christian came with us and, being French, pointed out the best wines and cheeses. On the flight back from Johannesburg to Mauritius, I invited Christian to sit in the co-pilot's seat. This was one of my favourite routes. It was a beautiful evening, flying over the Indian Ocean at sunset. Smooth flight conditions with very few other aircraft on our route.

We were approaching Madagascar when the SelCal alert chimed. The abbreviation SelCal stands for Selective Calling. Once you have established a code with air traffic control it allows the crew to take off their headsets and get some relief from the long-range radio that always had white noise in the background, which sounded like frying bacon. It is very hard on the ears on a long flight. If the ground station wishes to communicate with you, a light flashes and a chime sounds in the flight deck. This SelCal was from South African Airways, our handling agent, to say... "You have a bomb on board!" I looked across the flight deck at Christian. He had turned very pale. I said, "Did you understand that message?" He slowly nodded his head.

There are a series of actions required when you receive notice of a bomb threat. This call was classed as specific. The caller had named our airline and our flight number. As the threat was specific, we had instructions and training as how to proceed. We were closer to Mauritius than Johannesburg and elected to continue.

Mauritius air traffic was alerted to our situation. We were told to make a normal approach and landing, to stay on the runway and evacuate the passengers as quickly as possible. After we landed, passenger steps were positioned by the side of the runway, ready to be put into position.

I had briefed our chief stewardess, Marianne Garrioh, and she in turn briefed her crew. I asked her to have a casual look around the cabin to see if anything looked suspicious or out of place. She reported back to me that there appeared to be a metal object jammed behind one of the food lockers in the front galley. Blankets were packed around the locker and cabin crew were instructed to keep well clear. All the cabin crew acted calmly and professionally.

Immediately after touch down I made an announcement to the passengers that due to operational reasons they should follow the instructions of the cabin crew and vacate the aircraft as quickly as possible.

Having Christian on board proved a bonus. He made the same announcement in French. Shepherded by the cabin crew and pilots, the aircraft was soon cleared. The Mauritian Special Forces took over and searched the cabin. The passengers were whisked off to the terminal. The first thing they knew about it was when they read the papers the next day. We stayed close to the aircraft in case we had to move it when the all clear was given.

A huge Mauritian soldier, part of the Special Mobile Forces Team (SMF), appeared in the aircraft doorway. He proudly held up a shiny metal teapot! This had been judged to be the bomb. After a thorough search by the SMF the aircraft was declared 'clean'. Subsequently, the hoax call was traced to a bunch of drunks in the bar at Johannesburg Airport; they had been barred from flying because of their condition, so decided to take revenge with the bomb hoax.

We put the aircraft back in its hangar. Christian, Colin, Mark and

I went back to my bungalow for a couple of well-earned beers. Far from thanking me for the flight in our 707, Christian's only comment was that he felt much safer flying his small twin-engined aircraft for two hours, 300 miles out into the Indian Ocean with minimum navigational aids and without a co-pilot.

British Airtours

I returned from Air Mauritius to be seconded to British Airtours as a training captain based at Gatwick. British Airtours had been operating 707s for some time; they had none of the high lift wings and flaps. At about that time, there was a saying that the early 707s only managed to get airborne thanks to the curvature of the earth!

Now they re-equipped with a newer version designated 707-336. This aircraft was quite an improvement with more powerful engines, improved flaps and a greater range.

The route structure was a mix of charter flights, both long haul and short haul. It was a busy time converting pilots to the 'new' aircraft. More touch and goes! About this time, I experienced my first engine failure in a 707. Ironically, in a 'new' 707! We were cruising overhead Germany en-route to Heraklion. The No. 3 engine started to vibrate and continued to shake so violently it looked as if it would separate from the wing. Throttling back made no difference.

We shut down the engine and turned to land at Gatwick. We advised ATC of our situation and requested 'a return to Gatwick'. Immediately, the controller gave us clearance to turn onto a north-westerly heading. Remarkably, that initial heading remained unchanged until we intercepted the ILS for Gatwick.

It was subsequently discovered one of the fan blades in the core of the engine had broken; this made the fan oscillate out of balance, rather like an overhead fan in an old Asian rest house, but at ten times the speed! After ten years or more of good service the ageing 707s were gradually being replaced with Tristars.

So We Say Farewell to the 707...

On 2nd January 1984 I was privileged to be the captain of the last flight of British Airtours B707 G-AXXY. The co-pilots were John Macaulay and Hugh Beadle. The chief steward was Brian Forrest.

The engineering department organised this flight. The plan was to complete the flight, then have a 'farewell to the 707' party in a hangar at our base at Gatwick. The flight was extraordinary. Looking back, I am amazed that we were allowed to carry out such manoeuvres. It was more like flying an air show sequence. The 'passengers' were all staff members, including my wife and two daughters.

After take-off from Gatwick we headed towards Heathrow. We made a high-speed run at low level along the full length of the runway, pulled up and continued on to Newquay where we used to carry out our base training. It was an ideal airfield for training, having a long runway and little air traffic congestion.

The air traffic controllers were always most helpful. It was good to say farewell in style to such a base. We flew an ILS approach at high speed to a very low level along the runway and climbed away to return to Gatwick. As we were starting our approach, one of our flight managers, Ron Bridge, who had been sitting behind me on the jump seat, said, "What are we going to do at Gatwick?"

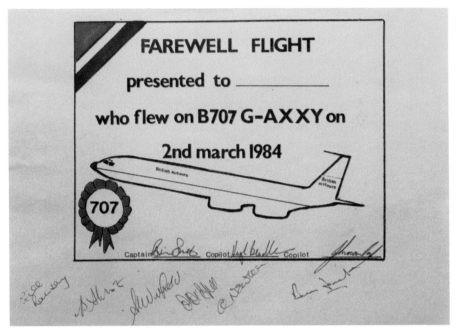

A copy of a flight certificate, given to every passenger. All 180 certificates were handmade!

Our instructions or flight plan were to come straight in and land. "We can't have that," he said. He grabbed the radio mike and asked air traffic control if we could do just one last low-level pass prior to our final landing. Their reply was, "You have to!"

After touchdown we called ATC to sign off, as it were. We thanked them for their help over the years and particularly for today. "It's been a pleasure. Goodbye and good luck," they replied.

The original plan was to taxi so that the nose of the aircraft was just inside the hangar. I understand our insurance company had something to say about this. We parked up just outside. Then the party started...

The engineers had transformed the inside of the hanger to make a mock-up of a country pub. A bar stretched the full length of the wall with a lean-to thatched roof complete with a pub sign '*The Glide Inn*'. There was a live band, and dancing went on all night. At one stage, dry ice covered the dance floor, giving the appearance of dancing on clouds. We were truly legless in more ways than one.

I was called back to Air Mauritius for two months. Two very interesting months as it turned out. This was quite a short but comprehensive period of training to convert Mauritian pilots to the 707. Yes, it was back to 'touch and goes'.

Air Mauritius wanted to train Dominique Paturau, their chief pilot on their DH Twin Otter aircraft, to become chief pilot of their 707 aircraft. Ranjit Appa was to be checked out as a flight engineer. Ranjit was the liaison officer between Air Mauritius and the BA crews. He had always met the aircraft when it returned to Mauritius from Johannesburg or Durban.

It was an important link as any problems could be sorted out there and then... more or less. Mark, our co-pilot, Colin, our flight engineer, and I had not been paid our living allowances for some time, six weeks or so and, as we explained, we had family to feed, including Café Crème, the dog. I decided to confront Ranjit and explain to him that we were very unhappy with this situation. I had a rant, and then he put his hands on my shoulders, gave a smile, and said, "Brian, you are looking at it with a European mind." He was right of course. The next day we were paid. We became good friends, and still are!

Base Training in Mauritius

As we did not have access to a flight simulator, all the training had to be done in the aircraft. It was expensive, but very exciting.

My previous experience of base training had been carried out in ideal conditions at Prestwick, Shannon or Stansted, that is, apart from my experience one night in Shannon (see Chapter 4). The base training consisted of hand flying only. No use of the autopilot, or automatics. The circuit is flown in a racetrack type pattern. A take-off, climb to 1,500', and then turn left or right onto the reciprocal track of the runway. At about four miles make a continuous turn on to final approach, hopefully with good visibility and calm conditions, followed by a touch and go landing. This is the ideal circuit in an ideal world. Now to Mauritius.

This is a view of an Air Mauritius B707, at that time it was operated by British Airtours. It is not the B707 we were flying for our crew training, but it does give a good view of the terrain. The name of the mountain in the background is Lion Mountain. 'Runway 14' points towards the sea and 'Runway 32' points towards the mountains that rise very steeply a few miles from the end of the runway. There is nearly always some turbulence associated with these mountains, making an approach towards the sea quite challenging. However, if you were making an approach to land towards the mountains for a touch and go landing, you would need to make a left turn immediately after take-off.

Typical weather for Mauritius at that time of year (February 1983) was rain showers associated with a change in wind direction and speed, which kept us on our toes. Some old timers would call it 'Good character building stuff!' I called it 'Not dangerous, or difficult, but *different!*' Overlaid on this is the consideration that the pilots flying were completing a conversion course onto the 707 from their previous light aircraft type. This would be the first time they had actually handled a large aircraft and carried out a landing. It was a busy time. We always had a fully qualified co-pilot and flight engineer on the flight deck. These extra pairs of eyes helped considerably. Visual circuits, as it says, require you to be able to see where you are going at all times.

I always looked for a prominent landmark to judge when to turn onto final approach. The Mauritius terrain consisted of green field after green field of sugar cane with no discernible features. It looked like a turbulent dark green sea. Ranjit, who knew this area like the back of his hand remarked quietly, "Do you see that white bungalow over there?" Sticking up in the middle of all the green fields was a large white bungalow. It was in exactly the right place… right on the extended centre line of the runway, about four miles out. "Incidentally," he said, "it belongs to your landlord!"

We completed the training in three days. Each pilot flying for about an hour and a half each day. The 707 is a noisy aircraft compared with the latest jets, and we were continuously going round in circles at a relatively low level. The thought crossed my mind that here we are, flying over a remote area that is normally very quiet and peaceful. I looked down at the workers in the sugar cane fields, they were all waving. As we flew over the beaches everyone was waving. My family standing on the beach outside our bungalow were also waving. We never had this reception at Prestwick or Stansted.

If you get the impression I seemed to flit between BA and Air Mauritius, that was exactly what was happening. 707 training captains were in short supply. One day I had a call to go to Abu

Dhabi to fly the sheikh's 707 for a short period while one of their pilots could take leave. I had heard much about this 707. It was fitted out like an executive jet, rather like *Air Force One*, the aircraft of the President of the USA.

I flew to Abu Dhabi where the immigration officer looked at my passport and asked me to stand to one side. Another officer appeared and took me into a small room. He explained I had an Israeli entry stamp in my passport; therefore, I must leave the country straight away on the next flight. Shock, horror! I had flown into Israel several times. The immigration authorities there did not stamp your passport but put a slip of paper in it with the Israeli stamp on it.

Somehow, my passport was stamped, not the slip of paper. I requested a phone call to my boss in London and poured out my story to him. "I don't believe it," was the reply.

"Well, neither do I!" I said. I then apologised for all the inconvenience I was about to cause.

"Well, you'll never believe it," he said, "I have just had a long conversation with a captain who is in Mauritius and very unhappy. He has requested to transfer to Abu Dhabi."

I found myself on the next flight to Mauritius and the other captain was soon on his way to Abu Dhabi. I am sure our flight paths must have crossed.

British Airtours 737. Abbreviated to KT, Our Radio Call Sign

Now the 707s were coming to an end, I wondered where I would go next, or what I would fly?

John Mason, the British Airtours Flight Manager, asked if I would like to fly the 737 at Gatwick. I was enjoying my time with British Airtours (KT). I thanked John and immediately started my conversion training to the 737. It was quite a change from the 707, with two crew, two engines (I nearly said 'only').

It reminds me of one of our senior 707 captains saying, "The only reason I flew the 707 was because there wasn't a *five* engine aircraft at the time." His reasoning was the more engines the better. At his retirement party we presented him with a model of a 707 with a DC10 engine in the tail. He had his five-engined aircraft at last.

'BOB, WITH HIS FOUR, FIVE
ENGINED AIRCRAFT

I soon learnt the reputation of the 737 as an all-round workhorse was true. The automatics made the day-to-day working environment easy. Two autopilots, with an auto throttle, two flight management computers, it was sheer luxury.

Initially, I missed not having a flight engineer. The 737, however, was designed to operate with two pilots, and making the transition was straightforward. Incidentally, most of our 707 flight engineers (F/Es) were retrained as pilots, and subsequently became captains with BA. Some became training captains. All of the

F/Es I flew with were very good 'airmen', a fully integrated part of the flight deck team. Not just 'flying spanners' from a bygone era.

However, one F/E I flew with, as an acknowledgement to past days, used to produce a large brass tap and attach it with a rubber suction pad to the side of the engine instrument panel. We were used to having passengers visit the flight deck on the 707. If he noticed a passenger staring somewhat bemused at the brass tap, he would whip out an oily rag and give it a quick polish!

Prior to departure on any flight a certain amount of paperwork, in the shape of load sheets, cargo and passenger manifests passed over the F/E's desk on its way to the front to be signed by the captain, then passed all the way back. To protest at this intrusion, another F/E had a rubber stamp made. The stamp read 'LES HEARN APPROVED'. He took great delight in stamping every piece of paper with a huge flourish. He gave me a rubber stamp: 'BRIAN SMITH APPROVED'. I still have it.

Funchal Airport

The KT route structure was varied, and some of the airfields were quite demanding. Funchal was an airfield that was definitely in the 'demanding' category. Funchal Airport is located on the south side of the beautiful island of Madeira. The airport is considered one of the most perilous airports in the world due to its location and its spectacular runway construction. This is a category 'Captains Only' allowed to land there, and only after a visit to the airport under the supervision of a training captain. He had to be experienced in the special requirements of the approach and landing of this demanding airport. In 1984 I made many landings as a supervisory training captain and lived to tell the tale!

What is so difficult or dangerous about Funchal? Firstly, it is the location. Mountains rise immediately to the north of the runway. R/W 05 requires an approach from the sea, pointing directly at the mountains.

The runway direction was roughly east–west. More precisely, in a direction of 050/230 degrees. There were many restrictions regarding the wind direction and speed. The wind from the north was particularly dangerous, sweeping over the mountains, swirling around the lee side and creating a tailwind at both ends of the runway. The two navigation beacons on Madeira code MAD in morse code for Madeira, and FUN for Funchal. I always thought FUN and MAD defined your feelings about landing at Funchal!

The shortness of the runway at Funchal affected our ability to lift enough fuel to fly directly back to Gatwick. As a result, we had to make a short hop over to Porto Santo Island, which was situated 70 kilometres north east of Madeira. The long runway there meant we would be able to uplift enough fuel to fly directly back to Gatwick.

These two photos are attributed to Peter Forster. Originally posted on Flickr as Madeira Funchal Landing Strip, 1990.

The runway is built on giant stilts, with the runway literally stuck on the side of a mountain. It was short. A runway length of about 1,600 metres with a 200 ft drop at each end.

Madeira Airport Runway. The concrete pillars of the 2,000'
extension completed to extend the runway, winning the 2004
IABSE Outstanding Structure Award.

Prior to departing Madeira, the passengers were informed of this brief transit stop. The turn round time on the ground at Porto Santo was usually about 20/30 minutes. We strived to make it as comfortable as possible for our passengers. The aircraft had air conditioning and cool drinks were served. As flight crew we developed a slick operation. The captain stayed on board giving the passengers a running commentary of our progress, and then completing the final load sheet and customs paperwork. The fuel truck would move quickly into position and started pumping fuel, supervised by the co-pilot.

So far, so good... However, on this occasion, out of the corner of my eye, I noticed the fuel truck had not moved from its position at the edge of the parking area, some 200/300 yards away. My uneasiness was confirmed by a call from the control tower. "Would the captain please come to the passenger terminal."

I hurried over to the terminal. As I entered the building, I was confronted by my co-pilot, a T.A.P ground attendant and the refueller, a giant of a man, clad in bright orange overalls, arms folded. They all had their arms folded. Not a good sign I thought! "Hello," I squeaked, "now, what seems to be the problem?"

"*He* won't refuel us," said my co-pilot, Geoff Bunn, in a loud voice.

I looked up at the refueller, all 6' 9" of him. I said in my best authoritative voice, "Now, listen my good man we need to be on our way, if you would be so kind as to refuel us I would be very happy."

"Non," was his gruff reply. The T.A.P girl explained there was some kind of industrial dispute going on, then shrugged her shoulders, and fled the scene.

I thought I could solve this problem quite quickly. Silly me. In pockets attached to the cockpit door there were various fuel carnets or business credit cards from Shell, BP, Esso, etc. Surely he would accept one of these and we would soon be on our way. Simple...

I headed back to the aircraft as quickly as I could, grabbed a handful of these carnets and rushed back to the building. "OK," I said, "choose a card, any card."

"Non," came the reply.

The co-pilot was beginning to snarl and looked like a dog about to bite someone (guess who!) Right, I thought. All is not lost. Maybe my personal bankcard would do the trick. I had them in my pocket. I waved them at the refueller. "Non," came the reply! Impasse? Time was running out and so was my patience. The chances of finding hotel accommodation for the night in Porto Santo for 180 passengers was minimal. Plus, all the cost and inconvenience involved did not bear thinking about. I thought I would give it one last shot.

"Cash?" I asked. A big smile came to his face. "Cash OK, cash OK."

"Right!" I said, "Get going." The co-pilot and refueller rushed off.

I set off across the tarmac for the third time. The passengers must have wondered what on earth was going on. This funny little man, who looked just like their captain rushing back and forth. I hated the thought of being held to ransom like this. I stood at the front of the cabin, facing the passengers. I look a deep breath. "Good afternoon, ladies and gentlemen. We have a slight problem. There is an industrial dispute that has just started at the airport, the only way we can get some fuel is to pay cash for it. If anyone would like to come up to the front of the cabin and make a loan, that would be much appreciated."

There was a stunned silence... I thought to myself, 'I've overdone this'. Suddenly, several passengers were jumping up and waving notes. "I've got money," they shouted. I recovered my composure, grabbed a sick bag for the loans and a clipboard. The first gentleman in the queue was very excited and said, "I've got money, lots of money."

"Thank you sir, how much would you like to let us have?" "Twenty pounds," he cried!

'Oh my gawd,' I thought, 'we'll be here all day.' We needed about £1,500 to pay for the fuel. Next in the queue was the spitting image of Del Boy from the *Only Fools and Horses* comedy. He was clad in a Hawaiian shirt, with gold bracelets on his wrists and gold medallions round his neck. "Ullow John," he said. "'Ow much d'want?"

"How much have you got?" I enquired.

He pulled a wad of notes from his back pocket. "Bout a grand," he said. I quickly grabbed the notes and stuffed them into the bag. Another gentleman gave £300, and so it went on.

We were on our way! A great cheer came from the passengers as we took off. It was as I settled down into the cruise that Geoff turned to me and said, "Can I say something?"

I wondered what was coming next. "Sure, go ahead."

"Well, I thought that was pretty good what YOU did back there... YOU did," he said. I got the feeling Geoff was exonerating himself from any repercussions.

"Go ahead," I said.

"How are these passengers going to get their money back?" Geoff asked.

"I have thought about that," I said, rather smugly. "I am going to invite them up to the flight deck and give each of them a personal cheque."

"How are you going to get your money back?"

"Well, I hope the company will reimburse me," was my rather feeble reply, getting bored with this line of questioning.

"D'you want to hear my idea?" persisted Geoff.

"Love to," I said.

"How about I call the company on the long-range radio and tell them what YOU have done. They can then meet the aircraft with a bag of money and reimburse the three passengers."

"Go ahead and make the call," I said.

Geoff made the call. "What did they say?" I enquired.

"They don't believe us. The airport manager will meet the aircraft."

We landed and parked the aircraft. I looked out of my side

window. The BA Station Manager was standing there in his uniform. He had a large paper bag under his arm. He pointed to the bag and smiled. All the passengers disembarked except for the three who had helped us out in Funchal. The manager reimbursed them there and then and they each received a voucher for a flight for two to any destination in Europe. This incident made the newspapers. Even as far as Zimbabwe. My mother-in-law living in Harare phoned my wife to say she had just read all about it in the local newspaper. Luck was on my side – they did not publish the captain's name. Incidentally, Funchal Airport is now known as Cristiano Ronaldo Airport.

Back to Abu Dhabi

The ruler, Sheikh Zayed bin Sultan Al Nahyan's private flight in Abu Dhabi required a training captain to train a captain and co-pilot for their B737. I presented my brand new passport to the immigration officer, no Israeli stamps this time! I was waved through. This B737 training was some of the most leisurely and enjoyable I have experienced.

After breakfast at my four-star hotel, I was driven in a limousine to the airport. The two pilots and I went to the aircraft and over coffee and biscuits we planned the day's flying. We had the luxury of a ground engineer that accompanied us. As well as being our technical backup, he also acted as our steward. The aircraft interior was one of the most beautiful I have seen. There was a master bedroom and a conference room, all decorated with carved wood, deep pile carpets, and silk furnishings throughout.

Although the two pilots were new to the B737, they were experienced in the Middle East. They suggested we fly to Salalah in Oman, some 1,200km south. Our training brief was to fly wherever we wished, but get the job done in three days. Money was no object. Salalah proved to be a good choice, with very little other air traffic, and the long runway allowed us to complete many take-offs and landings.

We had a break for a three-course steak lunch, served by our German engineer/steward. We were sitting in first-class style seats, at a beautiful inlaid table with full air conditioning and trying not to make a mark on the doeskin lined walls. It wasn't an easy life, but we made it look easy! Both pilots checked out in record time... I shall miss those lunches.

Their very first trip arrived within a couple of days. The sheikh had several aircraft but it was rumoured that the B737 was the sheikh's favourite. There was a conference due in Damascus to be attended by many heads of Arab states. Two of the private flight Airbuses were to take the ruler to the conference, one for the sheikh, and one as a back-up! The B737 was to carry the ruler's staff. The two new pilots, and me in the jump seat, were ready for anything! On the day of departure from Damascus we were required to be at the airport several hours before departure, standing by to be ready as soon as the ruler appeared.

The sheikh's chief pilot, Captain Denzil Beard, came over to our aircraft. We were positioned well behind the Airbus that already had the red carpet rolled up to it. Denzil popped his head in the cockpit. "Ready to go?" he enquired.

"Yes," we proudly replied, "all checks done."

"Just make sure you *are* ready. The sheikh likes the 737, he just might decide to come back with you."

At the scheduled time of departure, the band struck up, the soldiers stood to attention and then the dignitaries appeared. The sheikh strode quickly along the red carpet, turned right and headed straight for us. He galloped up our aircraft steps, robes flowing.

"Start number two engine," I called. The sheikh was on board! We taxied out and took off in record time. After landing at Abu Dhabi, our chief pilot came over and said, "What did I tell you?"

Not a bad effort for two rookie pilots.

10. HOT-AIR BALLOONING

On my return to British Airtours (KT) I was required to have a refresher check flight. I was scheduled to fly to Malaga with Fred Rivett, a senior training captain.

On the flight back to Gatwick he casually said, "We are going ballooning this evening, would you like to come along?" Little did I know that evening's ballooning experience would make a dramatic change to my life.

British Airtours sponsored the hot-air balloon.

The balloon was stored in a trailer at Gatwick and towed by a KT Land Rover. We met up at the hangar. The weather forecast was for clear skies and light winds, ideal for ballooning. I was to learn that balloonists suffered from wind! Either too much of it or not enough…

We drove to a field near Haywards Heath, south of Gatwick. The team started to assemble the balloon ready for flight. I was told to 'hold this or pull that'. I was just a spectator, I did as I was told. The balloon team looked highly efficient. A toy balloon filled with helium was released and everyone watched as it slowly climbed away. Its track was checked with a hand-held compass.

This was important, as the Gatwick control zone was close by. The track was judged to be well clear of any controlled airspace. The whole team watched as the balloon rose into the sky. Everyone stood silently with an arm outstretched at an angle of 45 degrees, like a flashback to WWII!

'Is this some secret society?' I asked myself. Later on, I learnt that if the toy balloon rises slowly above the outstretched arm, the wind speed is suitable for a flight; if *below* the arm, it is probably too fast. The team opened the trailer and pulled out what looked like a metre square laundry basket, followed by a large bag, smelling of cow manure and propane. The laundry basket proved to be the gondola in which the pilot and passengers stood, standing room only. The bag contained the envelope, some 77,000 cubic feet of it, equivalent in size to 77,000 footballs! The gondola was tied off to the front of the Land Rover, then attached to the envelope.

This was to restrain the whole contraption so that it did not take off until the pilot was ready and pulled the quick release. The envelope was spread out on the ground in a balloon shape. It looked huge and covered an area about the size of half a football pitch. A motorised fan was positioned beside the gondola and started up. A magical transformation then took place. The air from the fan blowing into the envelope made a rippling effect of the fabric as if a monster was coming alive. As the monster grew ever bigger and bigger, the team hurried around, tugging and pulling so that eventually it looked rather like a giant smooth ball. It was ready to fly! Ann Green, a very experienced instructor, was training Fred.

Fred was to inflate the balloon. He knelt down behind the burners and blasted a huge flame into the envelope. Great skill was required not to burn the nylon envelope. Before the invention of the motorised fan a brave crewman would stand just inside the mouth of the envelope and, using a broom, he would hold the mouth open with one hand, the other hand covering his 'crown jewels'. The flame would roar past him. As you can imagine there were not too many volunteers for this highly dangerous task. He was called 'Cremation Charley'!

Soon the balloon was standing upright. Fred was already in the basket and was quickly joined by Ann and a passenger. The 'before take-off checks' were completed, more heat was applied and the balloon slowly lifted off.

Over the years I have seen hundreds, maybe thousands of balloon take-offs. It is an exciting and emotional experience. Waving goodbye comes naturally. The ground crew watch the balloon ascend, checking the track with their compasses. It all looked very professional. We set off in pursuit. I followed in my car, as I was curious to see the landing. The retrieve team, as they were called, whizzed along the country lanes. After about an hour the balloon was found.

Fred, under the instruction of Ann, had landed in a pub car park! I thought to myself 'I could take up this sport'. The landlord came out with a tray of drinks and welcomed us.

It is a tradition, started by the French I believe, that the flight should be celebrated with champagne. As tonight's flight was a training flight we celebrated with best bitter. I said good night to the team and drove home. I was totally enthralled with the whole experience. The camaraderie, the ethereal effect, I could see this was a type of flying I had never experienced.

The next morning Fred phoned. "Well, what did you think of it?" he enquired. I said I very much enjoyed the whole evening's experience. "Good, we are going again this evening, would you be available to crew for us?"

I said, "Yes, but I don't know the first thing about crewing."

"Don't worry, we will teach you."

I became fascinated by the experience and retrieved many times.

One morning the balloon was about to take off, when Ann, the instructor said, "Right, Brian get in."

"No, No," I said.

"Don't be silly," she replied, "we have made a space especially for you."

"No, No," I insisted. I had studied this contraption carefully from Day One. Where were the engines and wings? Why would I agree to stand in a laundry basket, with destination unknown? No thank you! They then physically lifted me into the basket.

As the balloon lifted off, I had my eyes closed and I was gripping the rope handles in a vicelike grip. We settled down into level flight at about 1,000'. I opened my eyes and looked down. Fatal move!

"Don't look down," said Ann, "just look ahead." I did as I was told.

Suddenly... I felt a transformation. When the burner was not on, the peace and quiet was extraordinary. Any anxiety disappeared and I seemed to enter a world isolated from the real world below. We were moving so slowly you had time to take in everything. You could hear dogs barking and people talking. There is no wind effect felt in the basket. You *are* the wind, going along with it, not pushing through it as you would in an airplane. If you lit a match (not advised) it would remain lit.

Now I understood why every take-off, indeed every flight is different. Every time you take off in a balloon the destination is unknown. You are about to embark on an *adventure*. Waving goodbye is all part of it. I started to relax and watch Fred and Ann flying the balloon. Although you cannot control the direction, or turn round and come back, you can control the height, up and down. Ann was putting Fred through his paces. Many approaches and go-arounds were made.

As we made our approach to land, I was told to take my landing position. I took hold of the rope handles inside the basket and bent my knees. We touched down with a slight bump. Well done Fred! I noticed Fred was pulling on a red line as if his life depended on it, and it probably did! Although we had landed, the envelope still had some air in it and was acting like a spinnaker. We were still moving over the ground. Slowly, we came to a stop. The basket started to tip over. "Keep holding on," shouted Ann. I had no intention of letting go, there was too much excitement going on.

The basket ended up completely on its side. We ended up in a heap, arms and legs tangled. Fred was on top of me, all of him. Ann had skilfully manoeuvred herself to be on top of Fred. Fred was still hanging onto the red line. I subsequently learnt this was standard procedure until the envelope had totally deflated. "Stay in the basket until I say it is safe to climb out," said Fred in his best BA captain's voice. Fred gave us the OK. We wriggled out. Big smiles and handshakes all round.

The retrieve team had seen us land and the usual banter took place. "Anybody hurt?" they enquired. "Have you broken it?"

An important part of a balloon flight is the consideration for the landowner. Part of the balloon pilot's training is called Landowner Relations – learning how and where to land with consideration to animals and crops. Fred had chosen a set-aside field, no crop and no animals. Perfect...

Brian with grandsons Kambel and Smith about to go flying.

The retrieve crew, super efficient as always, had already spoken to the farmer and had obtained permission to drive in and pick up the balloon. It is a tradition that the balloonist should thank the landowner with a bottle of wine or something stronger. Having completed this little ceremony, we drove to the nearest pub. To 'pay' for my flight, it was my round. Fred and Ann were in deep conversation. I guess it was a de-brief of the flight.

They called me over. "Did you enjoy it?" asked Ann.

"Did I enjoy it? It was wonderful!" I replied.

"Good, the reason we asked you, is we need another balloon pilot and wondered if you might like to learn to fly?"

I did not take long to think about it. "Where do I sign up!" I quipped.

There followed a period of intense training. Fred and I flew together many times. After one flight Ann said we were progressing quite well... "but why do you airline guys always choose a field that is 10,000' long and 200' wide, on a 3 degree glideslope, as if landing a 737?"

The next day she showed us how to make a landing in very small spaces. She also taught us the Balloonist's Prayer:

May the winds welcome you with softness
May the sun bless you with his warm hands
May you fly so high and so well
That God joins you in laughter
And sets you gently back into
The loving arms of Mother Earth.

One morning we did quite a long training flight from our base in Sussex into Hampshire. We took off at dawn on a beautiful morning. The sun was already painting the sky a pale pink. Even the aircraft contrails in the sky were pink.

We landed in a set-aside field beside the A272. Our retrieve crew called to say they had us in sight and would go to find the landowner. We started to pack up the balloon. The crew called to say they had called at the farmer's house but could not raise anyone. It was still quite early in the morning. We were so close to the house, I said I would come over and leave a note for the farmer. I stood by the door writing the note when the door opened and out stepped the farmer. He was stripped to the waist, with half his face covered in shaving foam. "Yes?" he said in a gruff voice. Luckily, the crew had given me his name.

"Good morning Mr Mitchell," I said, "I have landed my balloon just across the road in your set-aside field."

"Oh, have you?" he said, glowering over the top of his specs.

"Well," he continued, "that is going to cost you. I would like £10 for the Save the Children charity." I explained I did not have £10, but I would send him a cheque as soon as I got home.

"OK," he said.

I must have been somewhat nervous, as I gave the most stupid reply. "Thank you Mr Mitchell, when we have packed up would you like us to come and say goodbye?"

He fixed me with a steely eye and sighed, "No. Just bugger off." We have landed on Mr Michell's farm many times and it is always, "£10, now bugger off." Inevitably, he has become known to the balloonists as 'Mr Buggeroff'.

The British School of Ballooning

One evening, after a particularly enjoyable balloon flight, I had arranged to meet Graeme Scaife, a friend of mine, in our local, The Cricketer's Arms. We had raced lawn mowers together some years previously. I arrived late, I apologised and then excitedly explained why. Graeme listened and said thoughtfully, "So, when are you ballooning again?"

"Tomorrow morning we plan to take the British Airtours balloon to tether at Lord Montague's house in the New Forest."

Tethering is to tie the balloon down with ropes and inflate it as an attraction. It is a good way to display the balloon and get the company name in front of the press cameras. The balloon does not fly away.

On the way home, I said to Graeme and Judy, his wife, "What did you think of it?"

The reply came straight away from Graeme. "Yup, I am going to buy one!"

"Whoa, hold on a minute, you haven't even flown in one yet," I said.

"I don't need to do that, I just know I will love it!"

The next day Graeme and I drove to the Thunder and Colt balloon factory in Oswestry. An order was placed there and then.

On the way home, Graeme said, "That's all set then. Oh, and you can teach me to fly it!"

"Well," I exclaimed, "there is only one problem… I haven't learnt to fly one myself yet!" That didn't seem to put Graeme off, and we started to fly together.

The saying 'the blind leading the blind' comes to mind. Why we did not kill ourselves I do not know! We would be flying along and one of us would say, "What do you think that does?"

"Dunno, pull it and see what happens. Oh dear! The houses seem to be getting bigger…!"

We did survive and went on to obtain our Private Pilot's Licence (PPL). The flying hours steadily increased. It seemed to be that after every landing the people we met asked the same questions: "How can I have a flight?" or "How can I learn to fly one?"

Graeme said, "I think there is a business opportunity here. Why don't we start a balloon school and a passenger rides business?"

Graeme, Judy, Cecilia and I met up and talked it over. We pondered over a suitable name. 'West Sussex Ballooning' or 'Southern Balloon School'? We were stuck until Cecilia said, "Why don't we call it *The British School of Ballooning*?"

"'Perfect," we all said. I did feel the name made it sound as if we were a huge outfit and that we knew what we were doing! However, we must have done something right to become one of the largest balloon operating companies in Europe.

In order to start flying passengers for 'hire and reward' we required an Air Operator's Certificate (AOC) from the Civil Aviation Authority (CAA). Every airline has an AOC. We were subject, quite rightly in my opinion, to all the rules and regulations, as if we were an airline.

BRITISH SCHOOL OF
BALLOONING
28 7 94 PM
Champagne Balloon
Flights
Flight Training
Tel: 0428 70730

In order to add some 'substance' to the company, I became a balloon instructor and shortly afterwards an examiner. An officer of the CAA checked me out as an examiner. He was to observe me carrying out a proficiency check on a commercial balloon pilot. When our passengers came to fly, we would ask them to dress as if they were going for a walk in the country. Our man from the CAA arrived wearing a smart suit and tie, complete with briefcase. Things were starting to look a little formal!

All the flight exercises were completed to his satisfaction. I assumed (never assume, always check!) things had gone well. I said, "Would you like to fly it?" He took over and made a good job of it. We made a landing in a field next to a pub. Surprise, surprise! I asked the CAA examiner if it was appropriate to have a drink and carry out the debriefing in the pub. This plan received instant CAA approval! He was so taken with flying the balloon. He learnt to fly with us and became a fully qualified commercial balloon pilot and worked part-time as one of our pilots. Ironically, I had to check him out for his licence. Small world!

One day when he and another man from the CAA were on a training flight with me, the balloon became becalmed. Interestingly, this can be the most dangerous situation to find yourself in. Strong wind is something you can cope with. More landing opportunities will open up as you whizz over the land, whereas there is always the possibility you may end up becalmed over power lines or a stretch of open water. It is hard to believe it can become so completely flat calm. On this occasion we were stuck over a field of wheat. Only by slowly inching the balloon up a couple of feet were we able to find a very gentle wind. We started to move at about one knot towards the A272, the main road between Petworth and Midhurst.

I had noticed there was a very wide verge on this side of the road. "Right chaps," I said, "we are going to land on that strip of land." Stony silence… followed by raised eyebrows. I called the retrieve crew and asked them to hold up the traffic. We landed on the grass verge and quickly deflated the balloon. The traffic was flowing in no time. The CAA men had to rush off to go to work at the CAA building at Gatwick.

Bob phoned later in the day. "Brian," he said, "I haven't done a stroke of work today. I have just sat staring out of the window, saying to myself, I am an officer of the UK CAA and I have just landed a hot-air balloon on a main road!" He then laughed and said, "When is the next flight?

Ballooning in France

One of our students, Bob Craig, whose wife is French, suggested we set up a ballooning business in France. A year later we were in operation, based in Bagnoles-de-l'Orne in Normandy. It is a beautiful area for balloon flying with large open undulating fields. As well as training pilots, we carried passengers. We employed a lovely English girl, Lucy, as our retriever. She spoke fluent French.

We rented a house by a lake.

The house was very old and in rather a dilapidated state. Without being unkind, that perfectly described our landlord, Olivier. He was in his 90s and rode his horse past our house every morning. Olivier had fallen in love with Lucy! There was probably 60 years difference in their ages. He would knock on the door. Lucy would hide. I would open the door. Olivier would look at me, smile and say quizzically, "Lucy?"

I would say, "Lucy not in."

He looked very sad, he then smiled again and said, "Whisky?"

Olivier had a glass of whisky at every house on his morning jaunt. At the end of his ride he would put his horse in the back of his ancient Citroen van and drive very slowly home. The local police knew Olivier well, and left him alone. He had fought in the French Resistance during WWII and was well respected.

One day, when he was driving his van home through the woods and country lanes, he heard a scraping sound coming from the back of the van. He ignored it. The police stopped him. They opened the back doors of the van and found the floor of the rusty old van had dropped out and the horse was trotting along inside! Fortunately, Olivier was driving so slowly the horse was unharmed. The police escorted him home, where they all sat down, had a whisky together, and laughed about the morning's antics.

Olivier passed away some years ago. In 2018, my wife, my daughters, Cymbeline and Kerry Ann, and I visited Bagnoles-de-l'Orne. We set out to try and find the house we had rented from Olivier all those years ago. We found the lake and beside it was the house, barely recognisable; it had been completely refurbished. There was no one around. We felt we should not intrude, and started to walk back to our vehicle, when along the road a car appeared. It turned into the driveway. The driver stepped out of the car and said to Kerry in perfect English, "I recognise you from the ballooning, I am Olivier's nephew." We stayed and chatted for some time and laughed about the story of Olivier and his horse.

Olivia Chalmel du Rozier .   Le 29.07.92
        La Dronière
61 600 La Ferté . Macé .
        France

                    Dear Brian,
        I knew that you were " one the Best Pilots"
of Ballooning -
        But I didn't know that, for me, you were
" The Best Doctor".
        In fact, to cure me :
        - you have prescribed " the Best Medecine
        - you knew" the Best Messenger" to administer
        it to me
        Under these conditions, don't doubt that I shall
be your " Best Patient" in taking your medical
potion - (especially as there's no limit to the
Prescribed dose).

        Many thanks, Dear Chap, Best Regards to
your wife . See you very soon, I hope -

                        Olivier

PS, I don't think that before you return,
I'll have another fall and need more medecine,
but who knows?

Olivier sent me this letter.

Nick Mason was one of our first students to start learning to fly in France. He was an accomplished mountaineer and was very busy on the lecture circuit. With so many commitments he did not complete his training in France. It was a pity as he had a great personality and was making good progress.

Cecilia and I were ballooning in South Africa (SA) when we had a call from Nick. He wanted to come out and complete his training in SA. Nick took to flying in SA and was soon ready to take his General Flying Test (GFT). We did the test one beautiful African morning. Calm winds and clear skies. Nick had passed everything except one last test. He needed to complete a solo flight to gain his balloon pilot's licence but there was a problem, the weather forecast for that afternoon and evening was for strong winds, too strong to send Nick off on his solo. Additionally, Nick was scheduled to fly home that night on Virgin Atlantic Airways. We were all very disappointed and in an effort to raise our spirits we went shopping. Nick was buying presents for his wife when I looked at the sky.

The wind had dropped dramatically. I made a quick call to the Met Office; they confirmed the winds would remain light. We rushed to our car and drove straight to the launch site. We rigged the balloon as fast as we could and launched Nick into the air. Off he went on his solo flight. Cecilia and I went back to our cottage and collected Nick's belongings. We also grabbed a bottle of champagne!

We saw the balloon land. In the time it took to drive up to the balloon, Nick was completely surrounded by several hundred children. Everyone was singing and dancing, including Nick. With so much help, the balloon was packed up in no time. Time was tight; we had to get to the airport as quickly as possible. We threw Nick in the back of the car, handed him the bottle of champagne and sped off.

On the way to the airport, Nick changed into clean clothes and consumed most of the champagne. We dropped him off at the airport terminal and parked the car. When we hurried back to say goodbye, Nick was standing with a huge smile, waving a boarding pass. "I have been upgraded to Upper (First) Class," he beamed.

"Well," we said, pulling his leg, "you're a balloon pilot now, you can do anything."

He gave us a huge hug, and then went off to board the aircraft. Cecilia and I looked at each other and said, "Phew, it's like the tide just went out!"

We went back to our cottage and fell fast asleep. The phone was ringing. I woke and looked at my watch, the time was 3am. Who could possibly be phoning at this time in the morning? I answered, it was Nick on the line. "Hello, hello, Brian? It's Nick."

"Hello, Nick, where are you?" I asked.

"I'm at home of course, I have got to tell you about my flight on Virgin," he said. He did not wait for me to answer. "Well, you know I was upgraded. I was shown up to the bar and given a glass of champagne by a beautiful stewardess. I turned to the fellow next to me and said, 'Hello, my name is Nick Mason, and I'm a balloon pilot.' The fellow replied, 'So am I, my name is Richard Branson.'"

It was all too much for Nick. He said, "Brian, I spent the whole flight drinking champagne with Richard Branson and Miss Venezuela. Thanks for everything, goodbye." Cecilia and I laughed about the whole episode.

However, 'The Nick Mason Story' as it became known, was not over yet! Some months later, Nick called. "Now listen Brian, I have gone about as far as I can go in ballooning. I would like to return to Normandy and do an advanced ballooning course."

"What on earth are you talking about?" I replied.

"Well, I have never ballooned at night. I have not flown above the clouds, I have not done a steep descent, or a splash and dash," he said. "I will pay for everything – for you, Cecilia, and your girls to come out and it will include your accommodation."

I said, "OK."

A couple of weeks later we all gathered in Bagnoles-de-l'Orne. Nick said, "I will see you at the launch site tomorrow morning, I have a surprise for you."

Very early next morning, Cecilia and I drove to the little grass airfield by a lake. Halfway there Cecilia stopped the car and said, "I need to put this blindfold on you." I wondered what was going to come next! She then drove on. I could feel the car bumping across the grass on the airfield. We stopped and Cecilia helped me out. She whipped off the blindfold, and there was Nick sitting in a dual seat sky chariot.

The dual seat sky chariot.

Nick was sitting on what could best be described as a garden seat, with the fuel tank underneath and the burners above your head. The balloon was completely inflated and ready to fly.

"Surprise, surprise! Get in," he said. I had not seen one of these before, but I strapped myself in and we took off!

It was the most beautiful morning; we were drifting along over the trees and meadows. Ten minutes into the flight, Nick said,

"What do you think?"

I said, "It's wonderful, how many hours have you flown in it?"

"Oh, this is its first flight," he replied, "I thought *you* must have flown one!" I did not know whether to laugh or cry. It seemed so incongruous to be flying along, sitting down on a garden seat, not standing in a conventional basket. Once I had got over the shock, we found it was easy to fly, and we landed in a field of wildflowers.

Nick was keen to get on with his 'advanced flying course'. The next morning the weather was perfect with calm winds and a thin veil of stratus at about 1,500'. Nick and I took off and climbed up through the stratus. I said to myself, that's number one task ticked off straight away! We continued climbing to 5,000', switched off the burners and allowed the balloon to descend. As we descended, the rate of descent steadily increased to a 'fast descent'. No. 2 ticked off. As we popped out of the stratus into clear air, there below us was the lake. How could we be so lucky! We did a 'splash and dash' over the lake. Three tasks in the bag!

That night Cecilia, Nick and I completed his night flight. The flight is planned to take off an hour or so before dawn, this allows you to land in daylight. You fly in darkness and land at daybreak.

Nick was pleased to have accomplished the whole thing, and said to me, "What a wonderful week, I did not know you had a night rating?

I replied, "I haven't got a night rating!" Smiles all round.

At the celebratory breakfast I said to Nick what an incredible few days it had been. "As a thank you for your company and generosity I would like you to take all the girls for a flight in our passenger carrying balloon, and I will retrieve for you."

Off they all went, Cecilia, Lucy and Kerry and Cymbeline, my two daughters. Nick was delighted to be the pilot. After the flight we went out to dinner to celebrate Cymbeline's birthday. The end of a perfect day…

One summer we were invited to a small balloon meet in Amiens. Jules Verne lived there from 1871 until his death in 1905. He wrote many adventure novels, including *Round the World in Eighty Days*; the tale of two adventurers' attempt to circumnavigate the globe in a balloon is of particular interest to balloonists. It's in a beautiful part of France, close to the Somme. This was a poignant area for me to fly over, as my father had fought in the fields below during WWI.

Based in our village in Sussex is a wonderful musical trio. They call themselves 'Les Anglais'. Vernon plays the musical saw, Dave the double base, and Pete Shade the accordion. Pete tutored Dudley Moore, which gives you some idea of their musical ability. We had decided to take them with us to the Amiens balloon meet.

After the first morning flight, we invited the other balloon teams for breakfast. We parked in a field and opened the trailer, rigged the burner and started to cook scrambled eggs, served with French bread. Our trio was playing in front of the vehicle. It all looked spectacular... The balloon teams were amazed by the whole scene. I was busy cooking the eggs, when round from the front of the trailer, the trio appeared. They started to play *I Don't want to Set the World on Fire!*

Ballooning in Ireland

A priest, Fr. Des Reid, started the Ballooning Club of Dublin in Ireland. He approached the monsignor and said that the boys were bored with table tennis, darts, etc. The priest said, "I have heard there is such a thing as a hot-air balloon, would it be possible to buy one?" Permission was given. Des asked an Aer Lingus pilot, Mike Alexander, to teach him to fly it. On their first landing, the farmer greeted them and gave a small bow. "You're very welcome here your grace, God bless you." The priest realised he was wearing his dog collar. He still wears it every time he goes ballooning. "It does ensure a friendly reception," he explained.

This year, September 2020, is the 50th anniversary of the Dublin Balloon Club and The Irish Hot-Air Ballooning Championships, which makes it the longest running balloon meet in the world. In 1986 we were invited to attend the 16th Irish Championships in Ballymahon, County Longford. Jim Kelly, Cecilia and I were booked into the Newcastle House Hotel. As we drove up the winding drive, the 'hotel' came into view. It looked like a film set for a horror movie! It had a gaunt stone front, with paint peeling from the walls and windows. We rang the bell. No one appeared. We slowly pushed the door open.

"Hello," we shouted.

Eventually, our host appeared, Mrs King. She welcomed us and was very charming. "I will show you to your room." She led us up the stairs, into a huge room. It was freezing cold and smelled of boiled cabbages. There was a single bed at one end of the room and a double bed at the other. I explained to Mrs King we had booked a single for Mr Kelly and a double for us. "Oh, I know you did, but we are full up, I am sure you are all good friends and won't mind sharing." Cecilia was not impressed, but I thought, well... I was Jim's best man at his wedding! Mrs King departed to prepare our dinner, hence the smell of boiled cabbages!

We sat on our respective beds and laughed. Jim suddenly

announced he had found an electric blanket in his bed; he looked very pleased with himself as he switched it on. We went down to dinner. We found the dining room by following the noise. We slowly opened the door. It was full of balloonists who had just returned from their flights, *via the pub*. We must have looked like three little children timidly peering round the door on their first day at school.

One huge American, with a long beard, stood up, pointed at us, and shouted, "New blood. New blood!" We were within an inch of running away. Looking back, I am so glad we stayed. They made us very welcome. The evening finished with each team providing 'entertainment'. This would be in the form of a song, poem or dance.

Over the years this has become a tradition for the last night of an Irish balloon meet. Eventually, we staggered off to our room. For the sake of decorum we agreed to put the light out, get changed and jump into our beds. Out went the light. Suddenly, Jim jumps out of bed, puts the light on, and shouts, "Jaysus... this bed is freezing cold and damp."

"What happened to the electric blanket?" we asked. Jim grabbed the blanket cord only to find no plug on the end, only three bare wires. Irish hospitality at its best! It was our first introduction to ballooning in Ireland. Anyone who has visited Ireland knows it is a magical place. By the very nature of ballooning, we were privileged to land in the most remote places.

Various tasks were set for each flight. At one meet, we were flying in an area of bog land in County Longford and every bog was alive with frogs. One task was to see how many frogs you could collect on your flight. I saw a balloon pilot scooping up frogs with a bucket on a pole!

As always, we ended up in a pub. This time it was Willie Donlan's pub in Killashee. Each crew came in with their frogs. Frogs were everywhere, all hopping about. You would hear the occasional 'plop' as a frog jumped into a pint of Guinness! The first balloonist through the door was Peter Dowlen.

The story goes: It was very early one morning, Peter had just landed his balloon close to the village of Killashee. In spite of the early hour, he decided to visit the pub. Willie was behind the bar, and although they had not met up for some time, he greeted Peter with a smile.

"Hello Peter," he said.

"Hello, Willie," replied Peter, "can I have 14 pints, please?"

"Sure," said Willie, quite unconcerned.

The doors burst open and the rest of the balloonists poured in.

Although the Irish Championships were competitive, to win the 'entertainment' for the evening was more fiercely fought for. The week flew by (no pun intended), and on the last night everyone gathered for the 'Survivors' Dinner', with each team doing a skit or sketch providing the evening's entertainment, accompanied by wonderful Irish music.

Our 'Pinky and Perky' team entered this competition many times and even won a couple.

A group photograph in Ireland.

We attended many Irish Championships. One of the most memorable was a meet based in the town of Trim, County Meath. Cecilia had been learning to fly our balloon and making good progress. It was suggested it would be special to take her check flight for her Private Pilot's Licence in Ireland. The check flight consists of flying with an examiner, who would expect you to carry out various exercises. If all goes well, the candidate lands the balloon, the examiner climbs out and sends the candidate off on their solo flight. It was a glorious evening, with light winds and clear skies.

I waved Cecilia off on her solo flight. As she climbed away another balloon drifted slowly past me. The pilot was Robert Zirpolo, an American friend of ours. He knew Cecilia would be looking ahead and concentrating on her flying, hoping she would not see him.

He flew his balloon closer, and closer then shouted to her, "Hey, did Daddy give you the keys to his car?"

"Go away," she replied.

We set off in our car to chase them. Both balloons were flying together now. We watched them land together side by side. The perfect end to a perfect flight. Cecilia had passed with flying colours! At end of the balloon meet she was presented with a personalized T-shirt as a memento of passing her test in Trim, Ireland. Inscribed was: *I passed out in Trim.* She is very proud of it.

As you can imagine there are many ballooning stories. This is my favourite... it's about an event that took place in Ireland. I'm not sure of the date and place and I don't want to get it wrong. Early one morning, my friend Ray landed in a field way out in the country, miles from anywhere. The farmer appeared. He was very elderly, dressed in Irish tweeds, wearing a cap and smoking a pipe, quite unconcerned about the balloon landing in his field.

Ray introduced himself and, in the course of conversation, he discovered the farmer was 94-years old. He lived in his broken-down house with two dogs and a cat. He had never been outside his village, he didn't have a car, or even a bike. Somehow, they hit it off, and clearly were well on the way to becoming good friends.

Ray said to the farmer, "It is a tradition that the balloonist should offer the landowner a flight in the balloon, as a thank you for allowing a landing on your property. This evening's forecast is for good weather, how about I come back this evening and take you for a flight?"

The old man immediately replied, "That'll be grand." Clearly, he had no idea what was involved.

That evening Ray returned to the farm. The old man was ready and waiting, still dressed as before. They climbed in the basket and took off. The old man was totally calm and spent most of the time gazing down at the countryside... his countryside. Ray enquired, "Are you enjoying it?"

"Oh, it's grand," came the calm reply.

Ray looked ahead and saw a large lake. He called his crew on the radio. "We're just going to do a 'splash and dash', I'll see you the other side of the lake."

He turned to the old man and said, "We're just going to do a splash and dash."

"That'll be grand!" was the reply.

A 'splash and dash' manoeuvre is achieved by allowing the balloon on a calm evening to descend very slowly over a stretch of water, the basket just touches or 'kisses' the surface, and then the balloon climbs away. If done well, it looks spectacular with the water droplets falling as you climb away. It is also very easy to get it wrong! In Ray's own words, "I completely cocked it up!"

The basket hit the water and started to sink, deeper and deeper until it flowed over the top of the basket! Ray immediately put both burners full on! Very, very slowly the balloon started to lift out of the water and shot up to 1,500' or so. Ray was completely soaked through. Mopping his brow, he turned and said, "Jesus, that was close!"

But the old man was not there – he had floated out of the basket! Ray looked down, and there he was, calmly swimming along in the water, still with his cap on and his pipe in his mouth. He even gave a thumbs up. Ray was in shock. He managed to quickly land the balloon on a spit of land on the far side of the lake. Ray rushed up the shore and hammered on the door of the nearest cottage. The door opened.

A splash and dash in Ireland.

"Help! Police, fire, ambulance! I have drowned an old man in the lake," Ray shouted to the startled owner. The man pointed to a phone, Ray grabbed it, and started to dial the emergency number. His heart was pounding. He looked out of the window. There was the old man... sitting on top of the balloon basket, still with his hat on and his pipe in his mouth. Ray dropped the phone and rushed down the beach. As he approached the old man stood up and calmly said, "Hello Ray!"

"What do you mean 'Hello Ray', I thought I had drowned you in the lake!"

The old man paused, finally took his pipe out of his mouth, and said, "Well, this fella came along with a boat!" He stretched out his arms, put his hands on Ray's shoulders and said, "Hey, Ray this splash an' dash 'tis a wonderful 'ting!"

The balloon in this picture was originally built to advertise the Inland Revenue, asking you to complete your tax return as soon as possible. I bought it second hand. I could visualize the little 'Hector' character could easily be changed to an old-time pilot's face. The balloon's radio call sign became 'Pinky and Perky'.

I realized that ballooning was a worldwide sport. Balloon meets were taking place in many countries and we started to receive invitations to attend these meets.

Greece

As part of the British Airtours team we attended the first balloon meet to be held in Greece. It was a short visit, but a memorable one!

Scheduled to take place at Agrinio, a Greek Air Force base, a huge crowd had come to see the event but it was far too windy to fly. Phil Dunnington, a balloon instructor and examiner, said, "We must try and put on some sort of a show."

As I was the least experienced pilot, Phil said it would be a good experience for me to tether our balloon so we tied a heavy-duty restraint rope from the chassis of a giant Greek Air Force truck to the balloon basket.

I was beginning to think we were pushing our luck. The wind was steadily increasing in strength. One of our crew patted the basket and said by way of reassurance, "You ain't goin' nowhere kid, you are well and truly tied off." The words '*Never assume, always check*' echoed through my brain.

Phil and I climbed into the balloon basket that was lying on its side. We looked like a couple of dogs staring out of their kennels. The balloon envelope, half filled with air, was thrashing about as if it were alive. I put the burner on fully. Giant flames started to fill the envelope with hot air. The balloon was about halfway inflated when there was almighty BANG! The rope had broken! We were off!

Phil and I were sliding down the runway at great speed with one of our crewmen hanging onto of the basket. The crowd cheered, they thought it was part of the show. "Rip, rip!" Phil shouted. I was already pulling the rip line as hard as I could. This line pulls the top of the balloon open, lets the hot air out and deflates the envelope. The noise was deafening. Everyone was shouting and cheering, plus the sound of the balloon basket screeching along the runway.

We eventually came to a stop. Mercifully, our crewman was still on top of the basket, and neither Phil nor I were hurt. "Phew," I said.

Phil looked at me and said, "Is that all you can say?" I was too shocked to say anything else. Balloon baskets are traditionally made of woven willow and cane, light and robust but not intended for tobogganing down concrete runways! However, the tatty side of the basket was soon repaired, and we were ready for more adventures!

India

We received a personal invitation from Mr Vishwa Bandhu Gupta MP, Secretary to the Ballooning Club of India, to attend a balloon *mela* or balloon event he was organizing in New Delhi, India. At that time, he was the only balloonist in India.

Rajiv Gandhi, the Prime Minister of India at the time, was also a balloon enthusiast and he came to meet all the balloon teams prior to the start of the *mela*.

Prime Minister Rajiv Gandhi with ballooning friends.

Judy and Graeme Scaife, Cecilia and I flew to New Delhi. The balloon was airfreighted free of charge, courtesy of British Airways. *'It's not what you know but who..."*

Our driver, an Indian soldier, met us at the airport and showed us to his Jeep. We squeezed in, suitcases on our laps. He drove off at high speed through the traffic, using the horn and brakes to weave a path round holy cows and cars coming at us on the wrong side of the road! Graeme muttered, "Holy cow!" under his breath and received a clip round the ear from Judy. All four of us clung together. As we approached a busy roundabout we slammed into the back of the car in front of us. It was an ancient Morris Minor. The boot flew open then slammed shut. The two occupants drove on, quite unconcerned. They had a sticker in the back window:

'British and Proud of it.'

Before the first flight we had a briefing from Mr Gupta. Our launch site was from Safdarjung Airport, located right in the city centre of New Delhi. The Delhi Flying Club was established there in 1928 with two de Havilland Moth aircraft named 'Delhi' and 'Roshanara'. Roshanara Begum was a princess and the daughter of the Emperor Shan Jahan, architect of the Taj Mahal.

The flight director explained that we should not fly *higher* than 500'. Most aviation regulations specify to fly not *below* 500'. When I respectfully questioned this. The reply was, "Was I not aware the people of New Delhi want to see the balloons?"

The first flight in India. Photo by Cecilia Smith.

The first flight was scheduled for early the next morning. The weather was slightly hazy with calm winds. Wood smoke drifting from cooking fires made it feel very atmospheric. We flew right across the city at roof top height. Many of the houses had flat roofs with people sleeping in the open and we were waking people up as we flew overhead. The children were rubbing their eyes in disbelief, some hiding behind their parents, other squealing with delight and waving furiously.

On landing we were engulfed by hundreds of children excitedly jumping all over the deflated balloon. With so many helping hands it was easily packed up.

Visit to The Baha'i Temple – New Delhi, 1986

The Baha'i Temple in New Delhi.

Written by Cecilia

Some years ago, I became a member of the Baha'i Faith. I was thrilled when Brian and I, together with Judy and Graeme Scaife, were invited to visit the newly completed Baha'i House of Worship on the outskirts of Delhi.

We were fortunate to be shown round by architect Fariborz Sahba, who explained the intricacies of the project.

The extremely complex design called for the highest order of

160

engineering ingenuity. Amazingly, in the absence of sophisticated equipment, much of it was built using traditional building methods – traditional tools and traditional equipment. Forty engineers and about 800 skilled and unskilled labourers from around the country were involved.

The natural light within the central prayer hall, together with the water feature of nine pools around it – representing the floating leaves of the lotus – accentuate the majesty of the temple, lending an atmosphere of natural beauty and serenity. The temple takes its inspiration from the exquisite lotus flower – a symbol of beauty, purity and divinity. It uniquely represents 'the Oneness of God, the Oneness of religion and the Oneness of mankind', expressing a unifying link in a land of myriad religions.

We were delighted when Mr Gupta, organiser of the balloon meet, enthused about Brian's idea of a hot-air balloon rising slowly and graciously from behind the temple on the dedication day, just as all the people were arriving for the dedication ceremony. He kindly agreed to facilitate this for us, as unfortunately we were unable to be there. This took place a short time after we left.

More recently the Government of India has chosen this (Baha'i House of Worship) temple as the symbol of India, as it is a symbol of the unity of the human race. It is now considered by many to be the 'Taj Mahal of the 20th Century'.

Flying in India

Luckily for us there was a balloon examiner, Chris Kirby, who was also at the meet, and available for any flight tests; this was an ideal opportunity for Graeme to complete his check flight with Chris and gain his Private Pilot's Licence (PPL). All went well on the check flight. Now it was time for the solo flight. The normal practice is for the candidate to land the balloon and the examiner then climbs out.

With a pat on his back Graeme was sent off on his first solo flight. We were way out in the Indian countryside. It was arid desert with small hills and dusty tracks rather than roads, but quite beautiful in its isolation. Our driver set off at breakneck speed, towing the balloon trailer, determined to be there when the balloon landed. Graeme's balloon must have been going at some speed as he was soon completely out of sight. We came to the top of a hill, and there he was, having landed safely in the valley below. We threaded our way through the hundreds of children gathered round. Graeme was standing in the basket, looking rather shocked at the reception he was getting.

Chris the examiner stuck his hand out and said, "Well done Graeme, congratulations." Graeme had passed the test with flying colours. (No pun intended!) We spent the next hour throwing children in and out of the balloon basket, and holding them up to let them operate the burner. Six-foot flames shot out. The noise was drowned by the delighted screams of the children. It was great fun, and excitement for everyone. Packing up 77,000 feet of envelope is normally a slow and laborious task. Not this time, however. We got the children to run up and down the envelope in their bare feet. It was completely deflated and rolled up in next to no time. It was very hot, the heat combining with the occasional aroma of curry, the fragrance of the earth, wildflowers, and many hot little bodies. As we drove away we had many children sitting on the trailer. We had to peel them off when we approached the main tarmac road.

Balloon flying always takes place at the two most evocative times of the day – the very early morning or late evening, just before sunset. The reason for this is that the weather needs to be calm with no thermal activity. Balloon flying in thermic conditions can be quite dangerous. You suddenly find the balloon erratically going up, then down, without any input from the pilot. Once the sun starts to heat the earth's surface, the air becomes unstable and creates up and down air currents. At the end of the day the sun's warmth has diminished and the air becomes stable again. I liken this to putting a saucepan of cold water on the stove. As you heat it up bubbles start to form and eventually it starts to boil. When you turn the heat off the bubbling stops and the water becomes calm again.

After the final flight of the meet, Mr Gupta, as he was known to everyone (and don't miss out the 'Mister'!) laid on a wonderful Indian meal for all the balloonists, complete with dancers and music. We were all presented with a certificate of participation. It hangs on the wall in my study. Mr Gupta still lives in New Delhi and is known as a social activist and was a prominent leader in the 2011 Indian ant-corruption group 'India Against Corruption'. We will always remember him as a fellow balloonist and a kind and generous host.

Some years later we flew in an Indian Army balloon, over Pune, formerly known as Poona. We landed on a barracks parade square. Everyone was completely unconcerned and were more than happy to pack up the balloon and wish us on our way.

Zimbabwe

As my wife is from Zimbabwe, we were looking forward to visiting Cecilia's folks for a short holiday. In the course of conversation with fellow balloonist Pete Bish, I mentioned our forthcoming trip. "Hey," he said, "take your balloon pilot's licence with you." He went on to explain that a mining company, Turnpan, had bought a brand new hot-air balloon. They did not have a pilot to fly it. He gave me the name and telephone number of the company. I thought to myself, could this really be true?

I made a phone call the minute I arrived in Harare. Not only was it true, the managing director came on the phone and said for me to come to look at it and fly it as soon as possible! I went to the offices of Turnpan and there in a back shed was the balloon. It was still covered in bubble wrap and clearly had not been touched since it arrived from the balloon factory in England. We unpacked the balloon. Some mice had eaten the foam and nested inside one of the crash helmets. We laid out the balloon envelope in the back yard. I inspected every stitch and panel. It was perfect. I then made a *big* mistake. Rather than taking the balloon out into the bush and flying it, I went to the Zimbabwe Department of Civil Aviation (DCA) to ask permission to fly. In England we are so regulated it seemed the correct thing to do at the time. There is a saying: 'If there are two Englishmen standing together, they will form a queue.' It is true.

I went to the DCA every day for a week. I was referred from one department to another. No one wanted to give permission for the first hot-air balloon to fly in Zimbabwe. On the Friday afternoon I was despondent. I was not making any progress. I called into the DCA's offices one more time. There I met Selwyn Lloyd, an operations officer, an easy name to remember, I thought. He said, "Mr Smith, I think you ought to go and fly it." I could hardly believe my ears. He added, "One proviso. I am your first passenger."

The next morning Selwyn and I met at dawn and went for a flight. It was a first for me to fly in Zimbabwe, a first for the Turnpan balloon to fly, and the first for a Zimbabwean to fly in a balloon.

Some years later I was talking to the Botswana Department of Civil Aviation (DCA) to obtain permission to fly balloons in Botswana. The conversation was going nowhere, when one of their officers said, "I think we should consult our balloon expert, Mr Selwyn Lloyd." I nearly jumped out of my chair!

"You mean Mr Selwyn Lloyd from Zimbabwe?"

"Ah, you know him?" he said.

"Yes, he is a good friend of mine," I replied.

The next morning, I was waiting with my balloon, and crew, outside the International Airport. A large black limousine drew up and out climbed my 'good friend', Mr Selwyn Lloyd. He was smiling. "So, now *you* are the 'ballooning expert' of Botswana?" I said.

"Ah, yes!" he said, and burst out laughing. He had had *one* passenger flight with me in Zimbabwe. After our second balloon flight together, things went quite smoothly obtaining permissions.

I returned to England and Jim Seton Rogers took over as the Turnpan balloon pilot. Jim was a Zimbabwean and worked for

Turnpan. All's well that ends well.

Balloon Meets in Zimbabwe

Back in England I thought about my ballooning experiences in Zimbabwe. I decided the time was about right to put ballooning in Zimbabwe squarely on the map. I was sure I would be able to find half a dozen or so balloonists that would come to fly in such a beautiful country, with wide open spaces and calm winds. I quickly discovered the jungle drums beat louder in England than Zimbabwe it seems, and before we could say 'Robert Mugabe' we had 20 balloon teams lined up.

The plan would be: Airfreight the balloons, find accommodation for a team of four balloonists, a company that sold propane or butane, pick-up trucks to transport the balloons around, and finally obtain permission to temporarily import the balloons. Clearly, we would need some sponsorship. We chose May for the festival as the month with the most stable weather.

Cecilia, her brother John, and I hired a conference room in a hotel, and advertised that we were planning a balloon festival and if anyone was interested in getting involved to please come along. We were very surprised at the interest. About 20 people turned up. Rhodesians have a reputation as a 'can do' nation – I should know – I married one! The ravages of the civil war meant they had become hugely resourceful and had to find ways to make or repair all sorts of items themselves. We could not believe the response.

One of the first in the queue was Ken Sparkes. He immediately volunteered his pick-up truck, and the use of his workshop. Also roped in were his wife Hilary, son Paul, daughter Therese and 'Big Paul', Ken's workshop manager. They were Ken's core team. We became good friends. Subsequently, Ken, Paul, Therese and Big Paul gained their balloon pilot's licence.

Some months later, in the course of conversation, we discovered that Ken and I must have flown together when he was an engineer and I was the pilot flying into the protected villages during the civil war. Other representatives from local firms volunteered their pick-up trucks, complete with a driver. One firm, Tanganda Tea, had a strapline '*Tanganda Tea, Up, up, up, it lifts you up!*' Perfect. Fortunately, Ken's company, TIG Welding were able to supply propane. Also present was Caroline Thorneycroft; she had a PR and advertising company in Harare. Caroline became one of our team and a good friend. She had many connections, and immediately set to work arranging customs clearances, and raising the public awareness of the festival. Cecilia and I agreed long ago if we ran any event, it had to have a charity element to it. The charity we chose was 'Special Olympics', raising money for handicapped children.

Balloons flying over the Sheraton Hotel, Harare.

The Sheraton Hotel in Harare very generously provided each team with two rooms free of charge. The hotel became our headquarters and they allowed us to park our balloon trailers and vehicles in their car park. At that very first meeting we had ticked many of the boxes.

Now, to find a company that would be prepared to airfreight the balloons. I approached Affretair, a Zimbabwean freight airline. Although based in Zimbabwe they had offices in Gatwick. I arranged to meet their sales manager.

Balloons are relatively easy to airfreight. All the parts fit into the balloon basket about a metre square. The flight cylinders are emptied and purged of propane. The whole thing weighs between

150 and 200kg, depending on its size.

Keeping up with the tradition of 'can do', a price was agreed and a date fixed. The balloonists had to deliver the balloons to Gatwick ready to be airfreighted, packaged and purged. I went to see the balloons in the cargo hangar a day before their flight. I felt very apprehensive as I suddenly realised I was responsible for their safe return. I phoned Affretair and asked if I could travel in their aircraft with the balloons. "Sure, be at Gatwick airport at 16.00hrs tomorrow," said their operations manager.

I was taken by minibus from the terminal to the aircraft, a DC8 freighter, which it would be fair to say was not in the first flush of youth.

There was a hive of activity around the aircraft; all sorts of items, including our balloons were being loaded. I introduced myself to the captain. He said, "You're very welcome, come and meet the rest of the gang, oh, by the way, there is nowhere for you to sit, the flight deck is full. There are seats for the three crew, but the flight engineer and I have our wives with us. All the jump seats are taken. You can stand at the back of the flight deck for take-off. You will have to take turns to sit down." He then gave me a huge grin and said, "You might get a chance to sit in my seat."

I had not expected any food or drink on the flight, so I carried a backpack with some sandwiches, biscuits and water, and a torch, which proved to be very useful in finding my way around in the dark cargo hold during the night flight. The sun was setting. The whole atmosphere was very relaxed. There appeared to be no scheduled time of departure. The crew, who were all well known to each other, calmly worked their way through all the pre-flight checks.

The very first DC8 flew on 30th May 1958. I started to get the feeling that this was one of the first off the production line. Having said that, the DC8 was a fine aircraft in its day, and many pilots who flew it felt it was superior to the B707. Many people feel it was the Concorde that was the first commercial airliner to break the sound barrier, although a story has emerged that it was in fact a DC8. On 21st August 1961, a DC-8-43 airliner on its pre-delivery flight achieved Mach 1 and broke the sound barrier. Escorting the aircraft was Chuck Yeager, who had broken the sound barrier on 14th October 1947 in the Bell X-1 experimental fighter.

On our DC8 I stood at the back of the flight deck for take-off. The aircraft must have been very heavy as we slowly climbed out of Gatwick. The residents of Russ Hill, situated about a mile off the end of the runway, were treated to a spectacular view of the underside of the DC8, and to the smoke pouring from its four Pratt and Whitney JT3C engines at full power.

In the cruise the routine of the flight deck settled into a familiar rhythm of radio calls and monitoring the navigation and engine instruments. We flew over the Mediterranean, and on to Africa. It was a beautiful clear night, as black as the ace of spades, with the Milky Way shining down, you felt you could touch it.

After a couple of hours, I was eventually upgraded to the jump seat behind the captain. He turned round in his seat and said, "Ah Brian, come and sit here, it's my turn to do the cooking tonight." He climbed out, and I took his place. The co-pilot was sitting quietly, hand flying the aircraft.

He smiled and said, "I like to keep my hand in, do you want to have a go?" The whole layout of the flight deck was very similar to the B707. "You have control," he said.

I replied, "I have control," hoping I really had. Quite some time went by and I tried to keep my flying smooth so as not to wake the wives who had fallen sound asleep shortly after take-off. Some delicious aromas were coming from the galley, and quite a lot of smoke too. The captain appeared and said to me, "OK, Brian what would you like for supper? There is steak and chips, sausage and chips and chicken curry. Hey man, have a good old Rhodesian steak." The next thing I knew a tray appeared with the food. It was an excellent steak. Now was the time to hand back control. The co-pilot watched me eat every mouthful. As he had 'the con' he could not eat until I had finished, with a cup of 'good old Rhodesian' coffee. My time in the captain's seat was up.

I thought I would go back to the cargo hold and find somewhere to sleep. I managed to squeeze through the giant cargo restraint net, into the hold. It was pitch dark. I switched on the torch and picked my way around the sleeping bodies of the crew. I climbed on the top of a large balloon basket and fell fast asleep.

After several hours I felt the engine note change, I knew we were descending. I went to stand at the back of the flight deck ready for the landing. We were making our approach over the bush type terrain for our landing on Runway 23 at Harare International Airport. The airport is nearly 5,000' above mean sea level. For some years it had the longest runway in the world of 15,500 feet. Now, I believe there is a Russian airport with a runway 17,725 feet long.

We landed about an hour after sunrise. I said goodbye to the captain and crew, it had been an experience I will never forget. The balloons were already being unloaded. I got a lift to Caroline's office. This was a tense moment for us. All the balloons had to be cleared by customs. Each balloon was valued and a deposit made to Zimbabwe customs. I had allowed three days for any possible hold ups.

We had just made a cup of GOR (good old Rhodesian) coffee when our handling agent walked in. He handed me a sheaf of papers and said with a heavy Rhodesian accent, "Bloody good." We raised our eyebrows. "Bloody good, they are all customs cleared." We could hardly believe our ears.

"Come on," I said to Caroline, "let's go to the Sheraton Hotel and celebrate, and I need to check the car park is clear for the balloons." We sat in the lounge of the Sheraton, overlooking the car park. Caroline said, "I have had a call from my friend Ivor who has collected your balloon from the airport and is on his way here." I had just raised a beer to my lips, when through the gates of the hotel came a most extraordinary sight: A small battered pick-up truck driven by an elderly man wearing a trilby hat, safari suit and cravat.

The pick-up was towing a two-wheeled trailer that looked like a Kontiki raft, some rough-sawn logs lashed together with ropes, and our balloon in its basket firmly tied down to the trailer. No lights, indicators or brakes were evident. The old man came into the hotel and sat with us and had what he described as a nice cup of GOR tea.

Ivor the Driver, as he became known, was a wonderful character. Looking like an elderly David Niven, he retrieved for us many times. One morning, we were coming back from a very early morning flight; Ivor was driving and falling asleep. In an attempt to keep him awake, I said, "I understand you used to be a skydiver, when did you last skydive?"

He thought for a minute and said, "I think it was last Thursday." He was 92.

We had some great help from John Ware and Roy Boulding – BA ground engineers who came to Zimbabwe, ready to help with anything to do with ballooning. We had organized a low loader to collect the rest of the balloons and bring them to the Sheraton Hotel. John, Roy and I raced to the airport to escort the driver to the Sheraton. The balloons had been carefully loaded with a large forklift truck. As we left the airport, we all gave a whoop of joy. We then looked at each other and said, "How on earth are we going to unload them without a forklift truck?" Each balloon weighed between 150 to 200 kgs.

Roy said, "Leave it to me."

We parked the huge truck in the hotel car park. Roy disappeared into the hotel and reappeared with all the hotel staff – waiters, cleaners, receptionists, and bellboys and gathered them around the truck. In his 'best Shona' he explained all the balloons needed to be unloaded. Many hands make light work. Ten or more hotel staff surrounded each balloon. With a loud collective grunt and a chant of 'bechanah', 'bechanah' (little by little) Roy took up the chant with his interpretation shouting 'pyjama', 'pyjama', and the balloons were soon whizzing off the truck onto the front lawn of the hotel. Twenty balloon baskets and their contents lay scattered everywhere. We lay flat out on the lawn, totally exhausted. Suddenly, there was a whooshing sound and all the sprinklers popped up out of the lawn and started to spray us and the balloons with water...

The balloon teams started to arrive at Harare Airport. We always went out to greet them and made sure they reached the hotel. We thought we would play a trick on our friends, Keith Sanderson, and Malcolm Findlay from Sussex.

The porter at the Sheraton Hotel had a small blackboard on a pole and used to walk around with chalked messages for the guests. We asked if we could 'borrow' his blackboard. Our plan was to write on it *'Message for Lord Sanderson and The Right Honourable Malcolm Finlay'*. We were going to stand outside arrivals at the airport, so that when they came though they would see the board. Just as we were putting the finishing touches to the board, Keith and Malcolm walked into the hotel...

The aircraft had arrived an hour early. The game was up. "Never mind," said Keith, "we will check in and see you in the bar in ten minutes." We waited in the bar.

Keith and Malcolm appeared. "You will not believe it, but they have put us in executive suites as 'Lord Sanderson and The Right Honourable Malcolm Findlay'." They had a bottle of champagne and fresh flowers delivered to their rooms every day!

One day, when we were all relaxing by the hotel pool, Keith appeared, looking rather shaken. "What's wrong?" we asked.

"Have a look at this, it was pushed under my door about an hour ago." He handed us an envelope. Inside was an embossed card. As I recall, it read: *'His Excellency the President of Zimbabwe Robert Mugabe invites Lord and Lady Sanderson for afternoon tea at 3pm on Thursday 20 May 1990. RSVP.'*

"What do I do?" said Keith. Kerry, our eldest daughter, grabbed his arm and said, "Well Keith, I could be Lady Sanderson!" We all got together and devised a note to say *'Thank you for the gracious invite. Unfortunately Lord and Lady Sanderson will be out of town on that day on a previous engagement.'*

All the crews had arrived now. We spent a morning preparing the balloons for the first flight the next day. As each balloon had a sponsor, much of the time was spent meeting sponsors and attaching their banners to the balloon envelopes. Before we had left the UK we approached Mothercare Ltd and asked if they would donate some nappy pins for our charity balloon festival.

Banners are a very effective way of displaying the sponsor's company name and logo. Made of light nylon, they are pinned or 'nappy' pinned onto the load tapes of the balloon envelope.

Some months before we had sent the sponsors details of the measurements and type of material required. Something was lost in the translation, as some of the banners arrived made of canvas, far too heavy to attach to the balloon. We were concerned the sponsors of these heavy banners would be upset that they could not have them on the balloon. It was agreed we would attach them to the fence surrounding the Sheraton Hotel. To everyone's surprise they looked good and attracted much attention.

We were making the final checks of the balloons, ready for our first mass take-off of the festival, planned for the morning, when suddenly, marching towards us appeared 20 security guards. Each guard had been assigned to a balloon, not that we were anticipating any trouble, but to act as a liaison or interpreter should we need it. They were a great addition to our teams, and quickly learnt how to rig the balloon. Our guard's name was Romeo.

A reception and briefing were organized for that evening in the Sheraton Hotel. As I was about to start the briefing, a note was handed to me. It read: *'Comrade XXXXX had died and tomorrow was declared a day of mourning.'*

We had planned to fly from the grounds of the Sheraton, and we were expecting several hundred people to come to see the mass launch. We had to come up with an alternative plan. After much discussion we felt we should respect the day of mourning, and launch our balloons way out of Harare, and fly away from the city.

All the teams and their sponsors were told the new plan.

The site we chose was a small village, Christon Bank, 39kms north of Harare. More by luck than judgment it turned out to be a perfect site. There were thatched African huts, with wood smoke from cooking fires, a backdrop of green rolling hills, a gentle breeze, and deep blue clear skies. A wonderful introduction to ballooning in Africa.

Pamazinda Game Lodge.

For the evening flight we organized a race. Each balloon was paired up with a vintage car.

The rules:

1. The cars park ten miles downwind from the launch site.
2. The balloons take-off from the launch site.
3. The pilot lands as close to his vintage car as possible.
4. The pilot jumps out, leaving the crew to pack up, and leaps into his vehicle.
5. The winner is the first one back to the Sheraton Hotel.

I was lucky to be paired up with a driver with a vintage Fraser Nash sports car, and he was determined to be first back to the finishing line at the Sheraton. Speed limits in the city were ignored. Luckily for us no one was arrested for speeding, and there were no accidents. I believe we were third.

I had promised the balloonists that the weather in Zimbabwe would be perfect for ballooning. This proved to be the case, and we flew for ten days consecutively.

I had arranged for a Met forecast to be available every morning at 5am throughout the festival. Each morning I would phone the duty forecaster at Harare International Airport for the day's weather. The weather had been very stable, giving a surface wind of 5 knots from the north east. On the last morning of the festival, I made the routine call to the Met Office. I thanked the forecaster and asked if the weather was going to stay like this? His reply, "Ah, yes until September." The date was 10th May!

On one occasion four men approached me to ask if they could parachute from my balloon. I agreed to their request as I had dropped skydivers in England. We drove about 20 miles out of town. The technique is to make sure the balloon is in a descent before they jump out. I briefed them, that they must only jump when I say go and, more importantly, one at a time. We climbed to 5,000' above the ground. I could feel they were getting more and more excited. I said,

"Go." I expected one at a time, but all four jumped together. The balloon shot up like a rocket, it was shaking and twisting, I clung on to the rope handles. I thought it was better not to touch anything and let it just stabilise, which it did at 12,000 feet. Phew!

I landed safely. Ken and the crew appeared, looking somewhat shaken, having witnessed the whole episode. After packing up the balloon, we set off along the dusty track towards the main road. As we approached the junction, there were the four skydivers sitting quietly, with their chutes on their laps, waiting patiently for the next bus to Harare.

Another exciting event happened when the manager of Charles Prince Airfield, a small general aviation airfield, invited the balloonists to attend the annual air show. He stressed that we must arrive early as there was only one small track in and out of the airfield, and we could be stuck in traffic for hours. I said, "How about we fly in? We can launch at dawn and be in the airfield before it gets busy then fly out at the end of the day."

"Great idea," he said, "you are all invited to breakfast in the Mashonaland Flying Club." We all landed in the confines of the airfield and duly went for breakfast.

The air show started. As I recall there was no programme of events. We were surprised to see an Affretair DC8 appear and give a very spirited display. I was standing with the Affretair manager. I said, "That was some show, how generous of Affretair to allocate a day for one of their aircraft to come to the show."

He replied, "No problem, because now it's on its way to London with 30 tons of freight on-board."

I said, "I hope they were not carrying eggs."

Next on the scene was an Air Zimbabwe B707. It is always a spectacle to see a large airliner close to the ground. The B707 did a low pass. It could not have been more than a couple of feet above the runway. I believe YouTube has a video of it. I thought what an exciting day it had been, but there was more to come.

The air show finished and we started to get the balloons ready to fly. Two men came up to me and said, "We would like to be the first to fly a radio-controlled aircraft from a balloon, will you take us?" I was intrigued, as I had not heard of this manoeuvre before.

We took-off and climbed to 2000' above the ground. They started to assemble their craft, it was a Piper Cub, with a six-foot wingspan. One of the men was the pilot with the controls strapped to his chest, the other was the handler. The pilot started the engine and nodded his head; the handler dropped the model over the side. Down it went, and suddenly it roared into a climb, and did loops and rolls around the balloon. They certainly knew what they were doing. We were now into open country. I asked a question. "How do you plan to land it?"

He replied, "I have a friend in a pick-up truck who is following us and with his radio link he can take over and land it."

I was impressed, these guys are professionals, I thought. He then said, "Oh dear, I have just contacted our man, and they are stuck in traffic, and cannot get out of the airfield." He then went on the say, "Not to worry. If you can land now, I think I can get it to land it beside you." He did exactly that.

What an end to a very exciting day.

We held three balloon festivals in Zimbabwe, 1990, 1993 and 1995. All raised money for Special Olympics Children charity. I do not know the exact amount raised, and I would not want to guess.

In 1993, Ken Sparkes was learning to fly. He loved low flying. We were flying very low towards the Harare suburbs. We could see some trees ahead, and a large house behind them. Ken put the balloon into a climb. Just as we cleared the treetops, we saw armed soldiers in the garden, pointing their rifles at us. We had flown over the president's residence. Ken was shaking with fright.

The residence is heavily guarded with all roads to it blocked off, and probably air space too. We finally landed way out in the bush. When we went back to Ken's office, his secretary said, "I have just had a call from a man that says he is the head of the Zimbabwe Department of Civil Aviation (DCA) and wants to talk to you." I quietly left the room, leaving Ken to talk to him. I waited outside.

After ten minutes or so Ken appeared looking dejected. I thought, this is where we go to jail. He said, "It WAS the head of the DCA on the phone. He was standing in the president's garden and saw us fly overhead."

I said, "And so... what's going to happen?" – expecting the worst.

"Ohhh!" he said. "He thought it looked wonderful. He wants to have a balloon flight!" Ken burst out laughing, and I joined in, more out of relief than humour.

The Final Flight – The Great Zimbabwe Long Jump

The final festival was in 1995. One of the tasks we set was to fly as far as possible from Harare in 36 hours. Starting with a morning flight and an evening flight, and a further flight the next morning.

It was called The Great Zimbabwe Long Jump.

There were only two rules:

Rule One: Anyone found taking it seriously, will be disqualified.
Rule Two: Do not forget Rule One.

People get up early in Zimbabwe, and there was a huge crowd to see us off. The start point was a mass take-off at dawn, from the grounds of the Sheraton Hotel in the centre of Harare. For the evening flight you were required to take off within 1km radius of the morning's landing spot. Then decisions had to be made: Do you camp out for the next morning's flight or do you wimp out and return to the hotel?

Most of the teams elected to camp out and took off with pots and pans and tents tied to the outside of their baskets. Fortunately, the wind direction on the evening flight took the balloons into the Mazoe Valley, a beautiful citrus growing area.

The Great Zimbabwe Long Jump 1995

I decided to hire a light aircraft and track the balloons. We had a VHF radio link between me and the balloons. I watched until they had all landed safely. Each balloon called in 'safe and sound'. One balloon landed close to a large farmhouse. I called the pilot on the radio to check if all was well, as his balloon appeared to be surrounded by a large crowd, several tractors and cars. Above the noise of the aircraft's engine, I could hear the singing. The pilot replied, "I am standing with the farmer, it is his son's 21st birthday today, and we are all invited to the party."

All pilots and crew were asked to write a report of their flight, and their overnight stay in the bush.

ZIMBABWE BALLOON FLIGHTS (PVT) LTD

316 Harare Drive, Msasa
P.O. Box AY 129, Amby
Harare, Zimbabwe
Tel / Fax 487035 / 6

May 1995.

Dear Reader,

As you read the flight reports of the 1st (ever!) Great Zimbabwe Long Jump, you will see a dream revealed.

The dream was to have fun, fly balloons, and raise money for 'Special Olympics', all at the same time! As you can see we have achieved our goal.

Thanks to the pilots who flew well and safely, but very special thanks to the retrieve crews, some of whom had never even seen a hot-air balloon prior to the festival. In many ways the success of the Long Jump was due to their unselfish and untiring efforts. They are all truly 'Golden Retrievers'.

This memento was produced in time for the survivor's dinner. Please send me any additional items, photos etc and I will pass them on, so you can add them to your copy. Best wishes

Brian Smith.

Directors: K. Sparkes B. Smith

Great Zimbabwe Long Jump – Flight report.

180

MAY 12, 1995

WE HAD ONE HELL OF A GOOD TIME! DRANK BEER
AND SLEPT IN THE BUSH! ATE THREE PLATES OF EGGS—
EACH — BACON, TOMATOES, TOAST AND PAPAYA. KNOCKED
OVER A TWENTY FOOT ACACIA TREE AND PLOWED A TEN
ACRE FIELD — GOT AN HOUR AND A HALF HORTICULTURAL
LECTURE AND TOUR — LOST ONE CREW MEMBER TO
THE NATIVES AND MOST OF OUR CLOTHES.
PLEASE INCLUDE US IN THE NEXT LONG JUMP. WE PRO-
MISE TO BE MORE SERIOUS!

P.S. WE STRONGLY RECOMMEND YOU DISQUALIFY ANY-
BODY AHEAD OF US!
   ALSO!!!
   THIS BULLSHIT OF TAKING OFF IN THE MIDDLE OF
THE NIGHT HAS TO GO!
                JUST A FEW COMMENTS
         WE THOUGHT OF REASONS FOR DISQUALIFICATION
            1) ANYONE WHO CAN'T GET IT UP BEFORE 3:30AM
            2) GPS — OR ANY OTHER ELECTRONIC DEVICE
            3) ONLY FLYING TWO OUT OF THREE FLIGHTS
            4) ANYBODY HOOKED UP TO A FUEL TRUCK
            5) SLEEPING AT HOME
            6) TALK SHOWS   RESPECTFULLY,
                                    Ed Weltshc

Balloonist's flight report.

Ken Sparkes gained his balloon pilot's licence in 1996. Ken and
I formed Zimbabwe Balloon Flights and commenced flying
commercially in the Harare area. Ken was very competitive. He

thought we should enter the South African Hot-Air Balloon Championships in Bethlehem, a town in the eastern Free State province, situated in a fertile valley with the backdrop of the Rooiberg Mountains. We were nervous about taking a hot-air balloon through the customs border post between Zimbabwe and South Africa. We thought it was best to take one of our oldest and most porous balloons in case it was impounded or confiscated. I called it the 'Green Tea Bag'.

Over a period of time the balloon envelope becomes porous due to the exposure to the strong sunlight, and the constant heating and cooling. Our Zimbabwe balloon was still safe to fly, but we knew the material was slowly deteriorating. The evening before the official opening of the championships, we decided to make a test flight. The balloon was laid out, and I was pulling the envelope material to make it into a balloon shape on the ground when there was a loud ripping sound, and the material split, leaving a two-foot gash in the top. Normally, that would ground the balloon but we were determined to fly. We patched it up with copious quantities of repair tape, which made it look like a giant Band-Aid or plaster tape.

The next morning the first task set by the organisers was a 'minimum distance flight'. This flight had to be at least an hour, and the balloon that travelled the *shortest* distance from the start point was declared the winner. Unusually, on that day, the winds at height were calmer than the low-level winds. Balloons were shooting into the sky and climbing high to find the calm winds. Knowing the delicate state of our balloon, Ken took off gently and remained at 20' above the ground for the whole flight. We were marked last in the task. However, when Ken made his report of the flight, as all were required to do, he stated he had seen many elephants, giraffes, zebra, and buck. The judges very generously gave Ken a special 'Safari' prize. It was a box of Band-Aid plasters.

Antelope Park – 'Lion Rehabilitation into the Wild Programme'

On our return to Zimbabwe we decided to take a few days off. We had heard about an impressive venture, rehabilitating lions into the wild. Antelope Park is 3,000 acres of open Savannah grassland situated near Gweru, three hours' drive from Harare. World Travel Awards voted it 'Zimbabwe's leading Private Game Reserve'. It has the successful and commendable programme of releasing captive-bred lions into the wild.

Over the last 40 years the African lion population has drastically reduced, particularly in African countries further afield. To offset the rapid decline, the Antelope Park Lion Rehabilitation Programme works to re-introduce the 'offspring' of captive-bred lions into the wild, in stages, developing the cubs' natural instincts, so that they can eventually have their own wild-bred offspring. To ensure the best possible chance of survival, there is a fenced and managed wild area, where the young lions are released, and where they naturally live and hunt their own food. (Young game are released into the area for them to find.) As I understand, the young of those lions have no human contact, and *their* young are eventually released into the wild. We met a number of charity workers who had come to Zimbabwe for work experience. They were full of enthusiasm about the project.

The game reserve offered a variety of activities. Topping them was the opportunity to 'walk with lions' in the early morning. After watching a video programme about the 'do's and 'don'ts', armed with a large stick, we proceeded to where two young lions had been assembled. The instructions with the sticks were never turn your back on the lions and if they DID advance towards you, bang the stick on the ground, repeating loudly, "No. No!"

We had two trainers with us. It was a beautiful morning and the two young lions ambled ahead, rising in the air in playful combat. They stopped to drink from a large puddle, and then continued towards the rocks ahead. One of them ascended a large rock and stretched out in the warmth of the early morning sun. To our amazement one of the trainers who had my iPhone for photos encouraged us to ascend the rock as well and kneel down behind the lion. It all felt quite natural, and not too scary – hence the extraordinary photo we now have as a record.

For further information about lion rehabilitation, see www.lionalert.org.

Australia

In 1988 Australia celebrated its bicentenary.

Ruth Wilson, a very experienced balloon pilot, and the event director, organised a hot-air balloon race. We were honoured to be invited to take part. Our team of four were Graeme and I as the pilots, and Rob Avelano and Kevin Cooper our crew. Our balloon was airfreighted from England to Perth. We flew to Perth and hired a car and flatbed trailer.

The plan was to take off from Perth, Western Australia, and in company with 78 other balloons to fly right across the continent to Sydney on the east coast, a distance of about 4,000kms. The idea was to complete the trip in 12 stages over 16 days. Each day flights were scheduled to fly morning or evening, and then drive on to the next town.

There were pilots from the USA, Canada, UK, France, Germany, Austria, Spain, Sweden, Finland, Brazil, Hungary, Belgium and of course Australia. All the teams were put up in a 4-star hotel in Perth ready for the start. The weather was to play a significant part in the whole trip.

All teams had to attend a mandatory briefing on how to survive in the outback. The ranger stressed 'Do not travel at night'. To make his point he said, "Kangaroos hop onto the warm tarmac roads at night and one night a car travelling at speed hit a large kangaroo. The kangaroo went through the windscreen. It was still alive, thrashing about right inside the car. All four occupants of the car were killed." After that story, we never travelled at night the whole trip!

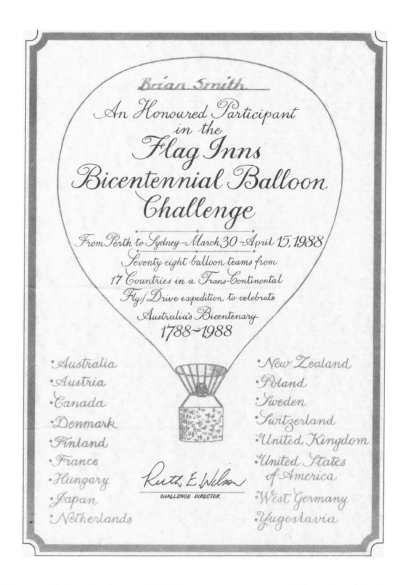

Brian Smith

An Honoured Participant
in the
Flag Inns
Bicentennial Balloon
Challenge

From Perth to Sydney—March 30—April 15, 1988
Seventy eight balloon teams from
17 Countries in a Trans-Continental
Fly/Drive expedition to celebrate
Australia's Bicentenary
1788—1988

- Australia
- Austria
- Canada
- Denmark
- Finland
- France
- Hungary
- Japan
- Netherlands

- New Zealand
- Poland
- Sweden
- Switzerland
- United Kingdom
- United States of America
- West Germany
- Yugoslavia

Ruth E Wilson
CHALLENGE DIRECTOR

Every flight had a task. Points were awarded and added up at the end. The target was a large red plastic cross, laid out in a field approximately ten miles downwind of the take-off site. The pilot carried a marker in the balloon basket. This was a strip of nylon material with a pocket of sand at the end for weight and marked with the balloon's assigned number. The skill was to manoeuvre the balloon by climbing and descending, trying to find a wind that would take you over the red cross. The marker closest to the cross was the winner.

We were flying with some of the most experienced competition pilots in the world. Graeme and I decided quite early on to not try and compete at this level and just fly for fun.

Kevin, Brian and Graeme flying high in a balloon over Australia.

After a morning flight at Norseman, we set off on the long drive to Eucla. Hour after hour went by on the dead straight Nation Highway A1. We had to get to Eucla before sunset. I started to put together a picture in my mind of what would await us. Maybe, a good pub serving cold beer and big steaks, and a nice little typical Australian town as was portrayed in the film *A Town like Alice*. We arrived in Eucla, population 53, just before sunset.

There were a couple of houses and some outbuildings, and a pub. That was it. Nothing else. The inside of the pub was lined with white tiles, and the air con was on full, but... they sold cold beer. The locals were friendly, and in good spirits (no pun intended). We thought we would join in the fun, and in our best English accent, we said to the barmaid, "Could we have four pints of warm beer, please."

She put her hands on her hips and said, "Jeez, if I sold warm beer, I'd have to leave town." The crowd loved it!

The next day, we drove on to Kimba. We made a lovely early morning flight over desolate ranges. Kangaroos were in abundance, quite unconcerned by a laundry basket floating by with two Pommies gazing down at them. At last we saw a road. A man was standing by his parked car, calmly smoking a cigarette. We were many miles from any habitation. He waved as we flew over him. We shouted, "Want to come for a flight?" He nodded.

To this day I don't know why I said it. Maybe, it was such a curious sight to see a man dressed in a smart business suit way out in the bush. We landed about 100 yards from his car. He ran up to the basket and jumped straight in. "G'day, me name's Bill," was all he said. Graeme and I looked at each other, shrugged, and we took off.

An hour later we landed. Our faithful crew were right there. We celebrated the flight with a couple of cold beers and we drove Bill back to his car. We were all excited by the flight and jabbering away with Bill. He explained he was part of the committee dealing with the bicentennial celebrations and had been visiting some Aboriginals nearby. We said our farewells and set off back to town.

We had travelled about ten miles, when suddenly, a man on a motorbike overtook us and waved us down. We stopped. He shouted, "Yer, lost yer balloon mate!" He pointed to our flatbed trailer. Shock! Horror! The complete balloon had fallen off! But when and where? We headed back along the road. After several miles we were beginning to feel despondent. With all the excitement we had forgotten to tie everything down. Eventually, we saw a car parked on the side of the road. A lady was standing with one hand on her hip and one hand scratching her head. She turned and said, "G'day, I knew you'd come back." There in a ditch was our balloon, completely unharmed. We started to thank her profusely. She waved us away, looked in the back of our car and said, "Yer got any beer left?" Another celebration took place…

One flight I well remember was a very early morning take-off over the Nullarbor Plain. In company with an American balloon, we climbed to 10,000 feet. Normally, there would be chatter on the radio between the two teams. This morning there was only silence. The scene before us overawed everyone. The desert of red soil and a few rocky outcrops seemed to stretch for miles, as far as the eye could see. The only features were the A1 road and the railway line that ran in a straight line right across the whole country. It is one of the most barren places I have ever seen.

We had another memorable flight at Broken Hill, New South Wales. I was pleased to visit this town, with its past connection to flying. Many years ago, its silver mines were so vast the town was renamed by many as 'Silver City'. This became the name of the airline that served the city.

We were told we 'must' visit Silverton, once a thriving mining town, now with just a population of 50. We made our way to a pub. It was the famous Silverton Hotel. Several films were made in and around Silverton. The old buildings and desert scenery were used in the production of films such as *Mad Max 2 and Razorback*, and many TV commercials.

At the entrance, there was a large handwritten sign that read *'Welcome balloonists, take the test and win free beer'*. Inside, it was packed with rowdy customers. We rushed to the bar. Graeme volunteered to be first to take the test. The barmaid appeared, with a large plastic funnel in one hand and an apple in the other. The funnel was stuffed down the front of Graeme's trousers, the apple placed on his head. The 'test' was to flip the apple into the funnel. Easy!

The barmaid asked Graeme to tilt his head well back, and on the word go, flip the apple. "Steady, steady," she said. Then suddenly she poured a bucket of freezing cold water down the funnel. The crowd roared approval, and Graeme had free beer for the rest of the day.

We realised we were facing a long journey back to civilization after spending many days flying and driving through remote areas, which were so peaceful and quiet, that arrival in Sydney quite overwhelmed us. We knew we had taken part in something really special – the country, the hospitality, and the memories that will stay with us forever.

On Return to England

I learned that my good friend Clive Ritchie had been diagnosed with cancer. He died within a few months, leaving his wife Cilla, daughter Olivia, and son Guy. I looked back at the times we had had and the hoops we had jumped though. I felt very sad.

It was about this time that our ballooning business was growing. Somehow, I felt I was torn between the airline flying and the balloon business. I had to make a decision. I decided to take early retirement from British Airways.

Ballooning from Wisborough Green

I live in a small village in West Sussex. It has been described as a quintessential English village with a 12th century church, two pubs, a duck pond and a beautiful village green, complete with a cricket pitch. It is an ideal spot to launch hot-air balloons.

In 1985 Richard Curtis, Jane Tewson and friends came up with the idea to use comedy to raise money and change lives in Africa and the UK. Comic Relief was born.

Wisborough Green Charity Balloon Event.

I could see a way we could use hot-air balloons to support this charity. The first event we organized was Red Nose Day in 1991. Twenty-two balloons took off from the village green, with each balloon carrying two or more passengers. Each passenger donated £90, all of which went to Comic Relief. The balloonists and crew gave their balloons and time free of charge. All the pilots, crew and passengers wore red noses. As you can see from the photograph it was a great spectacle for the whole village to enjoy.

We changed to various charities over the years. The event covered a whole weekend. Flights were scheduled on Friday evening, Saturday and Sunday morning and evening. Pilots and crews were accommodated with families in the village. Breakfast was served on Saturday and Sunday mornings in a large marquee on our back lawn and it became a very popular annual village event.

The CALA Balloon

I had a phone call from Neil Lindsay who ran a PR and advertising company. He explained he was about to sign a contract with CALA Homes, a large building and development company. As they were about to put pen to paper, one of the directors casually asked Neil if he knew about using a hot-air balloon for advertising purposes. Neil said no, but he would find out straight away.

True to his word, the next day he and I sat down and drew up an operating plan for CALA and our company. Things were moving fast and some weeks later Neil and I went to Thunder and Colt's balloon factory and picked up the CALA balloon, complete with its sign-written trailer.

We were given good advice by Thunder and Colt as to the best way of displaying the balloon. 'When it is brand new, take lots of publicity photos before the shine wears off.'

I see in my logbook that I wrote on 4th June 1988 – *The Inaugural flight of CALA balloon.* Very early that morning, we were driven to Leeds Castle in Kent, one of the most beautiful castles in England. The plan was to fly the balloon across the moat right in front of the entrance. We must have achieved about five or six successful passes when the chairman of CALA Homes and his wife drove up.

The photographer took photos of them in the basket. Then he said to me, "Could you do a 'splash and dash' in front of the castle?" The wind speed was starting to increase significantly, but I felt honour-bound to offer them a flight.

We took off... as the balloon descended towards the moat, a gust of wind caught the balloon and made the splash and dash more splash than dash! Into the moat the basket went, dragging across the water, over a stonewall and landing on the front lawn. Our basket slowly tipped over, we were all tangled up, and lying on top of each other.

There was a stony silence. I thought to myself, *'That's the end of a really good contract'.* Then the chairman and his wife burst out laughing and started to hug me. Their clothes were wet through and covered in mud and strands of weed. The chairman said he had just spent £50,000 on a speedboat advertising CALA Homes on the hull. The engine blew up after one run and he was given another bill of £50,000. He went on to say he had had more fun in ten minutes at a cost of £14,000 (the total price of the balloon). "Now," he said, "it is my turn."

He invited all the team over to his Rolls Royce and opened the boot to reveal a pile of bacon sandwiches and bottles of champagne. Thus started a relationship that lasted six years, and it is fair to say that it helped us set up BSB, the British School of Ballooning.

Derek Ridley was a director of CALA Homes. Derek could see the advertising potential of their balloon. He would contact me to put the balloon on standby for the following Monday evening. He loved coming to our village, Wisborough Green in Sussex and flying from the village green.

One evening Derek arrived with a lady reporter from *The Telegraph* newspaper to take her for a flight in the CALA balloon. They sat outside the Cricketers Arms pub overlooking the village green, a quintessential English scene. We prepared the balloon for them. They then walked over, and we took off... after an hour we landed at Knepp Castle, a beautiful estate of some 4,000 acres. The lady from *The Telegraph* was so enthralled with the whole experience, she wanted to take us all out for dinner.

After the meal we were driving home and I said to my wife,

"That went very well."

My wife told me the lady had said, "You need a write-up about the British School of Ballooning in *The Telegraph*."

Cecilia said, "Sure, but we cannot afford it."

"Oh, no," she replied, "I've had such a wonderful time, I'll put it in free for you."

The inaugural flight over Leeds Castle.

The next day, a half page article in *The Telegraph* was a write up about her flight. She described everything in great detail and was kind enough to say how the British School of Ballooning had given her a truly wonderful experience.

As Christmas was coming, this started us thinking about advertising. We wracked our brains to come up with something that would put us ahead of the other balloon companies. We decided to take an advert in *The Sunday Times*. It was very expensive for a very small piece of text.

We submitted the text, which read: *'For that original gift why not buy your loved one a balloon flight for Christmas?'* The next day we rushed out to buy the newspaper and see our advert. We could not believe our eyes. The advert read: *'For that original **git** why not buy your loved one a balloon flight for Christmas?'*

They had missed out the **F in gift**!

On Monday morning the phone in our office rang, and a voice said, *"Hello, I don't suppose I'm the **original git**, but I would like to buy a flight!"* The phone rang all day with original *gits* wanting flights. From this advert we had the best results we'd ever had. Graeme decided he would phone *The Sunday Times*. He pretended to be furious. They admitted it was their mistake and they put it in again the next week all free of charge.

We also had a little piece on the Esther Rantzen TV show about the 'git'... and then, the phone rang all the following day too.

About that time, I received another rather strange phone call. I picked up the phone and a gravelly voice said, "Are you the pilot of the CALA balloon?"

Mystified, I said, "Yes?"

"My name is Barry Sampson," came the reply, "I am the chairman of Seaward Homes, and I am fed up with seeing that bloody CALA balloon flying over our patch. We want one."

Graeme, my business partner, and I went to see Barry Sampson with costings and a visual of the proposed artwork for his balloon. Barry said he would think things over and give us a ring. Days and weeks went by. One day we received a phone call from Barry's secretary at Seaward Homes. "Hello, hello, well, it's here," she said excitedly.

"What's here?" we replied.

"The balloon of course. Can you come and have a look? We're not sure what to do with it." Graeme and I were mystified. Having heard nothing for weeks, it looked as if they had just gone ahead and ordered a balloon. We hurried down to their offices. In the drive was a new trailer all sign-written, and inside was their brand new balloon!

We drew up a very good contract and relationship with Barry and his team. They agreed that we could use their balloon for training pilots. As long as the balloon was flying, with all the publicity it generated, they were happy.

The Great British Long Jump

Anthony Smith (no relation), when he was the chairman of the British Balloon and Airship Club (BBAC), initiated the Great British Long Jump (GBLJ).

Anthony Smith wrote many books. One of his books had an unusual title, *Throw out Two Hands.* It documents his adventurous flight in a gas balloon from Zanzibar to East Africa, across the Ngorongoro crater in Tanzania. The title of his book refers to controlling the equilibrium of the balloon by the use of ballast. When flying a gas balloon you carry bags of sand. Throwing out two handfuls of sand will make the balloon ascend. To descend you open a valve in the top of the balloon.

I have never flown in a gas balloon. It is on my bucket list though! Reading Anthony's book gives you a good idea of what it is like flying a long distance in a balloon. His experience and enthusiasm were the inspiration for 'The Great British Long Jump'.

Rule 1. The flight must take place in the month of October only.
Rule 2. Fly the greatest distance in one continuous flight.
Rule 3. Anyone taking it seriously will be disqualified.
Rule 4. Do not forget Rule 3.

The UK airspace is crowded. There are many areas of air space that must be avoided such as airports, airways, danger zones… the list goes on and on. Balloons cannot be steered; they can only go where the wind blows them. They cannot turn round and come back like an aeroplane. At 2,000' the wind is different from that at 5,000' and so on. This difference gives the balloon pilot some steerage, but only about 30 degrees either side of the main track. By changing your height, up or down, you can change your track. Planning a long-distance flight is fascinating because of all the variables or unknowns you need to take into account.

In 1989 the Internet was not available. However, you could phone and talk to a weather forecaster. The first thing to consider was the weather forecast. A couple of days before our first long jump we knew the forecast wind was from the south west. Plan A was to drive down to the West Country, find a launch site, fly and end up in Suffolk or Lincolnshire. Simple! We contacted an RAF station in Devon. The duty forecaster was most helpful. He gave us all the information we needed – wind direction and speeds at various heights, visibility, and cloud heights. We were confident his forecast was just what we needed to make it to Suffolk. We thanked him and said we would phone him when we landed, long distance of course!

The night before the flight Cecilia and Judy made up lunch boxes for Graeme and me. We were anticipating a flight time of six or seven hours.

In answer to your inevitable question – we used a bucket and chuck it! We all set off in the early hours to drive from Sussex to 'somewhere' in Devon. More by luck than judgment we found a friendly farmer that did not seem to mind being woken up before dawn by four strangers, and our even stranger request. The take-off time is influenced by the landing time. Sunset was forecast as 5.50pm and thus deducting seven hours favoured a take-off around 10am. My logbook shows a take-off time of 10.40. We climbed to 5,000' to gain the best possible wind speed. As it happened this height gave us a perfect track to 'somewhere' in Suffolk. We had filled the balloon basket with extra fuel tanks, with an estimated endurance of about eight hours.

I was busy making calls with our handheld VHF radio, Graeme was flying the balloon. We were both navigating, as we did not want to stray into controlled airspace. We also had a walkie-talkie radio to talk to Cecilia and Judy, our 'golden retrievers', as I called them. We landed near Chatteris a small market town in Cambridgeshire. A flight time of 6h 20m, and a distance of 162.4 miles

The second long-distance flight that we attempted was a complete disaster! The weather forecast looked as if we could take off from Graeme's front lawn in Sussex and land in Devon. The forecast track would take us just north of west to avoid the Southampton Control Zone. Any track south of this point would take us too close to the south coast for comfort.

We were airborne at 8am on a stunningly beautiful morning. With such good visibility we could see the Isle of Wight. The trouble was we were heading straight for it! We started to climb to try and get a better track. If you climb in the Northern Hemisphere the track should turn you to the right. We continued to climb. The track stubbornly refused to change direction. We could not climb any higher due to controlled air space starting at 5000'. Graeme asked me, "How is it going?"

I replied, "Can you see the Needles, the western most tip of the Isle of Wight?"

"Yes, it's right on the nose."

I said, "That's the problem, it should be well off to our left. If we continue on this track we will end up in the Channel!"

We abandoned the flight and landed in a stubble field near Midhurst, just ten miles from our take-off point. Some long jump! It was still quite early in the morning when the farmer came over to see what was going on. We explained we were taking part in a long-distance flight. He sounded interested. "Oh, so where did you take off from?"

"Petworth," we replied. It did not take him more than a couple of seconds to work out that Petworth was only ten miles away.

"H'mm and where were you going to?"

"Devon," we quietly replied. He looked inside the balloon basket that was lying on its side. He saw the huge amount of fuel tanks, enough fuel for eight hours endurance, thermos flasks, and a pile of sandwiches.

"And you landed here?" He walked away shaking his head.

In spite of this setback, we had got the taste for long-distance flying.

Crossing the English Channel

A Frenchman, Jean-Pierre Blanchard, and an American, John Jeffries, made the first crossing of the Channel in a gas balloon on 7th January 1785. They flew from Dover to Calais in just over three hours. Halfway across they started to lose lift and the balloon drifted down towards the water. The only way to recover in a gas balloon is to throw out some ballast. In a desperate attempt to arrest the descent they threw everything overboard, including most of their clothes. Still, they were slowly drifting down. The story goes that one of them grabbed a bottle of champagne and was about to throw it overboard, when the other pilot said, "Don't be stupid," and took several swigs before it went! They made it to Calais.

I have made two hot-air balloon flights across the Channel from Dover to Calais. There is something special about flying over a large stretch of water, even if it is only 20 miles across! The first flight was with Graeme Scaife. It was a charity event. Several schools had sponsored their teddy bears to fly across the Channel so we took off with teddy bears all tied to the burner's uprights.

The second Channel crossing was with Ian Wadey and Jamie Palmer, both balloon pilots. Retrieving can be a lengthy business. Ian's wife Laura and my wife Cecilia proved they truly were 'golden retrievers'. They drove to the ferry from Dover to Calais and found us about 15 minutes after we had landed. As well as celebrating the flight, there are always two stories to tell. One is of the flight and the other is of the retrieve.

They can be quite different. We were not alone on this adventure. There were about 100 other balloons. It was reassuring to fly in company. We always try to take off last or at the back of the pack. This allows us to see the track of the balloons ahead to help with our track keeping. We crossed over Dover Castle, then out over the sea. There is always a moment of silence in the balloon at this point. You realise you are making a commitment.

Already the balloons were starting to spread out. It was very hazy in the early morning sun, with the grey of the sky and the green of the sea blending into one. Our GPS showed we were at 1,500 feet and on course. Halfway across, due to the poor visibility, we lost sight of the white cliffs of Dover behind us and could not see the French coast, which should have been ahead. It was as if we were in a vacuum, quite disconcerting. We put our faith in the technology. In ten minutes or so the outline of the French coast started to appear. Jamie shouted, "I can see Calais Port!" We celebrated with a cup of tea.

We landed south of the Channel Tunnel station in Calais. A flat stubble field near a road. A police helicopter appeared and hovered overhead for some time, then a police car came bumping across the field. We were still excited from our flight across the Channel and were hoping they would not ask what we were doing with what looked like a giant laundry basket and a huge bag of nylon material in the middle of a field. They dutifully scanned our passports and then went on their way. It was time for a proper celebration, French style. We opened a bottle of champagne. We recorded a crossing time of 1 hour and 50 mins in our logbooks. The tradition of celebrating a balloon flight with champagne started in France, the home of ballooning. The first manned flight was in Paris on 21st November 1783, 120 years before the Wright brothers made their flight in a powered machine!

I was slowly building my ballooning experience and felt now was the time to apply to be an instructor. While I was going through the process, I met Brian Jones. Brian and his wife Jo were running the operation of a balloon sponsored by Royal Mail.

The British Balloon and Airship Club (BBAC) have a very good training section. They regulate the training and examining of balloon pilots. Brian Jones became their training officer. His experience and personality were like a breath of fresh air. Every BBAC instructor has to attend an instructor day every two years. These days are organized and run by the training officer – Brian Jones. There is always a huge amount of work involved in running these days.

After one such day, Brian said he could do with an assistant, and would I like the job. I did not need to consider it for any length of time; I knew working with Brian would be interesting and fun. The Smith and Jones team was born! Little did I know what this would lead to some years later...

I found that instructing in balloons is different, and more difficult than I had been used to. Why? I feel it is a combination of two things.

1. The influence of the weather. You are at the mercy of the elements, particularly the wind. Once airborne, should the weather change for the worse, you cannot turn round and return. Your planned detail has to change with the wind!
2. Taking off with the destination unknown, you can only go where the wind decides to take you. Taking many factors into account, your planned flight might be long or quite short.

I have always enjoyed instructing. Looking through my logbook it is interesting and very satisfying to look back and see names of my students that have gone on to become commercial pilots, competition pilots and instructors.

One of our senior balloon examiners invited me to become an examiner. My reply was, "I am not sure I want to go off in a hot-air balloon with a complete stranger."

He looked somewhat disappointed and muttered something about, "No spirit of adventure?"

My instinct proved right. On my first flight as an examiner I had to fail the candidate. There were many reasons for the failure, too many to list here. It all stemmed from lack of preparation on the part of the candidate. The saying goes *'Failure to prepare is preparing to fail'.* The BBAC Training Manual lists the fail points. I have always thought I should be able to take control if I thought things were getting dangerous. Not in this particular case though.

By the time we took off, the candidate had already shown she was not as prepared as she should have been. Why did I let the flight continue?

Most examiners realise that the candidate can be somewhat nervous under examination conditions, and they make allowances for this. Indeed, I have found the second half of the flight generally goes much better than the first, once they settle down and realize it is not such an ordeal after all. Although it was an examination flight, there is still room to instruct. The UK Civil Aviation Authority (CAA) recognise this and approve it.

I hoped things might improve. I was wrong. It was an early morning flight. Correction, it was supposed to be an early morning flight. However, we were late getting airborne, due to the candidate's lack of awareness of the changing weather. Although the surface wind was relatively calm, the heat of the sun was causing the gradient wind or 1,000' wind to mix and gradually lower towards the surface. We took off. At 500' we entered this fast airstream. After 20 minutes the trees below were bending sideways. We were passing over field after field and, clearly, the wind speed would only increase the longer we flew.

I suggested it might be time to consider landing at the next available opportunity. I put it as diplomatically as I could. Without warning, she grabbed the rip line and pulled hard, and kept pulling. This rip line is connected to a large piece of material, known as a parachute, attached by Velcro to the top of the balloon. Pulling the rip line pulls the parachute down and opens a large hole at the top of the balloon. The flight manual recommends you open the valve for a maximum of *3 seconds.* The candidate was hanging onto the rip line for all she was worth.

As you can imagine, this huge loss of lift meant we were coming out of the sky like a grand piano! Mercifully, we were less than 1000' above the ground when we started on down. There was no chance of my prizing her hands off or firing the burner to try and arrest the descent. The only thing I could do was to turn off the pilot lights that fed the flames and shout, "Hold on. Hold on!" We hit the ground with an almighty thump. Apart from my sore back, no harm done. At the debrief, she was advised to carry out several more flights with an instructor, and with the emphasis on pre-flight preparation. She gained her PPL and has been flying safely and happily ever since.

I am pleased to report this was an isolated case and the many examination flights I have conducted since have been a pleasure.

There is one particular examination flight that will stay in my memory forever. It started with a phone call from Serengeti Balloon Safaris, asking if I could come to conduct a check flight in Tavernelle, Italy?

Tavernelle is a small village about 25kms south of Florence. Serengeti Balloon Safaris (SBS) is a commercial balloon company in Tanzania flying large passenger-carrying balloons over the Serengeti game reserve.

Early one morning, at the main SBS balloon launch site, Abeid Soka was standing close to the balloons, ready to take people on a game drive after their flight. He was looking at the excited passengers who were about to take-off, and he was about to wave them goodbye when the balloon pilot shouted for Abeid to come over to the balloon. Thinking something was wrong he ran over.

"Get in," the pilot said, and all the passengers shouted, "Yes, yes, get in, there is an extra space."

"I'm sorry, I am not allowed," said Abeid. They were insistent. Abeid climbed into the balloon basket, half in excitement and half fearful he might lose his job.

Immediately after the flight he set off to contact Colin MacKinnon, the co-founder of SBS. It was a drive of several hours. He found Colin's house, and knocked on the door. Colin, somewhat surprised, welcomed him in. Abeid explained what had happened that morning and he was so affected by the experience he had decided he really wanted to be a balloon pilot and would Colin be prepared to sponsor him.

Colin sat in silence for a few minutes. Abeid thought that any minute he might be sacked. The initial response was, NO. However, Abeid was persistent and for six months would hassle the co-founders of SBS. Eventually, the decision was taken that Abeid could be a member of the crew and help prepare the balloons for the morning flights. After nine months he was allowed to test inflate the balloons when balloons were due for inspection. On seeing that he was an excellent crewmember, quick to learn, with the right attitude, and comfortable with living in the bush, the decision was now, YES.

Abeid was shocked, he had taken such a chance, and now his dream was already taking shape. The first step was for Abeid to travel to Italy to attend a flight training school, learn to fly balloons and obtain his Private Pilot's Licence (PPL). He had not travelled out of Tanzania before. Suddenly he found himself flying to Italy. At Florence Airport he was met by Stephano and Neil, his instructors.

Anyone who has met Abeid will say, he has a 'presence', a calm, intelligent and dedicated personality. I would wholeheartedly agree with that statement.

When I arrived in Tavenelle I was told to go to the restaurant La Fattoria and to meet Abeid. I entered the tiny restaurant. Sitting in the corner eating spaghetti was a large young black African, surrounded by local Italians. It wasn't too difficult to guess which one was Abeid. He welcomed me and passed me the menu. Abeid had been in Tavernelle for about a week before I arrived. I asked what he would recommend. He said, smiling, "I don't know. I have had a different dish each day." We chatted about the flying training and I looked at his training logbook. The comments from his instructors all reported very good or excellent progress.

Later, one of the instructors let me into a little secret. A training flight had been arranged for Abeid the morning after he arrived. It was to be an early start. Abeid did not have an alarm clock. The instructor had given him a mobile phone with an alarm set for 4am. The plan was to all meet up at the launch site some three miles out of town. The instructor and crew arrived at the launch site on time. Abeid was not there. They called the mobile, Abeid answered. The mobile's alarm had not worked; their phone call had woken him up. They said, if they were not airborne in 45 minutes it will be too windy. "We will cancel your training flight for this morning, and schedule one for this afternoon."

They decided to make a flight anyway and started to take the balloon out of the trailer, when, to their astonishment, Abeid appeared running across the field. How could he possibly have covered the distance within minutes of their wake up call? Abeid said, "Oh, I stopped a car and a local farmer gave me a lift."

Once they had got over the picture of a large black African standing in the middle of the road in a tiny Italian village at 4am, waving down a car driven by an incredulous Italian farmer, they began to realise they had someone a bit special with them.

I should explain, the instructors were staying in Stephano's house about eight miles *east* of the launch site. The house was full, and accommodation was scarce around Tavernelle. A hotel was found for Abeid, three miles *west* of the launch site. The instructors had offered to drive over and pick him up. Abeid insisted he was happy to walk or run, and for them all to meet at the launch site.

We planned to arrange the check flight for the following

morning. The day dawned with light winds and clear skies. Ideal conditions for a balloon flight.

I offered to drive Abeid to the launch site. He said he was happy to walk. I decided to walk with him. We were about halfway, when I stopped and said, "Have a look around and tell me what you think is happening with the weather?" I wanted to check if Abeid was starting to think about the flight, or not. He described the weather conditions in detail – the wind, visibility and clouds. It was a good indication he was already concentrating on the flight ahead.

The check flight went well, Abeid completed all the tasks to a very high standard. I was happy to send him off on his solo flight. I climbed out of the basket, wished him luck and waved him goodbye. We followed the balloon, winding through the narrow Tuscany roads. After an hour we saw the balloon land in a large grass field. The balloon envelope was deflated and lay flat on the ground. Abeid was standing in the basket. He had a huge smile on his face and was talking on the borrowed mobile phone. "I am talking to my wife in Tanzania!" he exclaimed.

Then we were shaking his hand and offering him our congratulations. He described his solo flight in great detail, and how it was, to be alone flying over Italy, the peace and quiet, and the beautiful Tuscany scenery. He thanked us and said he would like to take us all out to dinner that night.

We all sat together at a huge table in a lovely restaurant. We asked Abeid to sit at the head of the table. There was much noise, lots of chatter and clinking of glasses, everyone telling the tale of the morning's adventure.

Abeid tapped a glass and stood up. Everyone went quiet. He then made a short speech. He thanked us for changing his life. It was all very emotional. The girls were in tears. I have to admit I had to dab my eyes a couple of times too. I felt if he had stood up and said, 'by the way I am the President of Tanzania', I would not have been surprised!

The longer I live the more I believe in the significance of

coincidences. About a year later I was in California visiting my daughter. A call came through from Colin. He explained that Abeid really needed to gain a Commercial Pilot's Licence to fly passengers in Tanzania. He went on to say he had heard of a balloon company in California who were prepared to train Abeid to commercial pilot standard. He then gave me the name of the company. Did I know them? When I explained I was actually in California, and the balloon company was about an hour's drive away, he was flabbergasted. Well, just another coincidence, I thought! Abeid enrolled there and gained his Commercial Pilot's Licence. He is now the chief pilot for Serengeti Balloon Safaris.

A quote from the gallery section of their website: *'Abeid is an exceptional pilot, with a deep understanding of local flying conditions based on his years of experience, and he arguably has the best smile in the business. A passionate advocate of ballooning over the Serengeti, he fully expects some of his four children to follow in his wake.'*

Photo from Abeid Soka.

11. BREITLING BALLOON FLIGHT ROUND THE WORLD

Bertrand Piccard and Brian Jones.

Brian Jones and Bertrand Piccard's book, *The Greatest Adventure*, describes their epic flight in absorbing detail. The build-up, the anxiety, excitement, endurance and finally jubilation are all there.

Introducing the Two Pilots

Brian Jones spent 13 years in the RAF. He started flying balloons in1986, then quickly became a balloon instructor, and an examiner. In 1990 he became the Training Officer for the British Balloon and Airship Club (BBAC). This involved organising the training of all UK balloon pilots. He worked on the *Breitling Orbiter 2* and was the project manager for *Breitling Orbiter 3*. He was also the 'back-up pilot' for the final project. When Bertrand's original co-pilot stood down Brian Jones joined Bertrand as his second pilot for the *Breitling Orbiter 3*.

Bertrand Piccard is a medical doctor specializing in psychiatry. He comes from a long line of adventurers. His grandfather, Auguste, took off from Augsburg, Germany on 27th May 1931 with co-pilot Paul Kipfer in a helium balloon and reached a record altitude of 51,775ft. They became the first human beings to enter the stratosphere and see the curvature of the earth. In 1960, Bertrand's father, Jacques, and Lt. Don Walsh of the US Navy made a record-breaking bathyscaphe dive to the bottom of the Pacific Ocean, the Mariana Trench. Bertrand originated the Breitling Orbiter project and was the command pilot for all three attempts.

Bertrand and Brian just prior to the launch of *Breitling Orbiter 3*.

I would like to try and give you a look at the way the control centre functioned during this record-breaking flight, and how

Cecilia and I became involved.

In the winter of 1998-1999 there was a period of intense activity with attempts to fly a balloon round the world. The Breitling Swiss watch company was a sponsor of many aviation projects and had already made two attempts to fly a balloon round the world. As they explained to Brian, they were prepared to give it just one more try. "There will not be an *Orbiter 4*. As someone once said, 'If it was easy, everyone would do it. It is because it is difficult that makes it a challenge.'"

Brian phoned us and said, "How would we like to join him and Jo in the Control Centre?"

Cecilia and I looked at each other and said, "Well, what an honour." Little did we know what a wonderful adventure we were about to embark on.

In the eyes of the press, we were to become 'Flight Controllers'. It sounded good, although 'communicators' would have been more accurate. We were to become the link between the balloon, the technicians, the Met men, and the air traffic controllers.

We did have some reservations. We felt we were not qualified for such a task. What if, due to my incompetence, I put their lives in danger? I phoned my friend Nick Purvis, a director of Cameron Balloons.

Cameron Balloons were building the *Breitling Orbiter 3* balloon. Nick and I had made several balloon flights together and were good friends. I explained my fears to him. He said, "Look at it this way Brian, you are not sending them up there. It's their choice. All you need is a cool head and a sense of humour." I was not too sure about the 'cool head' but I felt better.

Brian Jones was the project manager at that stage and reassured us that he and Jo would be in the Control Centre with us. More reassurance! Cecilia and I went to the Cameron balloon factory in Bristol to meet Bertrand Piccard and the rest of the team. At a meeting of technicians and balloon experts we began to see what a massive undertaking it was. I could see that Brian's experience, as the project manager of *Breitling Orbiter 2*, was having a huge influence on *Orbiter 3*, indeed on the whole operation. The pressure was on to launch as soon as possible. This appeared to be for two reasons:

1.   There were two other British balloon teams preparing to launch at any time. Both with experienced pilots.

2.   We learnt there is a season to fly round the world if you plan to launch in the Northern Hemisphere. During the late autumn and early spring, the jet streams are more in alignment, affording more of a chance of 'steering' in straight lines. To launch any later than February would be running a risk of the jet streams breaking up.

The Control Centre

The Control Centre was based in an area of the VIP lounge in Geneva Airport. We had a spacious room completely kitted out with desks, phones and computers. Once the balloon was launched, little did we know, this was to be our workplace for the following three weeks. Three couples were to work for three eight-hour shifts. At this time, Brian Jones was the project manager for *Breitling Orbiter 3*. He and Jo would be heading up the Control Centre team.

Then came a huge shock. Bertrand's co-pilot decided to leave the project. Bertrand immediately appointed Brian Jones in his place. Thus, Brian would be *flying the balloon*, and not with us in the Control Centre. As a result, Brian recruited a few of his fellow balloonists for the Control Centre.

Fortunately, Jo, Brian's wife, 'volunteered' to be in the crew room with us. Jo's experience of the Breitling project combined with her calm personality proved to be a real asset for the rest of the team. I believe the fact that we all knew each other helped considerably in times of stress or anxious moments during the flight.

The atmosphere in the Control Centre can best be described as 'the swan effect', serene and calm on the surface, but pedalling like mad underneath! Cecilia and I immediately volunteered for the night shift. More by luck than judgment, this proved to be the time when the Control Centre was quietest. That was until the press really started to take an interest, which was when the balloon looked as if it was going to make it round the world.

The Control Centre team.
Back row: Cecilia Smith, Sue Tatford, Brian Smith, Debbie Albury, John Albury. Front row: Alan Noble (Flight Director), Jo Sainsbury.

Brian Jones' influence was monumental. Among the many things he organized, and the ones that affected us most were:

1. He insisted we always have an air traffic controller on duty.
2. Any instructions were to be written on a white board. We could see at a glance any tasks that had to be to be completed, and ticked off when they were done.
3. All communications were to be by fax, rather than voice.

4. Copies of faxes had to be filed as a record of the flight. This meant that any instructions regarding Met information or track changes from Luc or Pierre could not be misinterpreted.

We also had what became known as the 'Big Red Book' and the 'Big Red Phone'. The big red book had the contact numbers of every air traffic control centre, restricted or danger areas that the balloon may pass over on the expected route. The big red phone was a direct link by satellite phone to the balloon – only to be used in an emergency.

We had comfortable accommodation in a good hotel immediately behind the crew room. We could have all our meals in the airport restaurant.

Somehow, we felt this contrast helped us understand what the pilots were going through. Although we could not physically be in the balloon with them, we could try and take the stress out of the many situations they encountered by working closely with the Met men and air traffic controllers. This became our goal…

On Standby

Prior to departure, the whole team was put on standby to fly to Geneva should a weather slot appear. As the balloon was sponsored by Breitling, the launch site was in Château-d'Oex, a beautiful village 3,000' up in the Swiss Alps.

David Niven, the famous English actor lived there from 1960. He died in 1983 and he is buried in the Château-d'Oex cemetery. Each year, the David Niven Cup, a flying competition for balloonists is held in the village.

We were called out at very short notice to fly on a British Airways flight from Heathrow to Geneva. There were six of us sitting in the departure lounge, when it suddenly dawned on me; that here was Brian Jones, a British citizen preparing to be the first person to fly non-stop round the world in a balloon. We boarded the aircraft and took our seats in Economy Class. I asked the chief steward if he would pass a note to the captain informing him that Brian Jones was on board, and to wish him luck. The chief steward took the note.

A few minutes later he reappeared and said, "The captain says, do you still race lawn mowers in Wisborough Green?" He leaned forward and whispered, "How many in your party?"

I felt there was a good chance he was going to upgrade us. "Only six, little ones," I replied. With that we were whisked up to Club Class and settled down in luxury. The captain made the announcement, wishing Brian the best of luck. Most of the passengers cheered or clapped, much to Brian's embarrassment. Two stewardesses came to give Brian their best wishes and gave him a BA teddy bear to take with him on the flight. It's the only teddy bear to have flown round the world! One of the stewards made all the cabin announcements mimicking Sean Connery. As a result, the bear was named Sean.

Back home, my boss and chief pilot, Fred Rivett, kindly gave me the time off from my duties with BA. Fred, also a balloonist, had been following all the Round the World (RTW) balloon preparations. There had been about 22 previous attempts. All had failed. Both Fred and I thought I would soon be back home from this crazy adventure. As the flight continued, I had to plead for more time off...

The Launch

Our job in the Control Centre did not really start until the balloon was airborne. However, we were privileged to be on the launch site throughout the night, as the giant balloon was being inflated. Our job was to keep the team of technicians supplied with hot drinks and sandwiches. The envelope, of 650,000 cubic feet in volume, covered an area the size of half a football pitch. Imagine 650,000 footballs all in one bag!

When the envelope was laid out on the ground, it covered such a huge area we used walkie-talkie radios to communicate. With this massive envelope, the slightest wind would cause the whole balloon to rock about and eventually become so unstable the take-off would have had to be abandoned. Through the early hours the wind speed steadily increased. Alan Noble, the flight director, had to order Brian and Bertrand to stay away from all the inflation procedures, and try and get some rest in the hotel. He planned to call them when the balloon was fully inflated. Brian and Bertrand could not wait for Alan's call and appeared in the early hours, fully dressed in their flying suits, ready to fly.

On the launch site at Château-d'Oex, 1999.

There was a short press conference. Brian and Bertrand said their goodbyes and climbed aboard the gondola to start their pre-flight checks, whilst at the same time being precariously thrown around by the wind. The whole balloon was being lifted off the ground. The noise of the creaking and crackling of the giant envelope with the scraping of the gondola on the icy ground was deafening. The balloon was tied off to a fire truck. It looked as if the

216

balloon was about to break free, or take the fire truck with it. Then...
Alan Noble sliced through the rope with his Swiss army knife, and
they were airborne. The crowd of onlookers went wild! People
were shouting best wishes, cheering and crying. I have to admit, so
were most of the Breitling team. The church bells were ringing and
the fire truck was sounding its siren. There is a photo of Jo, Brian's
wife and Cecilia looking up at the balloon with tears streaming
down their cheeks.

Flying at Last!

At 09.09 local time they were on their way! We drove in silence to
the Control Centre in Geneva to take up our posts. It was all set up
ready to operate, and we hurried in to join the rest of the team.
Inside were Alan Noble, the flight director, Debbie and John Albury,
and Sue Tatford. Also, there were the two meteorologists Luc
Trullemans and Pierre Eckert, and the air traffic controllers from
Swiss control, Greg Moegli, Patrick Schelling and Niklaus Gerber.
The Met men and the air traffic controllers were to play a pivotal
role in the success of the flight – as we shall see!

If you were to take off from Switzerland in an attempt to fly
around the world in a balloon, which direction would you want to
go? Most sensible people would say east or west. The balloon was
heading south! Luc and Pierre (known collectively as 'the Met men')
had noticed a low-pressure system over the Mediterranean. As
winds around a low-pressure system always blow in an anti-
clockwise direction, they knew this would eventually turn the
balloon on to a better track, taking them over the Sahara.

From the messages flowing to and from the balloon we were
aware of the problems the pilots were having with various
technical issues. It was frustrating for us not to be able to help.
However, we did have technicians available at the end of a phone.
This was to be an on-going theme throughout the flight – the pilots
and technicians working closely together.

In the Control Centre we were settling into a routine. We felt the three eight-hour shifts would work, partly due to the fact that we knew each other so well. A good example was the way each team interpreted the start and finish time of their shifts. Cecilia and I found it difficult to sleep. We desperately wanted to know what was going on if we were not in the Control Centre. It became a little ritual that teams would arrive early and leave late at the end of their shift. The conversation would go something like this: "Hello, you're early." Then, "OK, guys we've got the picture, see you later."

We had a photo of 'the boys' as we called them, on the desk in our bedroom. Cecilia would pray each night to keep them safe. We all agreed we wanted them to land safely, if they happened to fly round the world at the same time – that would be OK too! The balloon was making steady progress over Algiers and on to Libya. The concern was that some controlling authority would order them to land. On the good side the balloon had entered a jet stream. As a rule, a speed over 70 knots is classified as a 'jet'. On the not so good side was that the balloon's track was taking it towards the Aswan Dam, a prohibited area.

The big red phone in the Control Centre rang. Brian said the Egyptian air traffic controllers were demanding more and more information regarding the balloon's exact position. Greg Moegli, the Swiss air traffic controller was on duty. He calmly said, "Would you like me to talk to them?" Greg spoke on the phone for a couple of minutes. He put the phone down, smiled and said, "All OK."

"Wait a minute, what's the whole story?" we asked.

He calmly explained to the Egyptian controller he was sorry to give them so much trouble, but he totally understood, as he was an air traffic controller in Geneva. "You are a controller?" came the astonished reply. "OK. For you, I give you 15 miles. No make it 20!" They actually passed 20 miles south of the dam, the 'damn dam' as John Albury called it. This was just one example of how the Swiss controllers saved the day.

Approaching Yemen, the balloon was heading towards the edge

of a large danger area. Patrick was negotiating with ATC, but communications were very intermittent. While this was going on the balloon was getting closer and closer to the danger zone. I used the big red book to get the phone number of Salalah Air Traffic Control. I got though and asked for the supervisor. I was told, "He is saying his prayers, please phone back."

I phoned back some minutes later and was told he is still saying his prayers. I guess this delay must have made me somewhat stressed, as I said without thinking, "Well, he must have been very naughty then!"

"Standby," came the stern reply.

The supervisor came on the line. Before I could say anything, he said, in a cheery voice, "Hello, I'm not that naughty, how can I help you?"

I tried to pour out my story regarding the danger zone. He stopped me mid-sentence and said, "Mr Smith, I understand perfectly what you are saying. The zone is not active so early in the morning as the army do not start firing until later in the day. I wish you and the team success, Goodbye."

The power of prayer!

Throughout these ATC hiccups our Met men had been working flat out to find tracks or streamlines that would line the balloon up to enter Chinese airspace at exactly the right point, several thousand kilometres away. Only by changing the height can the track of a balloon be altered. Luc and Pierre used computer models from Met centres around the world to work out the optimum tracks. This is extremely skilful work. Luc took great delight in showing us how he interpreted all the lines and swirls on the graphs. I am sad to say that most of it went over my head. The reason the tracks were so important was the Chinese air space. This vast country lies in the way when you are trying to fly round the world. China had banned all flights above 26 degrees north of its territory.

It was like trying to thread the balloon through the eye of a needle. Luc and Pierre were attempting to do this when the balloon was still several thousand kilometres from the target.

The balloon was approaching India, when Mumbai ATC asked for our 'over flight clearance number'. The Breitling team had been trying to obtain overflight clearance for some months prior to the flight, but no replies were received. We consulted the big red book for any contact numbers for Mumbai ATC. Meanwhile the balloon was inching its way into Indian airspace. We found a number and Nik Gerber was soon talking to a Mumbai controller.

The Indian controller said he could not give permission.

"But who could?" I asked.

He gave Nik the phone number of Mr Saran, the Deputy Director of Civil Aviation. It was 6.30pm in Mumbai. What were the chances of getting hold of anyone? Mercifully, Mr Saran answered the phone.

Nik spoke to him for about an hour. Eventually, permission was given with the proviso Nik had to phone every half hour with the balloon's position. Once again the Swiss controllers had pulled off a miracle!

The balloon continued tracking towards China. I discovered that two years of diplomatic work had gone into obtaining permission to cross Chinese airspace. Bertrand had headed a party to fly to Beijing to meet with the Chinese Aviation Authorities. The Chinese were impressed by the Breitling team coming to see them.

Eventually, the permission came through, not only for the Breitling team but other balloon teams as well. Big thanks to Bertrand and the British diplomats in Beijing. This permission was granted on the condition that the balloon MUST NOT cross China any further north than 26th Parallel.

In the early hours of the morning the balloon entered Chinese airspace precisely 30 miles south of the 26th Parallel! This time it was the Met men that had pulled off a miracle. Their skill had steered the balloon over a distance of 13,000 kms and threaded the balloon through the eye of the needle. The tension had been steadily building as the balloon got closer and closer to the border.

Now, everyone was going crazy with excitement and, of course, relief.

Incredibly, the balloon flew right across China in a straight line! (Balloons never travel in a straight line.) The excitement continued.

After China, approaching the Pacific did not appear quite so daunting, until Luc stood up and said, "We have a problem!" I called it our Apollo 13 moment... We sat in silence as he continued.

Our Apollo 13 moment: Pierre Eckert and Luc Trullemans, our two 'Met men' show Jo and me the Pacific forecast chart.

The Pacific

Luc explained. "The jet stream we are in will eventually split into three parts."

1. The northern part will break into stormy weather. One of the British balloons had already ditched in this area. The pilots were unharmed.

2. The middle part – the winds will steadily decrease, making it impossible to cross the Pacific. A couple of days later, another British balloon became becalmed, and had to ditch by Honolulu.

3. The southern part will take the balloon to meet up with another jet stream and that will take them to America.

Luc continued, "I recommend they take Route 3." The silence in the room was deafening.

Up to this point the Met men's forecasts had been impeccable. Luc said, "They have to descend and slow down, head south, and in three days they will pick up the jet stream."

To try and get my brain round this I asked Luc to show me the 'new' jet stream on his computer. I thought that if I could actually see it, it would boost my confidence in Luc's prediction. In answer to my request, Luc calmly replied, "The jet stream has not formed yet. It will be born in three days' time!"

It may sound corny, but I felt the colour drain from my face.

The red phone rang, it was Brian. "What do you think of Luc's plan?"

I replied. "Well... up to now Luc and Pierre have been totally accurate with their forecasts. For what it is worth, I think we MUST trust them."

As if the Met situation wasn't enough to worry about, the burners were also causing more problems. Additionally, the balloon's track was taking them to two danger areas close to Okinawa. Again, the tension mounted. It must have been very frustrating for the pilots to see these danger areas on their charts, and to trust the Control Centre team were trying to sort it out. Patrick Schelling was already negotiating with Okinawa ATC. This did take time – you cannot just pull over and park up. The balloon was continuing to fly towards this prohibited area. At the last minute, Patrick's diplomatic skills came into play, permission to proceed was granted.

A very good piece of news came through. The balloon had just passed over the Mariana Trench, the deepest part of the Pacific Ocean at the exact spot where, in 1960, Bertrand's father with Lt. Don Walsh of the US Navy, made a record-breaking dive of 36,000 feet to the floor of the ocean.

One could almost write a chapter on the crossing of the Pacific. The pilots really suffered, both physically and mentally during this part of their flight.

Looking back, if we could have had better communications between the pilots and the Control Centre, and with ATC, that would have helped to ease the pain. At one point the fax and the telephone stopped working for two days. Over any ocean, if contact is lost for even 30 minutes, this would lead to concern and the possible setting up of a search and rescue operation.

Eventually, the pilots were able to talk to Oakland Radio on HF and were able to set up a link to pass messages between the Met men and Brian and Bertrand. Oakland advised them they were so far south they were out of the range of any type of rescue facility. That latest message added to the pilots' concerns.

The heaters had stopped working and there were storm clouds starting to form on their track. About two days later, 15 days into the flight, Cecilia and I were on the night shift carefully recording the balloon's steady progress south. Cecilia noticed a slight change in the track that was beginning to curve to the left.

At last, the balloon, now heading eastwards, was entering 'Luc's jet stream'. On a scale of 1 to 10, the tension went down to 5 or less. The next task was to obtain overflight clearance from a different set of countries due to our track change. Once more, the controllers swung into action. Greg Moegli's wife spoke Spanish and contact was made with aviation authorities in Mexico and Cuba. Permission was granted. On 15th March the balloon was on track for Mexico, firmly in the jet stream.

It seemed people all round the world were monitoring the progress of the flight. Now messages came flooding into the Control

Centre. One message came from a family in the USA. They had just had a baby girl, and named her 'Breitling'. They did not know, at the time, that it was the name of a Swiss watch company. The boys kept in touch with her and, some years later, when 'Baby Breitling', as she became known, was celebrating her 11th birthday Brian and Bertrand called her and presented her with a Breitling watch.

Just when we thought things were going well, further problems occurred. Over Mexico the jet stream's track changed to 110 degrees. A good heading for Venezuela but not so good for Africa! The speed also dropped dramatically. It would appear the balloon had slipped out of the jet stream! I'm not sure I understand exactly how a jet stream works. It is well known as a core of strong wind. It was either Luc or Pierre who explained that around the edges of the core the winds are likely to revolve or twist. The balloon is moving WITH the wind and not punching through it as an aircraft would. It would seem the balloon was spat out or, more accurately, 'eased' out of the jet. Luc was not fazed by this and predicted that within 24 hours they would pick up another jet stream that would take them all the way home. You have to admire his confidence! I believe Luc was also trying to raise the pilots' spirits as they were still suffering from the cold and technical difficulties.

The big red phone rang. Now Brian and Bertrand were having problems breathing. This was a very serious situation... Alan, our flight director, was getting advice from a doctor who was a specialist in aviation medicine, particularly high-altitude flight. The diagnosis was that the pilots were suffering from pre-oedema of the lungs, caused by breathing exceptionally cold air for several days. They could get some relief by breathing pure oxygen from the portable bottles they had on board. Clearly, this could only give temporary relief. The RAF Aeromedical Centre at Boscombe Down thought it might be carbon dioxide poisoning.

In response to these messages, the pilots re-pressurized the gondola. The 'new' mix of oxygen and nitrogen returned the cabin to a more normal atmosphere. They started to feel better, but it had been a huge shock to the whole team. Brian and Bertrand had coped with unimaginable problems throughout the flight. After 18 days the strain on their emotions was coming to a head. We had always thought their flight was dangerous. The number of teams that had failed confirmed how dangerous it was. Eighteen days of this roller coaster ride was also taking its toll on the Control Centre team. Each one of us coped with the stress in different ways... but no one threw their toys out of the cot. The question no one dare ask: "What do we do now to save the flight?"

Pierre Eckert came to the rescue with what looked like an extreme manoeuvre, but these were extreme times! "Go as high as the balloon will fly, it's our last chance to save the flight," he said.

Bertrand was on duty and put the burners on to get a rapid rate of climb. As the balloon climbed higher and higher, so the track started to change. Slowly it swung round to the left. They were now heading 080 degrees and away from Venezuela! Cecilia and I were lucky to be on duty and saw the reports from the balloon with the track changes on it.

Cecilia faxed up a message to the pilots: "C here, I wish you could see the map we have here that shows the jet stream lying just to the north of you. It extends right across the Atlantic and shows a steady increase in speed as you head east."

The balloon crossed over Jamaica. There was another morale boost with a radio call from what sounded like a very friendly lady controller at Kingston. She said in a lovely West Indian accent, "Bin outside, but I can't see ya, best wishes anyhow, and you take care up there." Bertrand fell in love again.

Heading towards Haiti the speed increased to 60 knots, better than forecast. Alan and the pilots planned a conference call to assess the situation regarding a 'go' or 'no go' for the crossing of the Atlantic.

The press were really taking an interest now and the Control Centre was becoming very crowded. TV cameras were set up and Alan put a call through to the pilots. Bertrand and Alan went through the agreed routine questions regarding fuel, the Met situation and how they felt about crossing the Atlantic. Finally, Alan said, "I think you can go for it."

Brian shouted to Bertrand, "Tell him we're going anyway!" Having made that decision to go and the relief that often comes when you make a decision, they found there was room for humour. They decided to consult the BA teddy bear that had been their constant companion on the flight. "Sean, if you don't want us to go for it, nod/shake your head." Of course, the bear did not move. They thanked him and said, "Thanks Sean. OK, Let's go!"

The Atlantic

The three air traffic controllers sent a fax:

> *Cher Bertrand, Dear Brian,*
>
> *Just to tell you how we three Controllers, along with all our colleagues at Swiss Control, are gripped by your voyage round the world. All of us are living through highly charged moments. We're being constantly interrogated at meals, and people are trooping around the big display board with its map of the world to check on your progress.*
>
> *We all wish you good health and the form, both physical and psychological, to attack this grand finale. And even if you decide to stop, you can be assured that you have given us the chance to take part in a huge, passionate and extraordinary adventure. All courage... and our best wishes, Niklaus, Greg and Patrick.*

Nik was already talking to New York Oceanic Control. There was a great deal of air traffic over that part of the Atlantic and the controller was concerned the balloon's altitude of 35,000' could conflict with commercial airliners. The New York controller insisted we stick to an agreement made some months earlier that the Atlantic crossing would be between 31,000' and 33,000'. "Just stick to the agreement," he said, and hung up. Nik was not to be put off. He knew how critical it was to stay at the optimum height. Nik was back on the phone. He emphasized if the balloon descended to a lower height, they would not make it and would have to ditch in the Atlantic.

The controller knew full well if the balloon ditched it would be in his control area, and he would have to organize a rescue mission. "Standby," he said. Half an hour later the crossing clearance was granted. The messages flashed back and forth. The meagre fuel supply was everyone's main concern now. If, and it was a big IF, the jet stream remained constant along with the present fuel consumption, they might JUST make the African coast. Mali and Nigeria could prove very difficult places to land. Libya was a no-go country. Egypt would be ideal. IF!

Just then a wonderful message addressed to the pilots came in from Pierre Blanchoud, the team's aeronautical adviser:

'Luckily we have the prospect of a fast, high-altitude flight, in a blue sky, without fear of CBs, because in winds of this speed CBs cannot form, and if one does climb to your height, it will soon disperse. Our maps show us a jet stream, which will take you to Egypt without any problem.

Brian – Your dream has become a reality, and you may well land in the vicinity of the Pyramids.

Bertrand – Profit from these unforgettable moments of the flight. You should talk to the wind, your ally, and thank it, just as the sailor thanked the dolphin, which saved his life. Observe how the clouds scatter from your route to let you pass, and how the cirrus above you shows you the route to follow the jet stream.

You must remain concentrated and vigilant, both confident and receptive of what your intuition tells you. Visualise your landing in the sand – and until we meet again, may God hold you in the palm of his hand.'

Over 20 years later, reading Pierre's message, particularly the ending, makes me cry.

The balloon was going like a rocket. Luc and Pierre were convinced that the balloon was right in the middle of the jet stream, with no danger of being ejected, as had happened over Mexico.

When flying for BA we only talked briefly to air traffic control and, as was the nature of things, we were passed from one control centre to the next as we whizzed through at 400 knots. The balloon, however, was going considerably slower so that we were talking to each controller for some time. One controller at New York Oceanic I had established a good rapport with was Mickey Dawson.

I answered a call from Brian. Could I check the sea state in the Atlantic Ocean? I immediately phoned Mickey. When he heard the request he said, "Holy cow! Is he planning to ditch?"

"No," I said, "He's just a bit cautious."

"OK," said Mickey, "give me ten minutes."

He called back. "Surface wind ten knots, with one metre waves, good visibility. All good."

The Control Centre was totally overcrowded with reporters. We had to fight to get through the crowd to our desks. Everyone was going crazy! John Albury and I had desks adjacent to each other. He and I had worked together through the stresses and strains since Day One, and we had formed a bond. I had no hesitation in saying to him, "It's going crazy here. I feel it could be very easy to lose the plot if we are not careful. I'm going to stay at this desk until we get three readouts from their GPS that says speed zero, and then we will know for sure they have landed."

He replied with a wry smile, "OK. Good enough for me."

As they got closer to the coast and the finishing line, both Brian and Bertrand started to reflect on what an incredible adventure it had been.

Bertrand wrote in his diary: 'During our three-week flight in our own magical world of the gondola, there has been no let-up in the suffering of the people on the planet that we have been looking down on, with so much admiration. There must be something we can do to alleviate all this suffering using the celebrity status that

228

we are bound to get. It would be a good idea to start a foundation of our own, which could give help every year to some charity that promotes greater respect, tolerance and harmony between people, and between people and nature. We don't understand why we are having so much luck up here... but, let's do everything we can to spread it around us. That led me to think about the prize of one million dollars, which the American brewing company Budweiser had offered to the first crew to fly round the world. The company had stipulated that half the money should go to a charity, and during the flight Brian and I had often thought how much we would enjoy choosing a recipient.'

Bertrand faxed Cecilia and me: 'Hello my friends, when we cross the finish line you will all be in the gondola with us. It will be the victory of passion, of friendship and of endurance – that's why it will be the victory of all of us.'

We replied, 'Thank you for your message. We've been with you all the way along, and we're not going to let you cross the finishing line without us. You should be in range of Canaries Control 124.7.'

As you can imagine, it was a very emotional time, heightened by the fact we were all totally exhausted. We all wanted to say to Brian and Bertrand exactly what we were thinking.

Cecilia sent: *'Dear Brian and Bertrand, this will probably be my last message. It now feels like the lull before the storm in here! I don't suppose I'll be able to get to the keyboard after this. I just wanted to say what a great honour it has been working with you both on this very special project. Smiffy and I have both said from the start how much we hoped the good guys would win. We felt it was so important that, as Jo has said so often, the prize must surely – HOPEFULLY – go to two balloonists who feel passionately about ballooning.*

'Now it seems that dream must come true. Much love from both of us – Cecilia and Brian.'

At 05.56 they crossed the African coast. Jo faxed at this time: *'Good morning Bertrand and Brian, according to our calculations you should be crossing the coast now. Welcome to Africa! I hope you will have a beautiful sunrise and a glorious day. Much love – and we are thinking of you both.'*

The speed of the balloon was now flying three times as fast as the speed we had used for previous fuel calculations, therefore, landing in Egypt was become more of a possibility.

They were heading for the finishing line, defined as 9 degrees 27 minutes west. Alan was organizing a press conference for the moment they crossed the line; it was to take place in the Control Centre. TV camera crews and commentators filled the place. Cecilia and I had to stand on our desks jammed against the wall, to keep out of the way. However, it did give us a grandstand view of everything! At this momentous occasion the red phone went dead! Everyone was waiting for news from the balloon. Alan faxed this message to the balloon: *'According to our poll report you crossed the line at 09.54 Zulu. Congratulations, you guys. You did it. Well done from everybody here at Geneva. Love you both, Alan.'*

The phone was still not working. Brian and Bertrand sent this fax: *'Hello to all our friends in Geneva. We can hardly believe our dream has finally come true. We almost got lost in political problems, in the slow winds of the Pacific, the bad headings over the Gulf of Mexico. But, each time, with God's help and great teamwork, the balloon got back on course to succeed. We are the privileged two of a wonderful and efficient team that we would like to thank from the bottom of our hearts, now that we are sharing with Breitling the result of five years' work. We are eternally grateful to the invisible hand that has guided us through all the obstacles of this fantastic voyage.'*

After a few minutes the satellite phone came alive. The press conference went ahead as planned. Brian and Bertrand said they could hear the sounds of the celebrations – people were laughing, crying, cheering and hugging each other. Many of the world's TV stations carried on broadcasting the event for over an hour.

The control team looked at each other in shock. They formed a circle, burst into tears, then joined in the celebrations. We were all interviewed. It was chaos. One reporter asked me what it had been like? I was at a loss to find a suitable reply, but I managed to spout out, "It was like holding your breath for three weeks!"

John, Debbie, Cecilia and I fought our way back to our communications desks... we were still on duty, and there we stayed for the next 24 hours. Alan, our flight director, left for Egypt. Thank God, Jo was still with us. She became our honorary flight director, but we didn't tell her.

Don Cameron, owner of the company that built the balloon, joined us in the Control Centre. Don is one of the most experienced balloonists in the world. It was a comfort to have him around at this stage

The Landing

Approaching Egypt, the Breitling balloon had already broken several records:

1. The absolute distance record.
2. The absolute duration record.

No other balloon had flown farther or longer.

There are rules governing exactly what constitutes a round the world record. In an attempt to understand these rules, I imagined the globe with a movable skull-type cap over it. If you took off from, say 80 degrees north, you could not fly in a circle round the North Pole and claim you have flown round the world. Fédération Aéronautique Internationale made up the criteria or rules to qualify as follows:

1. For circumnavigation at the northern latitudes, the chosen flight path must circumnavigate a circular cap with a radius of 3,335kms around one of the poles, but not necessarily with the pole at its centre.

2. The flight must start and finish on the same meridian or longitude.
3. Position checkpoints must lie outside the circular cap.

However, there was still the altitude record. John Albury was in the Control Centre when Brian faxed: "I hope the barograph is working. This is our last chance to get altitude using very little fuel, so we are going close to the ceiling to see if we can put the altitude record in the bag."

John's reply: "You arrogant little git! More records indeed! If you go for altitude, do NOT lose your track, as you need to stay as far south as possible, due to the likelihood of 18-knot surface winds near Cairo tomorrow am. Also, do not lose helium."

John and Brian share the same sense of humour! Brian pushed the balloon higher and higher. The maximum height achieved was 38,500' – a world record! Bertrand, who was asleep during this manoeuvre, eventually woke up and said to Brian, "You know, it's a pity we didn't go for the altitude record, and this was our last chance."

Brian smiled and said, "Don't worry, I did it while you were asleep!"

Our air traffic controllers came to the rescue once again. The Egyptian Aviation Authorities had previously given permission to overfly, but not land. This still had to be negotiated. I think it was Nik who was talking to the Egyptians. He had become an excellent diplomat over the course of the flight. He explained, "The balloon is running out of fuel. If the pilot doesn't have permission to land, he'll have to declare a full emergency, and you will be obliged under international law to deal with it."

The Egyptian controller replied, "OK, in that case I give you permission."

All the maps showed a green area near the city of Dakhla. Messages flashed back and forth. I thought to myself, 'Typical balloonists, every one of us had an opinion on the best place and way to land the balloon!' Apart from a last minute Met update from Luc, mercifully they were left alone to land. We had an agonizing wait as the balloon descended and made a final landing. Everyone in the Control Centre was on full alert. Waiting... Waiting...!

We subsequently had the full story from Brian. Brian had started the descent. The original plan was for Bertrand to land the balloon, as he had had the experience of *Breitling 1* and *2*. But as Brian was firmly in the driver's seat and well into the descent, they decided to swap roles. The descent profile was made difficult by showers of ice falling from the envelope. This made the envelope much lighter and caused the balloon to reduce its rate of descent. Brian opened one gas valve to lose some helium, to increase the rate. Bertrand opened the hatch of the gondola and climbed out on top. They were down to 3,000' and still travelling at 28 knots, too fast for a landing. As they approached 1,000' the wind decreased. The Breitling Canadair jet, with the Breitling rescue team on board flew by. Good communications were established between the balloon and the aircraft. With the team on board the jet was Jakob Burkard, the official observer from the Fédération Aéronautique Internationale, to record the precise moment of touchdown.

Brian had to operate the burners to control the approach and landing. This meant standing in the corridor of the gondola and peering through the portholes to be able to see. Not ideal. They hit the ground with a great thump and bounced back up in the air. Brian bought the balloon under control and made another approach and a smooth touchdown – as you would expect from the Training Officer of the British Balloon and Airship Club! The time was 06.00 Zulu on 21st March. The message came through: "The Eagle has landed, all OK. Bloody good. B." In the Control Centre we received the GPS signal from the balloon, indicating ground speed zero!

We were ready to celebrate, when I answered a phone call from a man who said he was an agent of some sort. The telephone line was not very clear and his name sounded like Mr Zigzag. Mr Zigzag, as he became known, was demanding double the amount budgeted by Breitling for a rescue helicopter; he wanted 30,000 dollars, otherwise the helicopter, already on it way, would be ordered back. I said I would phone him straight back. Time was short. Alan Noble, our flight director, had left the Control Centre to fly to Egypt as part of the recue team. No one had the authority to make a decision involving so much money. We started leafing through the big red book for the list of confidential telephone numbers. I found a number for the Swiss Foreign Minister. The phone was answered in seconds. I poured out our story as quickly as I could. He listened, and calmly said, in perfect English he would see what he could do. We all sat around the phone, willing it to ring. After what seemed like hours the phone rang. Much to our surprise it was Mr Zigzag! This time he said, "The problem has been resolved, now two helicopters and a C130 Hercules transport are on their way, furthermore there would be no charge." I have thought hard and long as to exactly what happened to have such a marked turn around. Hats off to the Swiss Foreign Minister...

Even so, it meant a seven-hour wait in the desert for Brian and Bertrand to be rescued. As promised the Hercules arrived, with a helicopter. The Egyptian crew helped Brian and Bertrand load all their kit into the helicopter. They and the helicopter took off and landed at Dakhla Airport to refuel. It seemed the world's press were there waiting. The throng engulfed the 'boys'. The people from Breitling were there too, Thedy Schneider, with the Governor of Dakhla, his officials, and the Swiss ambassador, who had flown down from Cairo to greet Brian and Bertrand.

There followed a five-hour delay while Alan Noble and Stefano Albinati returned to Dakhla. They had set off in a jeep across the desert planning to be the first at the landing site – but this was not to be.

The Governor of Dakhla treated Brian and Bertrand with wonderful hospitality. A shower, good food and a change of clothes were well received. As it was so late, a night stop in Cairo was organised. As the Breitling jet came to a stop, a huge crowd of journalists rushed to the plane. Bertrand was reunited with his wife

234

Michele and his children.

The British ambassador, Sir David Blatherwick came up to Brian and offered to carry Brian's bags. Fame at last! Sir David insisted Brian drive in the British Embassy's Rolls Royce to the Swissotel in Cairo. It was Brian and Bertrand's first post-flight press conference. They were completely exhausted and overwhelmed by this stage. They were asked many questions, but one philosophical question seemed to capture the spirit of the flight. "How did they feel about the flight as a human experience?"

Bertrand replied, how they had felt like flying in a 'peace bubble' above a world where there was so much fighting and suffering. In the eyes of the press this came to define the flight.

Heroes' Welcome

The next morning the team flew to Geneva in the Breitling aircraft to a heroes' welcome. The airport was thrown open to the general public. Thousands of people thronged the tarmac.

The aircraft came to a stop and the cabin door opened. A massive cheer went up as Brian and Bertrand emerged. Jo, Brian's wife, and Michele, Bertrand's wife, who had been patiently waiting, were nearly swept to one side as the crowd surged forward. At last, John, Debbie, Cecilia and I were able to give Brian and Bertrand a hug. Between the tears we all said, "Well done, well done!"

All Brian managed to say was, "Bloody good!"

They did a drive-by of the crowd in an open-top car, then on to another press conference. Bertrand's reply to one of the many questions was: "We all felt we were helped on our way by the good wishes of millions of people. That's why we decided to dedicate the flight to the children of the world. They'll be the adults of tomorrow, and they must know how important it is to have peace and tolerance on earth." He went on to say, "We're going to use the prize money from Budweiser to form a foundation which will promote the spirit of peace."

Bertrand finished with a phrase that has become famous "We took off as pilots, flew as friends, and landed as brothers."

They formed the charity 'Winds of Hope' using the prize money and other donations to provide assistance to children worldwide who are suffering from disease or the ravages of war.

We were to stay one more night in our hotel in Geneva. Cecilia and I stepped into the lift with Jo and Brian. As the doors closed it was the quietest it had been since Brian and Bertrand stepped off the plane. We all looked at each other, just smiling, not quite sure what to say.

Brian broke the ice with, "Bloody good."

Brian and Bertrand were feted round the world. They were presented with many awards and met many famous people.

I know one ceremony that meant a lot to them was held in Château-d'Oex, their launch site. Speeches we made. Brian expressed his feeling for the local people with a few words in French. "Aujourd'hui, ma femme Joanna et moi, sentons que nous sommes rentres a la maison." (Today my wife Joanna and I feel we've come back home.)

The air traffic controllers: Niklaus Gerber, Patrick Schelling and Greg Moegli with Bertrand and Brian.

This would appear to be the end of a wonderful adventure.

Twenty-one years later we still keep in touch. Every time we meet, there is a bond that keeps us reliving the flight. We seem to uncover details of the experience each time, either humorous or emotional events, through tears or laughter! Many of us felt Brian should now be 'Sir Brian' but it was not to be. One of our friends who had followed the flight from start to finish said, "Shame, but he is a National Treasure!"

After the flight many people asked the question, "How come the Breitling balloon succeeded when *22* other attempts failed?" My answer, for what it is worth, is the whole team were totally focused on the project as one, everyone working in harmony. I never saw anyone 'throw his or her toys out of the cot'.

12. BY BALLOON TO THE NORTH POLE

Introducing David Hempleman-Adams.

In 1998 David became the first person to complete the explorer's Grand Slam, a challenge that has seen him conquer the North and South geographical and Magnetic Poles and scale the highest mountain in each of the seven continents, including Everest. David was knighted on 30th December 2016.

About a year after the Breitling Round the World flight, Brian Jones called to tell me about an adventure that David Hempleman–Adams was about to attempt – to fly by balloon to the North Pole! He emphasized it was a low budget project. Brian was putting together a team to man the Control Centre. He was to be the co-ordinator, and manager. So far he had recruited Clive Bailey, a very experienced commercial balloon pilot. I had known Clive for many years; we had become friends, sharing various ballooning escapades. I was very pleased to hear that Gavin Hailes and Pete Johnson were also on the team. They were part of the Breitling Round the World project. Brian needed one more person to complete the Control Centre team.

"How would you like to join us?" Brian asked.

I didn't need to think twice about it. "OK," I replied.

'Hempie', as he became known, had also recruited Luc Trullemans, one of the top meteorologists in the world, who had been part of the Breitling project. It was a good feeling to be part of a team where everybody knew each other.

A few days later Hempie called a meeting of the team in the Globe pub in Bristol. Phil Dunnington, balloon instructor, examiner and one of the most experienced balloonists in the world, joined the meeting.

David outlined a trip he was planning as a workout prior to his North Pole attempt. He invited Phil and me to fly out to Resolute Bay to carry out various balloon flights inside the Artic Circle.

We flew to Edmonton. After an overnight stay we took a

Canadian North B737 to Resolute Bay. It was starting to get exciting. Little did I realize *how* exciting it was about to become! The Canadian North B737 was specially modified for flying in the remote areas of northern Canada. Many of the landing strips were covered in gravel to make a rough surface to land on, as opposed to smooth slippery ice. The engines had probes sticking out of the lower part of the nacelle. On landing, they would blow jets of air to keep the engines clear of stray gravel. The cabin of the B737 was divided in half. The front part was a cargo hold, mostly carrying mining equipment, with room for survival kit should we have to land in this inhospitable terrain. The rear part of the cabin had seats for a hundred passengers. The flight was full. As far as I could tell, all the passengers, apart from Phil and me, looked as if they were on their way for an audition for the film *Seven Brides for Seven Brothers*. Huge men, with beards, and dressed for the Artic. They all seemed to know each other, and there was much banter going to and fro. Phil and I were sitting right at the back of the cabin; this gave us a grandstand view of what was about to happen.

The B737 was at cruise height on our way to Resolute Bay. Suddenly, the man in the seat in front of us produced some matches and tried to set fire to his seat. He shouted in a loud voice, "God is in bed with the devil!" He jumped up and rushed to the back of the aircraft and tried to open the passenger door! The stewardess screamed and 20 or more giant miners rushed back and sat on top of him. Phil and I, our eyes out on stalks, squirmed deeper and deeper into our seats, trying to keep out of sight, and the fight.

The aircraft went into a very steep descent, and within minutes we made a landing at Cambridge Bay Airport. The 'gentleman' was led away by the biggest human being I have ever seen, dressed in the uniform of the Royal Canadian Mounted Police (RCMP).

The B737 captain appeared and slowly walked through the cabin, talking to the miners, thanking them and reassuring them we would soon be on our way. I had been talking to the captain in Edmonton; he knew I was a retired BA captain. He gave me a wry smile and said, "The paperwork is going to be horrendous." We were thankful to land at Resolute Bay.

Resolute Bay, at 74° North, 94° West, is an Inuit hamlet situated on the northern end of Cornwallis Island in Nunavut, Canada. It is one of Canada's northernmost communities and one of the coldest inhabited places in the world, with an average yearly temperature of -15.7 degrees Centigrade.

The hamlet is fascinating. Total population 198. There was a map in our 'motel'. Every house had the names of the inhabitants, but only their *first* names. The cold was so intense, we were told, 'If you go anywhere make sure your friends know where you are going and the time you plan to be back.' To emphasise this, about a week before we arrived a man was driving, at night, from the airport to his motel, a distance of ten miles or so. The car broke down and he was found some hours later, frozen to death in the driver's seat. The 24-hour daylight adds to this odd feeling, as it is not full daylight, rather more like permanent twilight. From 19th April to 23rd August there is no sunset.

We gave ourselves a day off to recover. We decided to visit Sir John Franklin's grave. In 1845, he led an expedition to find the Northwest Passage and to be the first to traverse the seaway that would connect the Atlantic and the Pacific Oceans. All 129 officers and men died on this expedition. I realized we were in an area where you need to tread lightly, cautiously, and with respect.

On 12th May, Phil and I took off from Resolute hamlet for a short balloon flight to check all was working properly. The weather was perfect. It was a great experience to fly in a hot-air balloon over such a special area. I proudly entered 'Resolute Bay' in my balloon pilot's logbook. We landed on the ice-covered sea, about 100 yards from the shore. The ice was smooth and thick, so we were able to push everything to the shore and pack it into a pick-up truck.

The next day we set about checking all the equipment ready for Hempie and Phil's attempt to cross the Northwest Passage by balloon.

Preparing the flight near Polaris Mine, on Little Cornwallis Island.

First Air is a commercial airline based at Resolute Airfield, operating DHC Twin Otter aircraft. These aircraft are ideal for operating in this rugged area. They are extremely robust, with a good short take-off and landing performance, and fitted with skis. Hempie had secured a contract with First Air to carry us and the balloon to and from the various launch sites, and co-ordinate any search and rescue operations. Morag Howell was their base manager, and a very helpful and efficient one too.

First Air had weather information available for their day-to-day operations and they were happy to provide us with forecast track and wind speeds for David and Phil's flight. The latest forecast showed a track from the north of Cornwallis Island to a position close to Somerset Island. This southerly track would take the balloon over the Northwest Passage. Plan A was, we would load everything into a Twin Otter aircraft and fly north to Polaris Mine on the southern tip of Little Cornwallis Island.

I saw them off and flew back to Resolute Bay. From the First Air office I was able to monitor their progress and landing point from a GPS position. I would like to emphasise that was *Plan A*. A friend of mine once said, "You have to have a plan, otherwise it can't go wrong." There was no Plan B.

With good communications established, and their GPS report showing a good track towards Somerset Island, they were well on course for the crossing. They passed south of Griffith Island and started to see the outline of Somerset Island. It started to become very hazy and the island looked somewhat rocky. The decision was to land on the ice before the shoreline.

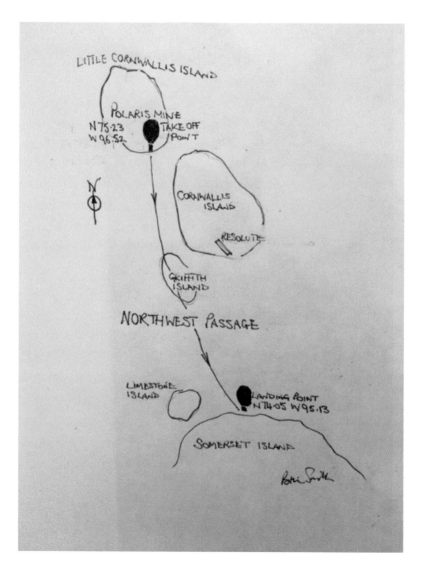

Once we had received a call that they were down safely, I joined the captain and co-pilot in the Twin Otter that had been in position ready for take-off, and we headed off in search of the balloon. We had the balloon's position showing on our GPS, plus, Hempie and Phil had laid out the bright yellow and blue balloon envelope as a marker. Through the haze we saw the balloon and Hempie and Phil standing waving. They looked safe and sound, and this was confirmed when we made contact on VHF radio with them.

However, surrounding the balloon, the sea had frozen into large blocks of ice. *Not* ideal for landing... then the weather instantly changed and went into 'whiteout'. Whiteout has been defined as 'a condition of diffuse light when no shadows are cast, due to a continuous white cloud layer appearing to merge with the white snow surface.' This is where the cloud and sea meet, so there is no definable horizon. It is very easy to get disoriented.

We flew low over the balloon and turned round to find a space beside the balloon to land. There was a loud bang. I thought we had hit the ground. Apparently, we had just 'touched' some ice rubble! We bounced back into the air, accompanied by much bad language from all of us. The captain told me that it was too dangerous to land. I was beginning to think that myself!

"We go back to Resolute," he said.

I thought to myself, 'No, no I want to pick up David and Phil and fly back to base and open the beers that Morag kept in the ops room.' I asked if I could talk to 'the boys' on the VHF radio. Permission was given. I said, "Congratulations on crossing the Northwest Passage. Now, the bad news is, the captain wants to, *is going to*, I should say, return to base due to weather. We will come back to pick you up tomorrow."

Hempie was the first to reply, "Great, we're fine. See you tomorrow."

To stay overnight in this inhospitable environment was something Hempie was quite used to. Afterwards, Phil confessed he was very apprehensive about camping in polar bear country, particularly when David said, "If you hear that sounds like a polar bear in the night please let me know."

Phil's retort was, "David! I live in Bristol, England, how would I know what a polar bear sounds like?"

I drove back to our motel and spent a sleepless night trying to think through all the possible scenarios... What if, what if, what if...?

Very early next morning I went back to First Air's operations room. Morag was already on duty. She said, "I have just spoken to David and the weather is still in 'whiteout'. The forecast is not good. We cannot fly out in the Twin Otter today, therefore I have contacted Nathan and Gary, local Inuits, and they are standing by with two large commercial skidoos, to go and pick up David and Phil, to bring them back to Resolute." She continued, "Nathan would like to talk to you, I suggest you go right now to his house."

There was no need to ask where he lived. I just looked at the hamlet map and found a house with the name 'Nathan'. I knocked on Nathan's door. He came out already dressed in his Artic clothing, ready to go. Gary, his son, joined us. I gave Nathan the balloon's GPS position.

"Do they have rifles?" he asked, "They are in polar bear country." I assured him they have good survival kit, including rifles, and distress flares. He said, "OK, we will be back in about ten hours. You stay here!" The way he said, 'You stay here' was more of a command than a comment. So, that is exactly what I did.

I was already wearing my Artic clothing, and I had stocked up on chocolate bars and water. I sat on the shoreline in the car and dozed and waited. Although it was very cold, it gave me a chance to run through the emergency plan, should they not find them, or have a breakdown... I mean their equipment, not me personally!

Right on schedule, I heard the sound of a skidoo's engine. Incredibly, they appeared out of the twilight right from the exact spot where they had left ten hours previously. It had been a hell of a ride. Once Nathan and Gary had picked up David and Phil they were ready to head for home as fast as possible. As well as the intense cold, the speed over the rough ice, with the skidoo leaping up and down, it made for a very rough ride home. Phil suffered from frostbite on his hands.

Gary, David and Nathan safely back at base camp.

As always, there were tales to tell both from the flight and the retrieve. Both teams lived through the mix of emotions. I felt that flying in the Polar region was best summed up in one word: 'DANGEROUS'.

Having completed these 'trial' flights we were ready for the big one!

The North Pole

I think it is true to say balloonists suffer from wind, either too much of it or not enough! Days, weeks and sometimes months can be spent waiting for the right wind for your balloon flight. This was particularly true of Hempie's attempt to fly from Spitsbergen, Norway to the North Pole, and hopefully, back! As well as wanting to be the first man to fly to the North Pole by balloon, David elected to fly in a Rozière balloon, a combination of helium and hot air, in an open wicker basket to pay homage to three Swedes who, in 1897, made the attempt in a gas balloon. David tells the fascinating story of both flights in his excellent book *At the Mercy of the Winds*. I would highly recommend the book.

Telemessage®

RDG5793 MSC1650 PFC0033 P052 BUCK0033 21 MAY 1999/1800

ST. JAMES'S PALACE
LONDON
SW1A 1BS

21 May 1999

TELEMESSAGE
MR D. HEMPLEMAN-ADAMS & MR P. DUNNINGTON
C/O COLD CLIMATE EXPEDITIONS LTD.
CORSHAM COMMERCIAL CENTRE
POTLEY LANE
CORSHAM SN13 9RH

    I WAS VERY IMPRESSED TO HEAR OF YOUR SUCCESSFUL BALLOON FLIGHT ABOVE
THE ARCTIC CIRCLE AND OVER THE NORTH WEST PASSAGE. THIS IS JUST TO
SEND YOU MY WARMEST CONGRATULATUIONS AND HEARTFELT BEST WISHES ON A
GREAT ACHIEVEMENT.

CHARLES,
H.R.H. THE PRINCE OF WALES.

TO REPLY BY TELEMESSAGE SEE REVERSE SIDE

246

From: Captain Neil Blair, LVO, Royal Navy

BUCKINGHAM PALACE,
LONDON SW1A 1AA

27th May, 1999.

Dear Mr Smith.

Princess Alexandra was delighted to be
informed of David Hempleman-Adams and
Phil Dunnington's achievements during their flight
over the North West Passage and in the high Arctic.

Perhaps you would be kind enough to convey
Her Royal Highness's congratulations.

Yours sincerely

Neil Blair

<u>Private Secretary</u>

Brian Smith, Esq.

I played such a small part in David's adventure, but I wanted to try and paint a picture of life in the Control Centre during the hectic days of David's flight.

It had taken two years of hard work, and by January 2000 David had assembled the launch and Control Centre teams, the meteorological expert, and TV crews and reporters.

Britannic Assurance sponsorship was secured. David was all set, with a take-off date of about a month's time. Then there came a message from the meteorological station in Spitsbergen: *'The forecast ground winds from March until June are more than 25kts on average.'* A speed above 5 knots would make it impossible to launch the giant balloon. This was devastating news. As well as the wind speed consideration, there is the Polar climate. Before April the Artic nights are long and days short, after May the ice cap will have melted and would not be able to take the weight of a rescue plane.

The delay in waiting for the right wind meant that most of David's team would have previous commitments. Also, although we all were contactable, we were scattered all over the world. I was the 'stand-in' in case Brian or Clive could not be in the Control Centre, but I had not been involved in all the extensive pre-flight preparations, as had the rest of the team.

Cecilia and I were in Ireland at the Irish Hot-Air Ballooning Championships when the call came from Clive: "Get here as fast as you can. Brian Jones has had to attend a ceremony in the USA and cannot take part. The balloon is about to be launched!"

I turned to Dave Triggs, our ballooning partner, and said, "Dave, I've got to go. Here's my balloon and here's my wife. Please take care of the balloon." Leaving my wife and friends, I dropped everything and drove to Birmingham as fast as I could.

Clive was in good form and welcomed me with, "What kept you? Now sit down and try and get a grip." Clive has a way with words. He went for a well-earned rest and I was very happy to talk to Hempie at last.

The Control Centre was set up in one of the offices in Britannic's

HQ. Claire and Denise, two secretaries, were also assigned to the project. As well as doing their normal 'day job' they handled all the communications and enquiries, and they kept Clive and me going with pizzas and coffee.

David Hempleman-Adams about to take off for the North Pole, 28th May 2000.

The messages flowed between Luc Trullemans, Hempie and the Control Centre.

It is well known with any project involving an extreme adventure that it is very easy to appear to the pilot that the ground crew are always nagging him. 'How much sleep have you had? Have you eaten anything? Are you wearing your harness?' This time the nagging paid off. Hempie had been going for four days with very little sleep and decided to try and take a nap. We suggested he put on his harness. I knew he hated wearing it, and I was expecting a retort from him. All was quiet; I thought he must be sleeping.

This seemed a good opportunity to have a snooze myself. I was wakened by a call from Hempie. "Brian! Brian!... I tried to climb out of the basket... I nearly lost it completely."

"You *what?*" I replied.

"I woke with one leg over the side… only the harness stopped me!"

Clearly, Hempie was on the verge of complete exhaustion. Clive spent some time talking him though all his safety checks. We all calmed down… but it had been a close call.

From the GPS readout it showed the balloon was slipping too far to the east. This did not make sense. Tom Shaw, a pilot and close friend of Clive's had called into the Control Centre just to say 'hello'. The three of us were puzzling about what it could be that was sending the balloon in the wrong direction. Tom said, "Ask Hempie to check the GPS setting. Is it on Grid or True?"

"Grid," came the reply.

Tom said, "It should be on True."

Thanks to Tom the flight was saved.

A left turn was immediately required. We called Luc. He understood the problem and responded with a height change. Slowly, the balloon's track and Luc's predicted track started to match.

Hempie was now less than 30 miles from the pole. He called us: "I am at eighty-nine degrees and thirty-nine minutes north."

It is virtually impossible to get 90 degrees north on the GPS. The True North Pole is a massive ice floe floating above a notional point to which all lines of longitude point and where every direction from the pole is south. Unlike the South Pole, there is no landmass.

At 12 miles from the North Pole, well inside the Polar Circle, the wind dropped to calm. Hempie tried various heights to see if he could get even closer. The balloon did not move forward an inch.

Clive said, "Why don't you call it a day, Hempie? You're closer to the pole than you ever dreamed you'd get."

Hempie was to write in his book 'The pole is in the bag!' *He had done it!* After consultation with the British Balloon and Airship Club, Guinness Book of Records announced they had recognized the flight as the first balloon flight to the North Pole. Time to go home…

Everyone was exhausted and elated at the same time. We

realized that now was the time for extreme vigilance. We know more people have died coming down from Mount Everest than going up. We knew at this point it is easy to drop your guard.

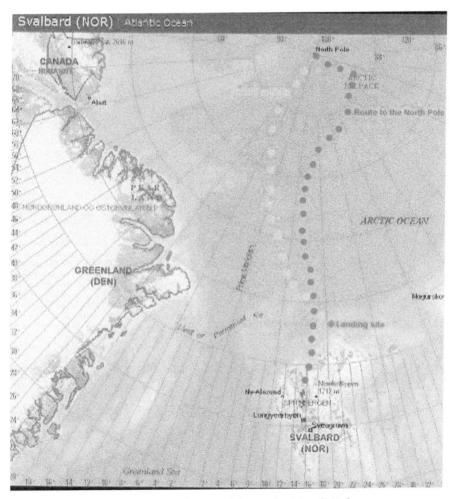

Hempie's track to and from the North Pole.

"So, what's the plan now, Brian?" asked Hempie. We discussed the plans:

Plan A: Fly south. When the weather clears, land about a hundred miles north of Spitsbergen.

Plan B: Fly to mainland Russia.

Plan C: Err. We don't have a plan C…

The original Plan C was to climb to 24,000' or so and fly on to Canada. This was not possible now as there was a problem with the oxygen supply.

Hempie was extremely tired. So Plan A it had to be. Clive talked to Hempie on a phone patch from Iceland Radio. "We've spoken to Luc. He says to stick to seven thousand feet. It's a perfect high-speed track to Spitsbergen. You should be home by 8am on Saturday."

Clive was then busy setting up the helicopter pick-up. I talked to Luc about the possible wind tracks to bring Hempie home. It seemed a miracle that Luc had found a straight-line track at 7,000'!

Clive called Hempie, "I suggest you set the autopilot and have a good kip. There's not much else to do."

Hempie replied, "I'm going to sleep. Speak to you in two hours." I watch the clock. Two hours is up. I have heard nothing from him. Should I let him sleep a little longer? I decided to wake him.

"Christ, Brian! Thank God you called when you did!" Hempie was so tired, he must have fallen asleep without switching the autopilot on. The balloon had slowly started to descend and would have continued until it hit the ice. I felt frightened. We were all on our 'beam-ends' and it looked as if we could lose the flight due to our exhaustion. Just one slip or omission from normal meticulous double-checking for every little eventuality could lead to disaster. I was about to reply when I realised my high-pitched voice would betray my fear. I took a deep breath, and in my best 'this is your captain speaking voice' said, "I'm going to be here all night. Grab as much sleep as you can. When you don't feel like sleeping you can talk to me. Luc is also asleep and he is happy for you to fly through the night." We ran through some logistics regarding the pick-up by helicopter, and the pre-landing checks.

When Hempie awoke he suggested a landing on the ice, east of

Spitsbergen. We knew that this is the worst area for polar bears. He has used his rifle once before on an overland expedition. In his book *Walking on Thin Ice* he describes an encounter with a polar bear.

Clive, Luc and I had a consultation. "We know the rescue helicopter is close to the balloon... why ask David to keep flying, when the isotherm map shows he is over solid ice?"

The reality was, the ice was not solid, but fragmented, with large leads of open water making it difficult to land on solid ice. Hempie then started his descent to land. Eventually, the only way we in the Control Centre would know he was down would be a call from the helicopter or Spitsbergen Radio.

Finally, the call came through. 'He has been picked up. All OK. Flying on to Longyearbyen.'

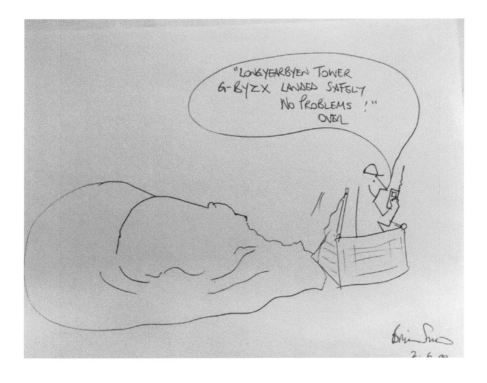

Clive and I looked at each other. With broad smiles, and tears running down our cheeks, we shook hands. "Bloody good!" we said in unison. "Now, we can celebrate."

We didn't have any alcohol in the Control Centre so we jumped into Clive's van and found a pub just along the lane. The landlord recognized the Britannic Assurance emblems on our shirts and said he had been following the flight on his radio. Several pints later we left the pub. When we got back to the Control Centre, I fell fast asleep. When I awoke, there was a note from Clive pinned to my pillow, it said: 'Bloody good. See ya!'

Britannic
ASSURANCE

Mr B Smith
Wheelers Farm
Wisborough Green
West Sussex
RH14 0BZ

Extension:	2645
Our Reference:	DIN
Your Reference:	---

21 June 2000

Dear Brian

Britannic Challenge

On behalf of Britannic Assurance and specifically the Britannic Challenge team, I should like to sincerely thank you for your contribution to the Britannic Challenge.

Your unparalleled experience was hugely significant during the execution of this trip and without it I am sure it would not have been the success that it was.

I know that having yourself together with the rest of the team was what convinced David that this miraculous flight was indeed going to be possible. So, many congratulations on helping to make this such an historic and memorable flight and my personal thanks for your great contribution.

Regards

Yours sincerely

David Newman
Head of Marketing
Britannic Assurance plc

The whole team back at base.

Some time after the flight, Hempie phoned to say we had been invited to Buckingham Palace to meet HRH The Duke of Edinburgh. Hempie briefed us on the correct procedure to be followed. He explained we would be escorted throughout by the Duke's aide-de-camp. The visit would be very short.

We assembled in a small room and were ushered to our seats. The duke entered through a side door. We sat in a circle. I was excited and somewhat nervous to be sitting up close to one of my childhood heroes. The duke put everyone at ease. You could see he and Hempie had a special regard for one another. The duke was extremely knowledgeable of everything to do with the North Pole flight and engaged with every one of us. Though we had been told the meeting would be very short, after 40 minutes we were still in animated conversation and reliving the flight.

Gavin Hailes politely asked the duke if we could have a photo with him and us together. There was a silence. Then the duke smiled, pressed a bell push on the wall, and shouted, "Harry!" Harry, the butler, duly appeared and took the photo.

While we were lining up for it, the duke looked at Gavin's tie and said, "When were you in the Grenadier Guards?" This observation added to the reputation the duke had for his intimate knowledge of the subject at hand.

Post-flight visit to Buckingham Palace.
Pete Johnson, Clive Bailey, Gavin Hailes, HRH The Duke of Edinburgh, Hempie, and Brian Smith.

13. THE ALBATROSS

I answered the phone to hear a voice say, "Hi, my name is Lt. Col John Stipetich the Third." I should have put the phone down, but curiosity got the better of me. John went on to say, "I have flown most things, but never flown in a hot-air balloon, how do I go about it?" John was a captain flying for Continental Airlines based in the USA, with a couple of days free in London. He travelled down to Sussex and I took him up for a balloon flight.

That was the start of not only a friendship, but also an introduction to more adventures. John wanted to get his type rating on a B737. Mike Pearce, a BA training captain, and I carried out his conversion course in the British Airways flight simulator.

About a year later, John phoned to tell me about a project he had become involved in. It was a complete restoration project to get an HU-16B Grumman Albatross amphibian back into flying condition. "Would you like to get involved too?" he asked. I started to get that feeling – another adventure was about to start!

My daughter Cymbeline and her two sons live in Los Angeles, so it seemed a good opportunity to visit her and take a look at this intriguing aircraft, which was being restored in Chuck Wootan's yard, in Tucson, Arizona. His yard backs onto the Davis-Monthan Airbase, known as the 'Boneyard'.

The Boneyard is the home of The Aerospace Maintenance and Regeneration Group – AMARG. There are over 4,000 US military aircraft stored there. They are all parked out in the open, on the desert floor, some to be broken up and others to be restored to flying condition. You can take a guided tour round the place. It is very interesting and I felt it would be poignant to see so many classic aircraft that may well end up as pots and pans. Strange to think that your frying pan could be part of the bomb bay of a B52 bomber!

I decided to drive from L.A to Tucson. When I told John, he said, "Why? There ain't nuthin' there." I thought I would see something of the real America... He was right. I saw a lot of US Highway 10, and not much else.

Chuck's yard was a mini boneyard, with bits of Albatross strewn everywhere. Chuck Wootan had spent about five years of his life restoring this aircraft. Over a period of an hour or so I was given the history and the future plans for it.

The Grumman Aircraft Engineering Corporation was founded in 1929 by Leroy Grumman. From 1947, 466 Albatrosses were built. They were designed as search and rescue amphibians and they could and did land on the open ocean.

One story I heard was that part of this particular aircraft finished its days with the Philippine Air Force. One of the many rumours, none substantiated, was that President Marcos had it filled it with gold bars just before he fled to Hawaii in 1986. It was then flown to Taiwan and abandoned in a farmer's field. After several years, the farmer's daughter realised it must be worth something and advertised it for sale. Bob Ryan bought it and had it shipped to Chuck's yard in Tucson. No gold bars were ever found!

It had been stripped down to bare metal. Bob had the engines taken off and sent for overhaul. The intention was to have it restored and used as a flying museum to educate children that a military airplane could be used to rescue people... It was to be called the Air Rescue Museum. I came away with my brain buzzing with ideas. What could I offer to help this project?

I remembered a story that some retired Qantas pilots and engineers planned to restore a former Qantas Constellation airliner that was 'mothballed' in the USA, and then fly it back to Australia. They contacted Lockheed Aerospace Corporation, who had made this aircraft in Burbank, California, and told them of their plans. Lockheed said that they would paint it in the original Qantas colours, free of charge. This story is told in a documentary *Affair with Connie.*

This got me thinking (always dangerous). Why don't I see if Grumman, now named Northrop Grumman (NG) would do the same for us? I telephoned Bob Ryan and told him of my plan.

"Good idea," said Bob, "see what you can do."

Why did I not keep these good ideas to myself? I was willing to give it a go, but where to start? I was telling a friend of mine, Jim Gavin about the project. He said, "I know Grant Rogan who lives in our village, he deals with Northrop Grumman, I will tell him your story." Grant took the story to Grumman, and they in turn agreed in principle to see if there was a way to get the Albatross painted. There was a long three years of emailing back and forth. Although it was an agonising wait, they were a pleasure to deal with, and one day they advised me it had all been approved and the Albatross would be painted free of charge in their paint shop in Palmdale, California. A huge thanks to Jim and Grant for the introductions.

A date was arranged for Bob Ryan and me to meet at NG Headquarters in Palmdale. As this was to be our first face-to-face meeting with their executives, I knew this was very important. It was our chance to convince them what they as a company would gain from their very generous gesture.

The day before the meeting, I asked my daughter Cymbeline if she would drive me out to Palmdale. Although it was a Sunday and her day off work, she willingly agreed. After a two-hour drive from LA, we pulled up at Northrop Grumman's main gates. She looked at me and said, "What now?"

I said, "That's fine. Now we can go home." To this day she will tell you the story how her father got her to drive two hours just to see a pair of locked gates!

I had not met Bob Ryan yet. By an extraordinary coincidence we both turned up for the meeting the next day at the main gate at precisely the same time. We were shown to an office and met Orville Dothage and Ian Hall. They were to be our contacts throughout the painting process. Over the months that followed we became good friends, and I still keep in touch with them.

I visited Chuck's yard several times and could see the day for its first flight was fast approaching.

Aer Lingus, the Irish Airline, have all their aircraft blessed by a priest. I thought, 'Why not have the Albatross blessed?' so I went to the church on the Davis-Monthan US Airbase. There I met Monsignor Lt. Col John Cusack. He was intrigued by the idea.

The next week, he came to the yard with his Book of Blessings. We stood in front of the aircraft and he read from the book, then walked round the Albatross blessing it with holy water. We invited him to have a look inside. We asked him to sign one of the bare metal panels. It's good to know that the aircraft started flying with his blessing and his signature.

The big day for the Albatross's inaugural flight arrived. The plan was to fly out of Davis-Monthan Airbase to Marana Regional Airport, about 15 miles to the north-west. Marana was to be its new home under the tender care of Bill Muszala, owner of ATW Aviation Inc. The airfield had a number of what we might call 'retired' aircraft ending their last days in the desert. The air is so dry they do not rust, they were just parked there on the desert floor, silent sentinels of another age. Among the many aircraft parked there was a Lockheed Constellation that caught my eye. Probably one of the most beautiful looking airliners ever built. The name on its nose was *Columbine II*. This aircraft was once the US Presidential transport for Dwight. D. Eisenhower. Its original call sign was 'Air Force 8610'. One day, in 1953, it was flying over New York City, when Eastern Airlines Flight 8610 was also flying in the same area, at the same altitude. A mid-air collision was narrowly avoided. To stop any further confusion, Air Force 8610 changed its call sign to 'Air Force One'.

There have been several Air Force Ones, but *Columbine II* was the first. *Columbine II* was restored at Marana Airfield, at about the same time as the Albatross. Both aircraft are now on display at the Mid-America Flight Museum in Texas. It's good to think that Connie and Albie are sitting side by side in retirement.

To get onto the Davis-Monthan Airfield from Chuck's yard, the boundary fence had to be taken down, and the Albatross towed across the apron to the runway. There were dozens of A10 tank buster aircraft parked with their pilots and crew sitting on them. They all gave us a wave and a cheer as they saw this ancient piece of aviation history trundle by and take off. On board were Bob, Chuck and Bob's son, Jordan. We watched the Albatross take off. We quickly jumped in our cars and raced to Marana Airfield. They were asked not to land until we were there to film the landing. The flight went without incident.

If the Albatross's first flight was not enough excitement for the day, Bob was itching to put it back on the water. The nearest large lake was Lake Mead near Las Vegas. It was formed as part of the Hoover Dam project. It is the largest reservoir in the USA. We refuelled ourselves at the Skyrider Coffee Shop at the airport. The speciality of the day was chalked on the menu board. 'S.O.S' was all that was written there. I asked John what it meant. "Well," he drawled, "It stands for 'Shit on Shingles'." I learned it was quite a well-known dish, consisting of mincemeat with gravy on bread, the bread being the shingle.

The aircraft was refuelled, and we were off to Lake Mead for water touch and goes. John Stipetich and Jordan were first to fly. I was lucky to be on board for much of this training and was put in charge of catering – back to the old job!

Landing on water opened up a completely new world to me. I felt honoured to be allowed to make a landing. Like many amphibians, written on the water-landing checklist, in bold letters is **LANDING GEAR – UP**. I was told that landing on the water with the landing gear DOWN is as bad as landing on the land with the landing gear UP. On touchdown, as the hull cuts through the water, you get this whooshing sound. Just as you are about to congratulate yourself on a smooth touchdown, suddenly you feel as if the whole aircraft is sinking. As you slow down, the aircraft settles quite deeply into the water. The throttles are positioned just above your head. Reverse is selected by closing the throttles and pushing one or both up a notch. On the water, even with the engines at idle they are still thrusting, producing enough power to move you gently through the water. You can steer on the water by selecting reverse on one side or the other, left to go left, right to go right. This is in addition to studying the wind on the water, the tidal flow, and 'water traffic'. There's a lot to take in.

The take-off technique is to get the aircraft on 'the step'. I found it a little disconcerting that when you open up to full power nothing seems to happen. It begins to accelerate very slowly as you are low in the water. As the speed builds up you feel the aircraft lift and you are on 'the step', skimming the water. Acceleration is quicker then, and at 80 knots you ease back on the control column and lift off. I was told that 105 knots is the critical 'engine out' speed, with an initial climb speed of 120 knots. Even with noise-cancelling headsets, the sound from those big radial engines right next to your ears is VERY LOUD!

We did several touch and goes at Lake Mead. Then Jordan, Bob's son, said he would like to go for a swim. We thought he was joking. After one landing he opened the back door and leapt into the lake.

We still had more training to do, so we took off, and after a quick circuit, landed back on the lake to pick him up. Jordan was nowhere to be seen. We taxied around in circles, but we could not see him. We made another sweep of the lake. We were beginning to get concerned. Suddenly, a speedboat appeared, driven by two pretty girls. Jordan was sitting in the back, giving us a royal wave and a huge grin.

Rescuing Jordon from Lake Mead.

We returned to Marana Airfield. The day had started with the inaugural flight from Davis-Monthan to Marana to Lake Mead, including several water touch and goes at Lake Mead. All through that momentous day, the weather had been clear and still, now we were treated to a golden desert sunset, with the cirrus clouds looking as if they were on fire. I turned to Bob and said, "What a great day. How did you ever get permission to land at Lake Mead?"

Bob looked at me, raised an eyebrow and said, "I have always thought it is better to apologise, rather than ask permission."

I was learning about the American way of doing things.

There was much discussion about how to get the Albatross into the paint hangar at Palmdale. The entrance to the hangar was wide enough, but the height of the giant concrete beam over the entrance was 25 feet. The Albatross tail reaches a height of 25 feet, 11 inches. Once it was past the beam the ceiling was very high and did not present a problem. John Stipetich and I borrowed a cherry picker (a mobile tower), climbed to the top of the Albatross's tail, undid the rivets and removed a metal crown or cap on the top. This only lowered the height by four inches. Seven inches still to go! One suggestion was to deflate the main tyres and jack up the nose wheel. When we went to the hangar the next morning, the Grumman crew had already hitched up two motorised tow bars to the main undercarriage wheels, ready to push it in.

The question of the height still remained, when one of the supervisors shouted to about six of the largest men who were standing watching, "Get in the back of the aircraft one at a time." They started filing on board, and, very slowly, it tipped onto its tail and they dragged it in. Pure genius...

On March 23rd 2012 it emerged from the hangar, resplendent in its US Air force colour scheme.

The inaugural flight of our Albatross in its new USAF colours was flown by Bob, John and Chuck from Palmdale to Fox Field Airport. My wife, Cecilia, daughter Cymbeline and my two grandsons, Smith and Kambel, drove up from LA to meet us. As a thank you, about a dozen of the painters were given a flight in the Albatross at Fox Field. Chuck Manning also joined us. I had time to sit with Chuck. This is his story.

Record breakers – Chuck Manning (Lt Col USAF Rtd.)

On 4th July 1973, Lieutenant Colonel Charles H. Manning, Major Paul M. Schaefer, and Technical Sergeant Edmund K. Schindler set an altitude record for amphibians of 32,881 feet.

Chuck said, "We stripped the Albatross of all non-essential equipment. We took off from Homestead AFB, Florida, and climbed to 28,000' or so; that seemed about as high as we could go, when I spotted a thunderstorm. We headed into it and it swept us up to 32,000 feet." This height was officially checked by the Fédération Aéronautique Internationale (FAI) barograph as 32,881 feet.

It was very cold; the outside temperature was 25 below zero. The *Air Force Times* reported that the cold caused the lens of Sergeant Schindler's watch to pop out.

Two weeks after the record-breaking flight it was flown to The National Museum of the United States Air Force at Wright-Patterson Air Force Base, Ohio, making the very last USAF HU-16 flight.

On 13th July 2020, I spoke by telephone to Chuck Manning. He is 96 years old. Although his eyesight is poor, his memory is still very sharp. He membered his record-breaking flight and our trip to Yuma Air Show.

From Fox Field in the afternoon, we set off from Palmdale to Yuma, Arizona, some 250 miles away. We had been invited to attend the Annual Yuma Air Show. James Palmer, a good friend of mine from the UK, joined us. At the air show we were a static display, which means we were not allowed to fly. However, this was the first time we felt we were promoting the Air Rescue Museum by showing the public inside our aircraft. This is what we wanted the youngsters to see – a RESCUE aircraft. We had some lapel pins or badges made to give to the children. They showed a cartoon Albatross with the name 'ALBEE'. It was Albee from then on.

After the air show, all the pilots wanted to leave at once. The executive and fast jets are usually first in the queue. We were amongst the tail end Charlies, the last to leave. It did mean we would be landing back at Marana Airfield in the dark. Normally, this would not be a problem. We settled down at cruise height above a thin veil of stratus with a glorious sunset. We flew so that the hull of the Albatross was skimming just above the cloud layer. It was a wonderful sensation. Everyone was very quiet in the aircraft, each with their own thoughts. It was as if we were coming home from a rescue mission. I thought about the history of this aircraft, and the airmen it had rescued. Having Chuck Manning on board made it all the more special. Bob and Chuck were in the cockpit. Chuck was flying the aircraft.

The logistics suddenly became very complicated. Bob and Jordan had driven to Marana Airfield to fly the Albatross to the paint shop at Palmdale. After painting, John, Bob and Jordan flew it to Fox Field.

Chuck, Jamie and I joined them at Fox Field and all six of us flew on to Yuma. This left us with only one small car parked at Marana. If we flew directly back to Marana, we would not be able to fit six of us in one car. Bob Ryan came up with a plan; to fly into Tucson International Airport, drop off Jamie, John, Chuck and me, leaving Bob and Jordon to fly to Marana.

The sun had set and it was quite dark now, a desert sky, and black as ink with no moon. We started our descent to Tucson International Airport. None of the cockpit lights were working as all the flying we had done so far had been in daylight. I stood between the pilots with a torch to light the flight instruments so they could fly by reference to them. The thought occurred to me. 'What happens if the torch battery dies?'

We landed at Tucson International Airport and advised the air traffic controller that we only need to drop off a couple of passengers, keep the engines running and take off for Marana, our home base.

The controller directed us to the Executive Jet Terminal. It must have been a bizarre sight to see this old propeller driven aircraft, with its squeaky brakes, throwing oil from the engines on the immaculate tarmac, taxiing among the sleek biz jets. We opened the back door and jumped out onto the tarmac.

The Albatross trundled off. We were left standing in the dark, wondering, what next? A golf buggy appeared, driven by a smartly dressed handling agent. "Good evening gentlemen, how can I help you?" he asked. We explained that we would like to hire a car. "No problem, I'll take you to the car rental." The end of another day.

Oshkosh Air Show

In May 2013 we flew the Albatross to the famous Oshkosh Air Show in Wisconsin. It is believed to be one of the biggest air shows in the world. Approximately 600,000 people visit, and up to 10,000 aircraft take part. It was a long journey, some 1,800 miles from

Marana Airfield. We flew via New Mexico, Oklahoma, Nebraska, and on to Iowa. The weather was good throughout the flight, some high cirrus clouds, and a scattering of fair-weather cumulus. Guess who was in charge of catering for the day? We set out at dawn with a refuelling stop at an airfield in Iowa, owned by one of the biggest crop spraying companies in the Midwest. We were the largest aircraft to visit, and probably the first amphibian. Most of the nearby town turned out to see it.

We arrived at Oshkosh Airfield just before sunset. Nothing can prepare you for the sight of so many different types of aircraft all flying at the same time. A full air show was taking place. Overhead, B17s, DC3s, Mustangs and Spitfires were flying back and forth. A banner on the control tower said: 'The Busiest Airport in the World', and I believed it. Meanwhile, aircraft were landing and taking off on another runway.

The control tower is so busy you are identified by your aircraft type, not your call sign as normal. I wanted to use our own call sign 'Seabird One', but it was not to be. The runway has three large, coloured dots painted on it, and, depending on your type, big, medium or small, you land on your assigned coloured dot. For example: "Silver Albatross land on the red dot." All the marshallers wear pink polo shirts, and you do *exactly* as they say. We were directed to our parking area, next to the camping site. There were hundreds of light aircraft parked side by side in an area about the size of four football pitches, each with its own tent.

The next day we made a short hop for a water landing on Lake Winnebago. On the edge of the lake there are many little lagoons filled with floatplanes. We landed and taxied towards the shore. A boat came alongside with two marshallers. They said we were too large to fit in any of the lagoons, but could we please taxi towards the shoreline for the folks to see us. Using a mud anchor, we moored up and shut down. The whole of the shoreline was covered in people, whistling and cheering. Dozens of small boats set out towards us. People were patting the Albatross and some climbed on board for a look. It was all very touching and quite overwhelming. As well as all the aircraft, there were hundreds of stalls, marquees, even aircraft for sale. One beautiful light aircraft had a banner that said: 'Your wife called, she says it's OK to buy it.' American aviation at its best. The show ended and we all went our separate ways.

I saw the Albatross depart to fly back to our base at Marana AIrfield. I did not realize that was to be the last time I would see it.

A few days later, Olya, Bob's wife passed away. About the same time, Bob was due to retire from the airline business. Bob was so affected by Olya's passing that The Air Rescue Museum project was put on hold.

Eventually, the Albatross was sold to The Mid-America Flight Museum, Mount Pleasant, Texas. If you look at their website there is a very good video clip of our Albatross flying and making a water landing.

It is good to know it is in safe hands.

Old albatrosses never die... In 2014 a company called Row 44 used an Albatross as a test bed for a satellite-based WIFI installation, now used on most civil airliners. It was chosen to be a better platform than a King Air or B737. Not bad for a 70-year-old aircraft. Dave Cummings, a director of the company, is a pilot and engineer specializing in Albatross maintenance. Not only was he able to convince them to install their equipment in an Albatross, no mean feat, he also flew the aircraft himself.

14. LAWN MOWER RACING

I am proud to tell you that I have raced against Sterling Moss and Derek Bell, two world famous professional racing drivers. However, I have to confess it was on lawn mowers.

This is how it all came about. One night in 1973 it was closing time in our local pub *The Cricketers Arms* in Wisborough Green, West Sussex. A group of car enthusiasts, who had been in the pub some time, were discussing the increasing cost of motor racing. Jim Gavin, who had been involved in motor sport for many years, and had organized several international car rallies, said, "What we need is a really low-cost motor racing sport. Why don't we start by racing lawn mowers?" Everyone present thought it was a great idea. At that time of night after consuming several pints of beer, any idea was considered great! Little did we know that some 47 years later it would still be going strong.

Back to the beginning. The next day Malcolm Cook and I went into the pub for a quiet Sunday lunchtime pint. The landlord said, "Hey, they are racing lawn mowers this afternoon, you guys ought to go and have a look." The idea appealed to our sense of the ridiculous. Boy, were we in for a surprise? When we arrived at the field, there was a track laid out with straw bales, and running round the track were about half a dozen men, each one holding onto an engine-driven lawn mower, the sort of mower you would cut your lawn with.

Jim's wife was ready with a chequered flag. We watched as she waved the flag to start a Le Mans style race. The 'drivers' ran across the track, started their engines and roared off round the track. Everyone was having fun, and there was much noise and banter. I waved at a friend of mine who was whizzing by with his lawn mower. "Hey, come and have a go," he said. I grabbed the mower, opened the throttle and off I shot. My friend Malcolm, not to be outdone, 'borrowed' another machine, and round and round the track we went. Malcolm and I were hooked. Jim Gavin and his wife

Mary, the founders of the whole affair, were already planning the next race meeting.

It literally took off. It grew and grew. Race meetings were organized in the local area. A farmer's field would be transformed for an afternoon into a racetrack, complete with a pits area. Jim and Mary eventually introduced a class or group system for mowers:

Group1 were 'run behinds': These mowers were just like the ones on that very first race back in 1973. Although the engine was running, the 'driver' was standing and running behind. Each entry was allowed an unlimited number of drivers. This class was for the young and fit. If you could recruit a local rugby team you were in with a chance.

Group 2 were called 'sit upons': These mowers looked like the type you would see with a groundsman gently mowing a cricket pitch. The main difference was that they could travel at 40mph. The driver sat on a seat towed behind the mower.

Group 3 were garden tractors: Ride-on tractors that you would see on a large estate or golf course.

For safety reasons, all cutter bars were removed. Soon team numbers on the grass box and the back of the driver's seat were required. Also, team names became all the rage. Some examples – *Smokin' Grass. Piston Broke.*

Our mower was *Smiffy's Flyin' Machine.* Number 35.

Our team consisted of First Officer Pete Hopper, Flight Engineer Frank Warburton and me. The airline connection was strong. My wife Cecilia was a BA stewardess, as was Mary, Jim's wife.

It was great fun for the drivers, and the number of crashes also gave the spectators a thrill. If a driver fell off his mower, the mower often carried on, at full throttle towards the spectators. Eventually, a safety device was fitted. This consisted of a cord from the driver's belt to a pin attached to the top of the spark plug. If you fell off, the line would pull the pin out and the engine would stop. That was the theory. In practice, the line or the driver's belt would often break, the mower would continue at high speed. The crowd loved it.

Malcolm Cook and I – ready to race!

Jim was full of good ideas, and still is, by the way. "I have had a great idea," he once said. "How about a World Championship?" I tried to explain to Jim that teams would have to come from further afield than the next village in Sussex to make it 'world'.

"No problem," he said, "I can get a team from Canada, Australia and Hong Kong. How about a committee meeting next week?" I had to say I was sorry, I would be in Zimbabwe. Not to be put off, he replied, "Great, don't come back without a team from Zimbabwe!"

Whilst there, one evening I was having a drink with the cargo manager of Air Zimbabwe (AZ). I told him of Jim's idea. He looked me in the eye and said, "He ought to be locked up, you too!"

The next day he phoned to say, "Right, I have handpicked your team, they will be flying into Gatwick next weekend." He explained that Rhodesia had been through a terrible civil war, and now the war was over, everyone needed something to brighten up their days.

Air Zimbabwe (AZ) operated a B707 from Harare to Gatwick. The crew stayed over for two days at a weekend, then returned. On their first visit, my wife drove to our nearest railway station to pick up the AZ team, consisting of Captain Roy Downs, and three crewmembers. One of the crew, a stewardess named Amanda proved to be a 'natural', and the fastest one on the team. I had arranged for them to drive my mower for the day. I painted it in Zebra stripes and on the grass box wrote: 'On lease to Air Zimbabwe'. They took to the racing like a duck to water. At the end of the day we all went to The Cricketers Arms to celebrate. We managed to throw them on the last train to Gatwick Airport. It had been a great day.

A couple of days later the phone rang. "Hello Brian, it's Roy here – we want one."

I replied, "Sorry, one what?"

"A racing lawn mower of course," came the reply.

To cut a long story short, Roy Downs and his team would fly the Air Zimbabwe B707 from Harare to Gatwick with their racing lawn mower in the hold. They would spend the weekend racing, then take their mower back with it wrapped in bin liners. Like most lawn mowers, they were not built to race. Maybe roaring round a track for hours at 40mph meant you inevitability ended up with a bag of bits. The next weekend, they would be back with their mower ready to race again.

Jim came up with another great idea. "Why don't we have a 12-hour race?"

The Air Zimbabwe team entered. Their pit was built like an African hut, complete with a canvas washbasin, and a towel hung on a nail. The driver would come into the pitstop, have a wash and a glass of sherry. Then the next driver would take over.

The 12-hour race started at 8pm with a Le Mans type start and went throughout the night until 8am. It was great fun to watch the 'drivers' race across the track, jump on their mowers, and roar off into the night. The winner was the mower completing the greatest numbers of laps. Racing through the night made it that much more exciting. Once you were away from the lights of the pits, it was very dark out on the track. If you crashed and fell off, the mower carried on. Although there were track marshals to help put you back on the track, some time was spent trying to 'capture' the run-away mower that probably had the throttle wide open.

A driver changeover was done Formula 1 style. Mechanics were ready as the mower came into the pits. It was refuelled, tyres and wheels checked, then it was on its way. The whole family was involved. We used the youngest members as lookouts, watching to see if the mower had stopped out on the track. They would sit for hours wrapped up in a blanket, eventually calling out, "Dad, the mower's stopped." We would rush out and carry the broken mower into the pits. The camaraderie among the competitors was incredible. Anything would be offered to get you going again, nuts, bolts, split pins, wheels, just about anything you needed.

One night the call came. "The mower's stopped." When we got the mower back in the pits, we discovered the one-inch diameter main drive shaft had sheered. We thought that was the end of the race for us. Henry Nicholls, a local farmer and a good friend, quietly said, "I can weld that."

Henry's farm was five miles from the racetrack, where the welding machine was. We loaded our mower into the back of my estate car and, in the middle of the night, all four of us drove like maniacs to Henry's farm. We ran into his barn; it was completely dark. "Has anybody got a shilling?" asked Henry. "I need to put some money into the electricity meter to get power." We stood there open mouthed, fumbling in our pockets. Somebody found a coin, the lights and power came on and Henry started to weld. Soon we were back in the race.

Prior to one race, I loaded piles of spare parts into our pit tent. There were boxes everywhere. I asked Pete and Frank to take a look and familiarise themselves with what each box contained. They thought I was starting to take the whole thing far too seriously. I walked round the tent saying, "Now, these are the clutch bits, these are the brake parts." They patiently followed me, shaking their heads. I pointed to one box and said, "What's that?"

Frank immediately replied, "That, that my friend is a bottle of scotch!"

How nice to work with professionals, I thought.

The lap keepers were housed in a double decker London bus. There were about a dozen lap keepers, mostly ladies as I recall, each responsible for recording the laps of four or five mowers. The laps were written on what looked like a till receipt. Mary collected the strips and marked the results on a large chalkboard. She also kept the lap keepers supplied with refreshments throughout the night. The wives and girlfriends of the drivers and mechanics kept up a steady stream of refreshments, finishing with a bacon and egg breakfast.

Prior to one 12-hour race Malcolm, my lawn mower racing pal, who was very competitive, told me about a man that could tune mower engines. We drove over to his workshop to have Malcolm's engine tuned. Sitting outside the shed was a race-prepared mower. We remarked to the mechanic how good the machine looked. "Take it for a drive," he said. Malcolm climbed on, he happened to be wearing his best suit, and set off across the grass field. When he returned the mechanic said, "Take it out again, and open it up this time." Malcolm roared off once more. As he reappeared, we took one look and dissolved into laughter.

He had been going really fast over the grass, when he drove over a huge cowpat. The rollers plastered him in cow manure from head to toe. He then had to drive home in his new BMW. Pam, Malcolm's wife, was not impressed, as they were about to go out to dinner that evening.

One race meeting was organised in Sevenoaks, Kent. We put Malcolm's mower and mine in my estate car. It was a tight fit. The grass boxes had to be tied onto the roof. We were late leaving home. When we arrived at the field, the first race was about to start. Jim said, "Hurry up guys, we will hold the start for two minutes for you." We pleaded with him to go ahead and start the race. "No, no, we will wait for you."

We threw our mowers together. The start flag dropped and we were off! I was roaring down a hill fast approaching a sharp bend. I tried to close the throttle to slow down; nothing happened, it had jammed wide open. I whizzed round the bend, hit the straw bales and flew in the air, leaving the mower embedded in the bales. I lay on the ground unhurt. The crowd were all cheering and clapping, clearly they thought it was all part of the show. After the last race Malcolm said he was going out to dinner (again!) that night and we must depart as soon as possible. We stuffed the mowers into my car and put the large grass boxes on the roof. In our haste… we forgot to tie them down.

As we were driving at speed down Sevenoaks High Street, we saw both grass boxes bowling along on the right-hand side of the road overtaking us. That incident delayed us considerably as we tried to explain to the nice Sevenoaks police lady what we had been doing all day.

As time went by, the British Lawnmower Association was formed. Its motto is *'Per Herbam Ad Astra'*. I believe the translation is 'Through Grass to the Stars'. I smile every time I see that motto.

15. THE SPITFIRE SIMULATOR

There have been so many books written about the Spitfire. I am not going to subject you to another one.

There is a saying: 'Cometh the hour, cometh the man.' It sounds like a line from a Shakespearian play, but it is attributed to Cliff Gladwin, who struck the winning run for England in a cricket match between England and South Africa in 1948. I believe this phrase could well be applied to the Spitfire.

'Cometh the hour, cometh the Spitfire.'

The Spitfire's first flight was on 5th March 1936 at Eastleigh Airfield, now Southampton Airport. The pilot was 'Mutt' Summers, Chief Test Pilot of Supermarine. There was a rumour that Mutt had gained his nickname from his habit of urinating on the tail wheel of a new aircraft he was about to test fly. Whether he carried out this little ceremony on the Spitfire is not known. After the test flight he is reputed to have said, "Don't change a single thing," indicating that it's not perfect, but good enough to hand over to another pilot.

The Spitfire was the only aircraft to operate in front line service throughout the whole of the WWII.

Martin Davidson and James Taylor, authors of the book *Spitfire Aces*, wrote:

'In an age that has become jaded, even cynical, about historical myths, uneasy about the sentimentalities they play on, the Spitfire legend is impressively resilient. There IS something special about the Spitfire, something that goes beyond how good it looked or how iconic it became in the British imagination. The Spitfire deserves its status as one of the great artefacts of British history. Of course much of this is symbolic, but symbols are powerful too, and the Spitfire is one of the most powerful.'

My brother Johnnie was a crewman on the air sea rescue launches. During the war years, the crews of the launches saved over 13,000 lives. My brother assisted in rescuing many pilots that had been shot down. Some in dinghies were lifted on board, others were wearing only a life preserver.

Many of them had serious injuries, broken or missing limbs, some had succumbed to the freezing water. The life preserver or life jacket was known throughout the RAF as a Mae West, named after a famous American actress, singer and sex symbol. She was renowned for her remarks or innuendoes, such as: "I used to be Snow White, but I drifted!"

When listing the uniform worn by RAF aircrew, a quote from one issue of the BBC's magazine *The Listener* in 1940 read: '*Then comes a life saving waistcoat. This can be inflated in a few moments by the wearer, and for some obscure reason is known technically as a 'Mae West'.*' I am certain every RAF aircrew knew *exactly* what the Mae West referred to.

After the war, I asked my brother, "Did you pick up anybody, and did you pick up any Germans?"

He said, "Yes, we picked up anyone in the water."

I wanted to know more. "Did you have any problems?"

"Well," he said, "there was one occasion when we picked up a German pilot. We were just about to lift him into the boat, when he pulled out a pistol, and tried to shoot us."

"What did you do?" I asked.

"We got cross!"

"What! He is trying to kill you and you got cross?"

"We told him to stop, in German."

"Then what happened?" I enquired.

"Well, then we got really cross."

I thought their reaction would be to leave him in the water.

"We had to hit him over the head with a boathook to get him on board."

The photo below shows a Type Two HSL (high speed launch) with a Hawker Hurricane flying over it. The HSL had a crew of nine, with a top speed of 36kts. It was operated by the Marine Branch of the Royal Air Force whose motto was: '*The sea shall not have them.*' This motto was the name of a 1954 British war film starring Michael Redgrave, Dirk Bogarde and Anthony Steel.

Photo from the Imperial War Museum.

Johnnie saw action throughout WWII. Although I was very young, I can remember some of the pilots that called at our house and listening to their stories.

The Spitfire was gaining its reputation. Ask anyone to describe the flight path of a Spitfire without using their arms and hands? It is impossible.

One Christmas, I was given a wooden model of a Spitfire. In the film *The Battle of Britain* there is a scene where two boys, each holding a model Spitfire, run through a bombed-out building, waving their models and mimicking the sound of the Merlin engines. I played in our street in the East End of London for hours with my pals and my model. However, I did not grow up with a burning desire to fly a Spitfire, but a seed was sown. It must have been a very slow-growing seed, one that was not to flower until many years later.

It was 28th April 1971. I was flying B707s for BOAC. On a day off, I went to Shoreham Airport for a cup of coffee. It was a beautiful spring day, calm winds and clear skies. It was very busy, it seemed everyone wanted to go flying.

I was looking towards the hangars, when the huge doors slowly cranked open and a Spitfire Mk IX G-AVAV was pushed out. The coffee shop quickly emptied as everyone rushed out to see it. It had just been painted in its original WWII colours. It looked stunning in the bright sunshine. I was one of the first to reach the hangars. I recognised one of the mechanics. "Hello Brian," he said, "great to see you, would you do us a favour and taxi it over to the pumps and fill 'er up?" There is a saying for such occasions, '*You could have knocked me down with a feather*' comes to mind. I looked at him to make sure he was not pulling my leg. "Well, you're a pilot aren't you? Come on get on with it!"

Although I had not flown a Spitfire, I had been around them. At that time I was a first officer with BOAC. One of the captains I got to know was Pete Jarvis. One day he phoned and said, "I have just lost my driving licence, I was at an RAF squadron reunion party and a friend was so drunk I said I would drive him home. I was stopped by the police, breathalysed and only just failed the test."

I immediately said, "Don't worry Pete, I can drive you to and from the simulator."

"Oh," he said, "I am not worried about that, I want to get to Duxford Airfield to fly the Spitfire!" I assured him I would take him anytime.

Duxford Airfield dates back to the First World War and is now the home of the Imperial War Museum and the American Air Museum. Many warbirds live and fly from there. Two days later, Pete phoned to say, "Can we go tomorrow?"

When we arrived at Duxford Airfield, sitting on the tarmac were three warbirds. A Spitfire Mk IX, a Kittyhawk and a P51 Mustang. I was introduced to the other two pilots who were to fly them – Mark Hanna and Carl Schofield. They were experienced warbird pilots. The plan was to fly down to Redhill Airfield to meet a group of Second World War veterans, members of the famous Guinea Pig Club. To become a Guinea Pig you had to be aircrew and had to have had two surgeries performed by Sir Archie McIndoe. At East Grinstead Hospital, McIndoe performed miracles with plastic surgery on badly burned airmen.

I was lucky to sit in the back seat of the Kittyhawk flown by Mark Hanna. He performed a low-level flyover of the hospital. After the 'beat up', we returned to Redhill Airfield to refuel. Finally, home to Duxford. Pete Jarvis flew the Spitfire; I was in the back seat. What a day out! I felt very privileged to have been given the opportunity to experience these historic aircraft, particularly the Spitfire.

Now, back to Shoreham… I felt if I dithered about any longer, before taxiing the Spit, someone else would do it. I jumped in, did up the straps, and took a long look around the cockpit. I cannot remember the mechanic's name, but together we went through the start-up and taxiing procedures. He started the engine for me. I took a deep breath, waved the chocks away, opened the throttle about an inch and we started to move.

The long nose of the aircraft stretches out before you and blocks the forward view. To see where you are going you have to weave from side to side, holding the stick hard back, as it is easy to tip it on its nose. Braking very gently is the key. I was totally unaware of anything or any person near me other than the task of delivering this magnificent, priceless work of art back safe and sound. I pulled up by the fuel pumps, applied the park brake and shut down. Phew!

The refueller came out of his hut. I remember him as a miserable old man, who hated any student pilots. I took great delight in giving him a royal wave and saying, "Just fill her up old boy." I will remember the look on his face forever. I really cannot remember taxiing back to the hangar; I guess it went OK though.

After all these years, the whole experience seemed like a dream.

I had to look at my pilot's logbook to check if it had really happened. It is all recorded there.

I went to many air shows and always admired the way a particular pilot displayed the Spitfire. His name is Brian Smith, my namesake. We both joined GB Airways as training captains at the same time. We said to the Chief Pilot Fred Rivett, who is also a balloonist, "It might be confusing to have two training captains with the same name, spelt exactly the same."

"Oh no," he said, "you will be 'Balloon Smith' and he will be 'Spitfire Smith'." And so it was, and it worked very well.

The Reunion

On 24th July 2012, it was 50 years since my first training flight with Joan Hughes at White Waltham. Jim Kelly phoned to say we should celebrate the occasion with Lou Daley. Lou also learnt to fly at White Waltham. He retired as a training captain with Cathay Pacific.

I said I thought the reunion was a good idea. "Great, you can organise it then," said Jim. I thought it *should* be celebrated, and as we had had our first flight 50 years ago at White Waltham why not go back there? We planned to hire an aircraft, go for a flight, and then take our wives out to lunch. I phoned the West London Aero Club and booked a trial lesson for each of us, in a Piper Cub aircraft. I also booked lunch for us at the Royal Oak pub, run by Michael Parkinson. We were determined to make it a memorable day.

Beforehand, there was much discussion between the three of us as to whether we should tell our instructor we had flown before. A 'trial lesson' implies you are a complete novice. I said straight away, "Oh well, I'm going to tell him."

"Why?" enquired Jim and Lou.

I replied, "I don't think I could bear it, if, after the 'trial lesson', my instructor said to me. 'Well, Mr Smith, I don't think flying is really for you.'"

The day we were due to fly was very windy with rain forecast.

However, as we had booked lunch and a hotel, we hoped it might be possible. The chief flying instructor said there would be no flying that day, and that was that. A young instructor, Ray Ling, who was standing close by could see our disappointment, and said, "If you have an hour or so to spare, why not visit the Air Transport Museum in Maidenhead."

We discovered his 'day job' was a chief steward with British Airways. What a coincidence. We spent some time chatting to him about our background as stewards with BEA and learning to fly at White Waltham. He knew what the celebration flight meant to us. He offered to be our instructor when we re-booked. I think between Jim, Lou and I we had already begun to see he was the man for us.

When we checked into the museum, the lady at the desk said, "Would you like to fly the Spitfire Simulator?" We raced up the stairs, and there was a replica of a Spitfire cockpit. We all really enjoyed flying it.

We had booked rooms for the night at the Monkey Island Hotel, near Maidenhead. This was a trip down memory lane for Cecilia and me. It was where we had had our first date (see Chapter 5. 'Cecilia'). This time I had enough money to pay the bill!

The next morning, we went our separate ways, but agreed to keep in touch and arrange to have the flight at a later date. Some months were to pass before we were able to organize the flight.

On 30th October 2012, Jim, Lou and I each flew a Piper Cub at White Waltham. Ray Ling was our instructor. It was quite an emotional experience for all of us. When I asked Ray to sign my logbook, he said, "Sure."

When I handed it to him, he stared at the page, and said, "I cannot sign on the same page as Joan Hughes!"

"Of course you can."

Proudly, I now have those two special signatures in my logbook, exactly 50 years apart.

On the way home my wife said, "You're a bit quiet?"

Deep in thought I replied, "I'm going to build one."

"One what?" she asked.

I said, "A Spitfire simulator, of course!"

Cartoon by Dave Coverly. Speedbump.com

The seed that had previously been sown had started to bear fruit! We live in a 16th century farmhouse, with a couple of barns attached. One of the barns was in disrepair and full of junk – the perfect place to house the simulator. I set to work to clean it up. I could visualise it as a WWII RAF crew room.

I had the most incredible help from not only friends and family, but also all sorts of technicians that just seemed to appear out of nowhere. I started to see why this was happening. It was nothing to do with helping me, it was the idea of the Spitfire that attracted them.

We started to clear the barn. Eventually, we were left with just the shell of a room. John Nicholls, whom I had known all his life, and was the son of Henry, my lawn mower racing pal, set to work on the old tiled roof and fitted a new door. Jamie Palmer, a ballooning pal, and I lined the walls and ceiling with hessian.

The floor was concrete, last used by cows passing through on their way to be milked. Dave Saunders of the West Sussex Antique Timber Company put in a lovely oak floor, free of charge. Friends and family donated WWII memorabilia, RAF uniforms, WWII telephones, flying jackets, ration books. The room was starting to take shape.

Oak floor not laid.

Now for the simulator. I contacted Ed Grant who had put together the Spitfire simulator at Maidenhead. He put me in touch with Niall Paterson, owner of Creative Cockpits, who would supply the full-size Spitfire cockpit. It arrived by road as a flat pack. My only experience of flat packs was IKEA, and I usually ended up with some vital bits left over. Fortunately for us, Niall had also supplied detailed notes on how to put it together. Jamie, Peter Edmonds, Ed Grant and I worked 12-hour days for about a week putting it all together. Cecilia kept us supplied with tea and sandwiches throughout.

At the end of each day, I insisted we all went down to the Cricketers Arms for a pint. This was a tradition I inherited from my father, not so much of going to the pub, but sitting down at the end of the day all together, discussing what had happened that day and what the plan was for tomorrow. The cockpit shell had to be painted in camouflage colours, but if we did, how would we ever find it again! Sorry, I had to slip a Tommy Cooper joke in there somewhere!

Most RAF Spitfires have letters on the fuselage. Two letters identify the squadron and the third letter identifies the aircraft in alphabetical order.

Example: XT (the squadron) and A for (Able) or B (Baker) and so on.

Douglas Bader, the famous RAF pilot, had his initials 'DB' painted on his aircraft. After a couple of dogfights, he quickly realised this was not such a good idea as it made him a target for the Luftwaffe.

Our simulator has two letters on each side – MV on one side and JH on the other. MV are the initials of Mary Villiers, and JH for Joan Hughes. Both flew Spitfires in Air Transport Auxiliary (ATA), ferrying them from the factories to the frontline airfields and landing grounds.

Mary told me a story of a friend of hers, a very attractive 22-year-old girl, who landed a brand-new Spitfire at Coolham, an Advance Landing Ground (ALG) just prior to D-Day. The ALGs were all grass fields, most covered with perforated steel mesh runways. This covering was known as Sommerfeld tracking, ironically named after a German engineer, Kurt Sommerfeld. It was nicknamed 'tin lino'. All buildings were temporary, the accommodation was in tents.

It was a very hot day and all the airmen came out of their tents, completely naked to see the Spitfire. The girl had her helmet and oxygen mask on, and they assumed it was a man flying it. She was well aware of what was going on and decided to have some fun. She kept the Spitfire gently bumping along the runway with the airmen running alongside. Eventually, she stopped and pulled her helmet off and let her blonde curls down. For a second or so the men stopped and stared in disbelief, then rushed off to put their trousers on.

47" TV SCREENS IN PLACE AND WORKING THANKS TO DAN

There were many ALGs dotted about southern England in the build up to D-Day. Six fighter squadrons operated from Coolham ALG – three Mustang and three Spitfire. Their pilots and ground crew came from many nations – Poland, Britain, Canada, New Zealand, Australia and Belgium.

A war memorial stands outside the Selsey Arms pub in the village as a tribute to the allied airmen who lost their young lives while flying from Coolham.

Work in Progress

The Spitfire fuselage was ready. So far it had involved a fairly straightforward job of basic carpentry and painting. Now, it was time for the technicians to take over.

Mike Dacey, now a captain with BA who I have known since he was 16 years old, called one day to say he had built a simulator in his bedroom, and would I come over to see it and help him to check out the flight instruments. I drove to Mike's house, wondering what I might see. It is not every day you build a simulator, and particularly not in your bedroom. Well, not at the age of 16.

Mike's mum, Jacqs, showed me in and we went upstairs to Mike's room. We had to push the door open as his bed was propped up behind it. There, against one wall, was a full-size Cessna 172 cockpit, complete with flight controls and flight instruments. We flew it around, and I came away very impressed. He had done a great job of putting it together. I could clearly see Mike's computer skills.

Mike's simulator set up in his bedroom, reminded me of a TV programme for children that was broadcast many years ago. It may have been an early *Blue Peter* type of programme. This particular sequence went something like this: The TV presenter said, "We are now going over to British European Airways simulator flight training centre at Heathrow." The TV cameras panned to a view of a BEA Trident cockpit. There appeared to be two pilots in uniform sitting in the pilots' seats. Closer inspection revealed they were schoolboys. Sitting behind them was a BEA training captain. The scenario started with the training captain saying that the boys had built the simulator, and, in his opinion, they had done a very realistic copy of a Trident cockpit. BEA had donated checklists and headsets, and the boys set to work reading through the start-up procedures. It came to the engine start up point. One of the boys picked up a mike and called Heathrow Tower for clearance to start up. His R/T procedure was quite correct. He went on to say, "Heathrow Tower, this is Speedbird 123 on stand Zulu 1 with information Alfa. Request start." The camera then pans down to the kitchen. The boy's mum is seen washing up, complete with apron. She picks up a mike and replies, "Speedbird 123 cleared to start, call when ready to taxi." I laughed out loud. It was so well done. The following week, the training captain took the boys to the Trident aircraft simulator and let them fly the real thing.

Several weeks later, Mike came to our barn to set up the

computers, graphics and flight instruments for our Spitfire. He then handed over this work to Dan Froughi, who became our No 1 techie. Dan has steadily improved the realism by setting up the huge visual display we have now. We were advised to install the largest visual display the room would accommodate.

We were puzzling over exactly how we would attach three huge TV screens to an old wooden wall, and to have them in the right place at the right angle. The width of the barn was a restriction on the size of the TV screens. The centre screen was to be bolted flat to the wall, the left and right screens had to be on hinges at the correct angle to stop any distortion to the scenery. We were successful, finishing up with a wraparound view of approximately 160 degrees.

Jack, a young friend of ours, came to have a look. He said, "My Dad, Jock, is a master carpenter. He builds sets for film studios. He would be able to fit the screens for you." Jock did a really great job. He fixed the centre screen in position, then fitted giant hinges to the side screens, which allowed us to be able to adjust them. We then had to find the correct TV screens to fit.

Tim Worrall, the owner of Airwave Ltd in Billingshurst, supplied us with three 47" TV screens at cost. The computers were installed and Dan got to work linking all the flight instruments to the visual display.

Associated with the myth or legend of the Spitfire is the sound of the Merlin engine. You know when there is a Spitfire in the sky when you hear that distinctive sound. Jamie Palmer, who had been on 'the build set' since Day One, happened to be a fully trained sound engineer. His company name 'Gorgeous Audio' gives you some idea of his expertise in this area. He fitted the Merlin engine sound and it has worked perfectly from the first time it burst into life. The sound is also linked into the movement of the gear and flaps, and on touch down you hear that distinctive 'screech' as the tyres hit the runway.

The flight controls came as a modular unit. Spitsim, a company in Devon, run by Jon and Wendy Fellows, supplied them. The controls were an exact replica of the real thing. Jon and Wendy came and fitted them.

THE FLIGHT CONTROLS ARRIVE

I think it is true to say, when you start up a Spitfire the whole airframe shakes. It changes from a sleek aerodynamic airframe into a 'Fergie' tractor. We had heard about a device that would vibrate the simulator. It is called a 'Butt Kicker'. Mike Sherwood, one of our instructors installed it. When fitted to the seat, it not only kicks your butt, but it replicates any change of engine note, and the sound of the gear and flaps retracting and extending.

The seat in our simulator was fixed in position. We knew the seat in the aircraft was adjustable. In our striving for realism, we searched high and low to find one. There were several for sale, ranging from £3,000 upwards – just outside our price range.

Mike Sherwood and I phoned a local scrap yard and explained what we were looking for. They were very helpful and said, "Come along and have a search around."

Mike and I must have spent an hour or more looking in dozens of old cars and vans. We needed a seat with a mechanical ratchet, not an electric one. We then set off to scour the yard; I was at one end, and Mike the other. The day was gloomy, overcast with a low cloud base. I was just beginning to think we were wasting our time, when the cloud broke and a shaft of sunlight beamed onto a van in the distance. On top of the van was a car seat. I ran over and took the seat down; it was *just* what we wanted. I know it sounds spooky, but that is what happened. Two days later, after much toil, tears and sweat, it was fitted and working.

We were constantly striving for realism. One day, when Dan Froughi and Marty Sweet, our two techies, were upgrading the graphics, I was standing in the background watching in awe at their skills. I thought I might have some fun so I said, "Excuse me, can I have my input?"

They turned and looked at me with their eyes raised to the heavens. "What do you want?" they asked.

I explained that when you start up a Spitfire or any propeller driven aircraft, you get some airflow or prop wash. "How about we fit two fans each side under the TV screens?"

Just shaking their heads, they turned away.

A week later they had fitted the fans. The airflow on start-up and taxiing is now part of the experience. The speed of the fans is controlled from the instructor station. As the propeller turns and bursts into life, the fan speed is turned fully on – enough to part your hair.

I had thought hard and long as to what to do with the simulator when it was finally up and running. I decided to ask potential customers to donate £30 per session. All proceeds were to go to the RAF Benevolent Fund.

Our open day was 1st April 2013. The following two photos show the youngest and the oldest pilot to fly the simulator to date.

OPEN DAY 1st April 'OUR VICAR FLYING HIGH'!

OPEN DAY.
FOR FRIENDS
AND FAMILY

"PREACH FOR
THE SKY!"

" DOG FIGHTING IN A DOG COLLAR - WHATEVER NEXT! "

6½ YEAR OLD GRANDSONS GET THEIR FLIGHT CERTIFICATES.   MAR/2014

Grandsons Kambel and Smith, aged 6, with their flight certificates. We had to prop them up on several cushions, to be able to reach the flying controls.

try Spitfire simulator

Bill Lucas at the Spitfire simulator controls with organiser Ian Davis - picture submitted

Bill Lucas, 97, a former squadron leader operated 81 flying missions in Wellingtons, Stirlings and Mosquito bombers. He was full of life and really enjoyed flying the simulator.

One of the simulator manoeuvres is to fly under a bridge. Bill was making his approach to the bridge; it is a tight fit and you have to line up by passing over a small island that is on the centre line. I said to Bill, "Can you see the island OK?"

He nodded.

Jokingly, I said, "Can you see the girl on the beach?"

"Yes," he replied. He flew under the bridge right on the centreline, and then pulled up and did a victory roll. Everyone cheered.

I said, "That was great, Bill!"

He smiled and said, "I just kept thinking about that girl on the beach!" Not bad for a 97-year-old. I asked Bill to sign the inside of the Spitfire simulator door. We have adopted this little door signing ceremony for any veterans. We recently had a former Luftwaffe pilot come to fly the simulator. He wrote in our scrapbook: 'I don't like to remember the time of war but it was interesting to fly an aircraft of the other side.'

One of our first simulator instructors, Peter Edmonds, who had been part of the team from Day One, came up with an idea for raising funds by running what he called a 'Dawn Patrol'. The idea was to fly the simulator, visiting 30 former WWII airfields with a change of pilot at each one. The 30 'pilots' would donate £30 each to the fund. A marquee was set up on our front lawn, and tea and cakes were served throughout the day. In the evening we all had a 'Battle of Britain Dinner' together at the Cricketer's Arms. There was to be a prize for the best fancy dress. Most of us wore RAF uniforms. However, one person came as a Nazi spy, dressed in long black coat, trilby hat and false moustache. It looked so good I awarded him first prize, a bottle of champagne. One of my friends who had had quite a few drinks, said to me, "Oi! Brian. Is this 'do' called the 'Battle of Britain Dinner?'"

"Yes," I replied.

"Well," he snorted, "how come you have given the champagne to a German?"

We have run two Dawn Patrols and were planning a third this year. That has had to be postponed until spring next year, due to the Coronavirus pandemic.

In autumn 2020 we had a call from the RAF Benevolent Fund confirming that, to date, we have raised £100,000 for the fund.

Unfortunately, at this time, the simulator is also closed due to the Coronavirus. It is an extremely frustrating time for us. The simulator is housed in a very small barn, designed to look like a WWII RAF airfield dispersal hut. For many reasons we cannot comply with the government guidelines regarding the virus. We plan to remain closed until autumn 2021.

Every year the RAF benevolent Fund has an award ceremony. I received an email from them to say The Spitfire Experience had been nominated for an award. They sent out a press release:

Royal Air Force Benevolent Fund

Immediate release

Fundraiser who generated £100K for RAF charity shortlisted for national award

Caption: Brian Smith in his Spitfire cockpit. Photo: RAF Benevolent Fund.

Charity supporter Brian Smith has been recognised for his incredible fundraising efforts for the RAF Benevolent Fund, after he was shortlisted in the charity's annual awards.

Brian's project, The Spitfire Experience, has been shortlisted in the Outstanding Support from an Organisation category after raising more than £100K for the charity, including £30K in 2019, alone.

Brian, a former RAF Physical Training Instructor who went on to become a commercial pilot, created the Spitfire Experience when he retired. He built the Spitfire simulator around a restored Spitfire cockpit in a barn at his home in Wisborough Green. All the profits generated from 'pilots' who take a flight in the iconic Second World War fighter plane are donated to the RAF Benevolent Fund.

Eighty-two-year-old Brian said: "I wanted to do something to raise money for veterans and to support the RAF in some way and this seemed a very good way to do it. I am delighted we have been able to raise so much.

"As well as myself, I have six volunteer instructors who give their time to support the Fund. We really feel like we're part of the RAF Benevolent Fund family."

As well as running the Spitfire simulator experience, Brian and his wife Cecelia have held Battle of Britain dinners and attended Goodwood to raise funds for the charity.

Mike Straney, Director of Fundraising and Communications at the RAF Benevolent Fund, said: "Brian and Cecilia's nomination for this award is well deserved – what they have done for the Fund is nothing short of incredible.

"Undoubtedly their contribution to the Fund has allowed us to continue to make an impact on the welfare of the whole RAF Family, particularly during this challenging year."

Now in its eighth year, the RAF Benevolent Fund Awards recognise the outstanding contributions of its supporters, personnel on stations and corporate partners who support the charity each year. The winners of eight categories will be announced during a virtual ceremony on October 13.

The RAF Benevolent Fund is the RAF's leading welfare charity, supporting RAF personnel past and present. If you know an RAF veteran in need, go to rafbf.org to find out how the Fund could help.

For more information and high-res images please contact:
Rebekah Sharrock, PR Manager, RAF Benevolent Fund
E: rebekah.sharrock@rafbf.org.uk | T: 020 7307 3305 | M: 07595 657979.

RAF Benevolent Fund: The Royal Air Force Benevolent Fund is the RAF's leading welfare charity. We exist to support current and former members of the RAF, their partners and dependants, whenever they need us. In 2019, we spent £28M supporting.

This year's *virtual* award ceremony was held on 13th October 2020. I am delighted that the Spitfire Experience (not Brian Smith) won an award. It was a true team effort: Dan Froughi, who has been with us from Day One, and claims to have aged ten years sorting out the numerous computer 'glitches'. Marty Sweet, whose computer skills fit perfectly with Dan, as result they make for a great team. Jamie Palmer, the soundman. The sound of the Merlin engine has worked perfectly throughout. The instructors: Jerry Sirley, Peter Edmonds, Peter Allison, Mike Akers, Mike Sherwood, Phil Polwin, Alan Crabbe and Chris Hebbard. They give their time entirely free.

The date now is 29th October 2020. As it is approaching Halloween, I thought it appropriate to share a ghost story with you. It also seems a good way to end the book.